Longman e

practice kit

A-level
Mathematics

Cyril Moss
Michael Kenwood

SERIES EDITORS
Geoff Black and Stuart Wall

TITLES AVAILABLE
A-level
Biology
Business Studies
Chemistry
Mathematics
Psychology
Sociology

Addison Wesley Longman Ltd.,
Edinburgh Gate, Harlow,
Essex CM20 2JE, England
and Associated Companies throughout the World.

© Addison Wesley Longman 1997

First published 1997

ISBN 0582-30389-3

British Library Cataloguing-in-Publication Data
A catalogue record for this book is available from the British Library.

Set by 32 in 11/13pt Baskerville
Printed in Great Britain by Henry Ling Ltd., at the Dorset Press
Dorchester, Dorset

Contents

How to use this book

This Exam Practice Kit was written to help you achieve a high-grade pass at GCE A-level or AS-level in mathematical subjects involving Pure and Applied Mathematics and Statistics.

The book is arranged in four parts.

Part I of the Exam Practice Kit gives suggestions about how to prepare for the examination.

Part II gives an easy to use outline of the theory you require for each of twelve major topic areas. This theory is followed immediately by worked examples which closely mirror the questions that you will get in the actual examination. These worked examples are further reinforced by practice questions at the end of each topic. If you have any difficulty with answering the practice questions you should turn to Part III and look at the hints given for each question. Try not to look at the answers until you have completed your own answers.

Part III provides hints and outline solutions for each practice question followed by answers to each question.

There are also three timed practice examination papers in Part IV of the Exam Practice Kit. Separate examination papers are provided for Pure Mathematics, Mechanics and Statistics. These are followed by answers and examiner comments for you to check your own answers against. It will be helpful to time yourself on these examination papers before the real examination.

We have modelled all of the questions on past examination papers but we have deliberately not used actual board questions. As experienced examiners, we firmly believe that the questions we have set are relevant to the style and standard of your examination board. It is essential that you try the question first before looking at the answers. Use the answers, by all means, but preferably only when you get into real difficulty and when you wish to compare your final answer with that given.

Preparing for the examination

The best preparation that one can do for an examination in any subject, but particularly mathematical subjects, is to work steadily and carefully throughout the whole of your course. We wish to suggest a number of things that should, hopefully, make the examination easier, more enjoyable and certainly lead to higher marks and consequently a better grade.

Planning your revision
Everyone has their own ideas on how to revise, but you may find the following recommendations useful.

1 Do not leave revision until the last few days or weeks. Start at least eight weeks before your examination and build up gradually.
2 Do not approach revision in a haphazard way. Make a weekly plan and stick to it. A planner is provided with this book for this purpose.
3 Do not leave out topics you do not like or spend a lot of time practising questions you are good at.
4 Each time you have revised a topic, practice answering questions on it first from this Exam Practice Kit and then from past papers. You must at all costs avoid passive reading.
5 Do not start learning new material at the last minute, but do practise topics you do not like or are not very good at.
6 Do get as much of your work marked as possible. It is surprising how often you think you have done something correctly when you have missed a point. It happens to us all!
7 Do make sure that you ask your teacher about any point you do not understand. That is what they are there for.
8 Try to anticipate what will be in the examination by being familiar with your syllabus and with past papers. There are never any new examination twists.
9 Keep the week before the examinations to go over awkward or difficult topics one last time.
10 Try a mock examination – even if you sat the same paper some weeks before. Part IV of this Exam Practice Kit provides you with timed practice papers in Pure Mathematics, Mechanics and Statistics to practise working to the set time. Solutions are also provided to check your answers against.

Preparation is also about anticipation: both of what will be expected of you in the papers and of how you may react and of what not to do when actually in the examination room.

What to do
1 Be familiar with your examination board's syllabus.
2 Look at past examination papers and examine them alongside the syllabus; they also indicate the standard required.
3 Be familiar with the rubric, i.e. the instruction at the start of the paper, noting in particular which questions are compulsory or optional, how many questions have to be answered, how much time is allowed and what materials are supplied.
4 Do a rough calculation to find out how much time you have to spend on a question or section. For example, a $1\frac{1}{2}$ hour paper worth 100 marks means one mark $= 0.9$ minutes, so an eight mark question $= 7$ minutes.

5   Get used to working in a neat and orderly manner. It not only saves time but undoubtedly leads to higher marks and fewer errors and consequently less panic.

6   Get used to showing all of your working. Do not cut corners. Remember a wrong answer with no working attracts no marks. *This is particularly relevant to the use of calculators.*

7   Make yourself familiar with the formula booklet, but *do not depend on it exclusively.*

8   Work through at least four past papers, preferably in the last eight weeks before the A-level examination and have your answers marked by a teacher/lecturer.

9   Most importantly, use this Exam Practice Kit in the ways we suggest on p. iv, 'How to use this book'.

What not to do

1   Do not write your answers in red or green ink or in pencil. Use only blue or black ink.

2   Do not waste time doing the following:
   (a) underlining your answers;
   (b) writing out the question before starting your answer;
   (c) drawing diagrams with excessive use of drawing instruments – learn instead to draw freehand.

3   Do not write down an answer without showing your working.

4   Do not amend or alter a symbol; it is better to cross it out and replace it with a new symbol to avoid confusion.

5   Do not write an essay telling the examiner how you would answer the question if you only had time. Such pleading does not gain marks!

6   Do not draw diagrams at the foot of a page you are going to turn over – instead draw it at the start of a clean page.

7   Do not make the mistake of saving your best topic to the end. Make it your first question.

8   Do not fail to include your rough working in the answer book.

9   Do not spend too long on any one question. If you have not answered it in your time allocation, leave it and come back to it later, time permitting.

In the examination room

There is no need to panic: just compose yourself and work steadily.

1   Read through the whole paper to get an idea of what each question is asking you. Do not discard any question at this stage, since in mathematics you never know how difficult a question is until you try it. Once you have selected the appropriate number of questions to attempt, pick out the question that looks most familiar and you feel most confident about and attempt this question first. A good start invariably leads to a good result.

2   Make sure that you follow precisely the instructions given on the paper.

3   Make sure that you read each question carefully, paying particular attention to signs, indices and equations. When you have copied the information into your examination book, check again. A second or two spent here can save a lot of time later. Each year many marks are lost through miscopying information.

4   Do not cut corners.

5   *Do use brackets*. More mistakes are made through the omission of brackets than anything else.

6   When you have completed a solution, read through the question on the examination paper again to make sure that:

(a) you have not omitted any part of it, and

(b) you have given the answer in the form required, e.g. 3 sig. figs; 3 dec. places; radians rather than degrees, etc.

7   Remember that, unless instructed otherwise, you can leave your answer in terms of π, e, etc. Do not waste time expressing an answer in the form $y = \ldots$ unless the wording of the question requires it.

8   Do use diagrams, especially in Applied Mathematics, and transfer the information given in the question to the diagram – check at least twice!

9   Remember that when a question says 'Hence or otherwise . . .' the word 'hence' is only suggesting a method. It is, however, usually the most suitable method, though an alternative will be accepted. If a question merely says 'Hence', it means that other solutions are not going to be accepted by the examiner.

10   If you cannot complete a question, leave a space and come back to it later.

When difficulties arise

At some stage in the examination room you may well experience difficulty with a question. Do not panic and do not continue with your solution. Proceed as follows:

1   Go back and read the question again to make sure you have used the correct figures and information. If you have time, go quickly through your solution and try to find the error. If you cannot find the error, leave the question until later and come back, time permitting. If, though, you do have time to spare, start the question again – errors often only come to light when the solution is restarted. *Do not cross out any of your previous working*. Work not crossed out must be marked, but crossed out work subsequently replaced by other attempts may not be marked. You will not lose marks by leaving incorrect work which is replaced by correct work.

2   Most questions, particularly the longer ones, are structured with intermediate answers given along the way. If you cannot get an intermediate answer then do not continue to struggle with your answer. Instead take the intermediate answer given on the question paper and try to complete the next stage of the question. That way you will be able to get all of the remaining method and accuracy marks.

part II
Topic areas, worked examples and practice questions

1 Algebra

✓ **TOPIC OUTLINE AND REVISION TIPS**

Surds

Rationalisation of the denominator of a surd
You must be able to rationalise a denominator involving surds.

Example

$$\frac{2 - \sqrt{3}}{\sqrt{3}} = \left(\frac{2 - \sqrt{3}}{\sqrt{3}}\right)\left(\frac{\sqrt{3}}{\sqrt{3}}\right) = \frac{2\sqrt{3} - 3}{3}$$

For more complicated denominators simply multiply the denominator and numerator by the number in the denominator with the sign changed.

Example

$$\frac{1}{3 - \sqrt{2}} = \left(\frac{1}{3 - \sqrt{2}}\right)\left(\frac{3 + \sqrt{2}}{3 + \sqrt{2}}\right) = \frac{3 + \sqrt{2}}{3^2 - 2} = \frac{1}{7}(3 + \sqrt{2}).$$

Identities

Identities are true for *all* values of the variable or variables. You must be familiar with these

$$(a \pm b)^2 \equiv a^2 \pm 2ab + b^2,$$

$$(a + b)(a - b) \equiv a^2 - b^2,$$

$$(x + y)^3 \equiv x^3 + 3x^2y + 3xy^2 + y^3,$$

$$x^3 \pm y^3 \equiv (x \pm y)(x^2 \mp xy + y^2).$$

Basic processing

You must be able to expand, factorise and manipulate brackets with ease and confidence. Do use brackets and remember that when removing brackets a negative sign before the bracket changes the $+$ and $-$ signs inside the bracket to $-$ and $+$ respectively. More mistakes are made by the failure to use brackets than any other process.

1. **Simplify**
$$a(b - c) - c(b - a) + b(a - c) = ab - ac - cb + ca + ba - bc$$
$$= 2ab - 2bc = 2b(a - c)$$

2. **Factorise** $\quad x^3 - 4x \equiv x(x^2 - 4) \equiv x(x - 2)(x + 2)$

3. **Factorise** $\quad 6y^2 - 5y - 6 \equiv 6y^2 - 9y + 4y - 6 = 3y(2y - 3) + 2(2y - 3)$
$$= (3y + 2)(2y - 3)$$

Equations

Equations in general are true for some (or perhaps *none*) of the values of the variable or variables. Here are the strategies with which you must be completely familiar.

Simple equations

Find the final value of x for which $\dfrac{3x+7}{11} - \dfrac{8-x}{3} = 1$.

Insert brackets, multiply by 33, the common denominator, to obtain

$$\tfrac{33}{11}(3x+7) - \tfrac{33}{3}(8-x) = 33$$
$$\Rightarrow \quad 9x + 21 - 88 + 11x = 33 \quad \Rightarrow \quad 20x = 100$$
$$\Rightarrow \quad x = 5$$

Simultaneous equations

To solve a set of two linear equations in two unknowns it is necessary to eliminate one of the variables by either adding or subtracting multiples of the equations. Experience shows that fewer errors are made when adding than subtracting.

Worked Example 1

Solve the simultaneous equations $2x - 3y = 11, \quad 5x + 2y = -1$.

Working

The y terms have opposite signs so eliminate y.

$2x - 3y = 11$ [1]

$5x + 2y = -1$ [2]

Multiply [1] by 2 to give $\quad 4x - 6y = 22$ [3]

Multiply [2] by 3 to give $\quad 15x + 6y = -3$ [4]

[i.e. do tell the examiner what you are doing by labelling your equations.]

Add [3] and [4] to give $\quad 19x = 19 \quad \Rightarrow \quad x = 1$

Substitute in [2] to give $\quad 5 + 2y = -1 \quad \Rightarrow \quad y = -3$

Always check your answer using the other equation.
Check in [1]:

$\text{LHS} = 2 \times 1 - 3(-3) = 11 = \text{RHS}$

Worked Example 2

Solve the simultaneous equations $x - 2y = 7, \quad x^2 + 3y^2 = 28$.

Working

$x - 2y = 7 \quad \Rightarrow \quad x = 2y + 7$ [1]

$x^2 + 3y^2 = 28$ [2]

Substitute [1] in [2] to give $\quad (2y+7)^2 + 3y^2 = 28$

Hence $\quad\quad\quad\quad\quad\quad 4y^2 + 28y + 49 + 3y^2 = 28$

$\Rightarrow \quad\quad\quad\quad\quad\quad\quad 7y^2 + 28y + 21 = 0$

Always be on the lookout for a common factor which could make your working easier. Here divide by 7 to give

$y^2 + 4y + 3 = 0 \quad \Rightarrow \quad (y+3)(y+1) = 0$
$$\Rightarrow \quad y = -3 \text{ or } -1$$

Substitute in [1] to find the corresponding values of x.

When $y = -3, \quad x = -6 + 7 = 1 \quad \Rightarrow \quad x = 1, \quad y = -3$
When $y = -1, \quad x = -2 + 7 = 5 \quad \Rightarrow \quad x = 5, \quad y = -1$

Do pair your answers, and again check.

$$\text{Check:} \quad x = 1, \quad y = -3 \quad \text{LHS of } [2] = x^2 + 3y^2 = 1^2 + 3(-3)^2 = 28 = \text{RHS}$$
$$x = 5, \quad y = -1 \quad \text{LHS of } [2] = 5^2 + 3(-1)^2 = 28 = \text{RHS}$$

Quadratic equations

The most general form of the quadratic equation is

$$ax^2 + bx + c = 0, \quad a, b \text{ and } c \text{ constants.}$$

It can be solved by either factorising or using the formula

$$x = \frac{-b \pm \sqrt{(b^2 - 4ac)}}{2a}$$

Worked Example 3

(a) Solve $x^2 - 8x + 15 = 0$.

Working
$$x^2 - 8x + 15 \equiv (x - 5)(x - 3) = 0 \quad \Rightarrow \quad x = 5 \text{ or } 3$$

(b) Find to 2 decimal places the roots of the equation $2x^2 + 3x - 7 = 0$.

Working
$$2x^2 + 3x - 7 = 0 \quad \Rightarrow \quad a = 2, \quad b = 3, \quad c = -7$$

$$\Rightarrow \quad x = \frac{-3 \pm \sqrt{[9 - 4 \times 2 \times (-7)]}}{2 \times 2} = \frac{-3 \pm \sqrt{65}}{4} = 1.27 \text{ or } -2.77$$

The formula $\dfrac{-b \pm \sqrt{(b^2 - 4ac)}}{2a}$ for the roots of the quadratic equation $ax^2 + bx + c = 0$ shows that

1 roots are real provided $b^2 - 4ac \geqslant 0$,
2 roots are equal provided $b^2 - 4ac = 0$,
3 roots are complex (not real) provided $b^2 - 4ac < 0$.

Worked Example 4

(a) Find the value of k given that the equation $2x^2 + 3x - k = 0$ has equal roots.

Working
$2x^2 + 3x - k = 0$ implies, for equal roots, that $b^2 - 4ac = 0$. Hence

$$3^2 - 4 \times 2 \times (-k) = 0$$

$$\Rightarrow \quad k = -\tfrac{9}{8}$$

(b) By completing the square find the greatest value of $5 + 4x - 2x^2$ for all real x.

Working
To find the greatest value we need to incorporate the negative sign in a perfect square and, to complete the square, it is safer to take out the 2, the coefficient of x^2, as a common factor.

$$5 + 4x - 2x^2 = 5 - 2(x^2 - 2x) = 5 - 2[(x - 1)^2 - 1]$$
$$= 7 - 2(x - 1)^2$$

which has its greatest value when you subtract the minimum value of $2(x - 1)^2$ i.e. $5 + 4x - 2x^2$ has a greatest value of 7 when $x = 1$.

Inequalities

Expressions of the form $x > 6$, $2x^2 - x + 3 \geqslant 0$ are known as inequalities. Their solutions consist of a set of values of the variables concerned and may be represented on a number line as follows.

$x > 3$

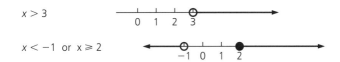

$x < -1$ or $x \geqslant 2$

Note: open circle for $>$ or $<$, solid circle for $\geqslant$ or $\leqslant$

Worked Example 5

Find the set of values of x for which $3x^2 + 2x - 8 \geqslant 0$.

Working
First solve the quadratic to find the critical values.

$3x^2 + 2x - 8 = (3x - 4)(x + 2) = 0$ when $x = \frac{4}{3}$ or -2 (critical values)

Now draw up a table to show the signs of the factors around these values, and finally combine the factors.

	$x < -2$	$-2 \leqslant x \leqslant \frac{4}{3}$	$x \geqslant \frac{4}{3}$
$(3x - 4)$	$-$	$-$	$+$
$(x + 2)$	$-$	$+$	$+$
$(3x - 4)(x + 2)$	$+$	$-$	$+$

The solution is $x \leqslant -2$ or $x \geqslant \frac{4}{3}$, i.e.

Modulus signs

Inequalities may involve modulus signs. The notation $|x| < 2$ means $-2 < x < 2$, i.e. the numerical value of x is less than 2.

The expression $|2x - 3| < 5$ means $-5 < 2x - 3 < 5$, so it is necessary to consider two inequalities: $-5 < 2x - 3$ and $2x - 3 < 5$. Now,

$-5 < 2x - 3 \quad \Rightarrow \quad 2x > -2 \quad \Rightarrow \quad x > -1$, and

$2x - 3 < 5 \quad \Rightarrow \quad 2x < 8 \quad \Rightarrow \quad x < 4$

The complete solution is, therefore, $-1 < x < 4$.

You may also be required to graph an inequality.

Consider $y = |x|$

To sketch $y = |x|$ simply draw the graph of $y = x$, but take the mirror image in the x-axis of any parts of the curve below the x-axis i.e. the dotted part of the straight line in the figure.

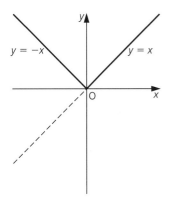

For $|2x - 3| < 5$ sketch the graph of $y = |2x - 3|$, i.e. first draw the line $y = 2x - 3$ taking the mirror image of any parts of it in the x-axis.

Then draw the line $y = 5$ and find the x coordinates of the points A and B where this line intersects the graph $y = |2x - 3|$, i.e. $x = -1$ and $x = 4$.

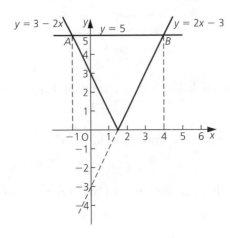

The solution to $|2x - 3| < 5$ is that part of the x-axis between $x = -1$ and $x = 4$, i.e. $-1 < x < 4$.

Always avoid squaring when solving modulus inequalities. Often you will introduce false extra solutions if you do.

Indices

You must be familiar with the rules for indices

Rules

1 $\quad a^m \times a^n = a^{m+n}$

2 $\quad \dfrac{a^m}{a^n} = a^{m-n}$

3 $\quad (a^m)^n = a^{mn}$

4 $\quad a^{-m} = \dfrac{1}{a^m}$

5 $\quad a^{1/n} = \sqrt[n]{a}$

6 $\quad a^0 = 1$

7 $\quad (ab)^n = a^n b^n$

8 $\quad \left(\dfrac{a}{b}\right)^n = \dfrac{a^n}{b^n}$

Never mix up the plus or minus signs when dealing with indices with the rules for multiplication and division.

$$(a + b)^n \neq a^n + b^n \quad \text{or} \quad a^n b^n, \quad \text{and}$$

$$(a - b)^n \neq a^n - b^n \quad \text{or} \quad \frac{a^n}{b^n}$$

Worked Example 6

(a) Given that $a^k = \sqrt[4]{a^3}$, find k.

Working

Use rule (5) above to express the RHS in the same form as the LHS.

$a^k = (a^3)^{\frac{1}{4}} = a^{\frac{3}{4}}$

Once in the same form we can compare indices, giving

$k = \frac{3}{4}$

(b) Given that $64^{x+1} = 16^{2x-3}$ find the value of x.

Working

This time the two bases 64 and 16 must be reduced to the same number. Both are powers of 4: $64 = 4^3$ and $16 = 4^2$.

$64^{x+1} = 16^{2x-3} \quad \Rightarrow \quad (4^3)^{x+1} = (4^2)^{2x-3}$ and by rule (3)

$4^{3(x+1)} = 4^{2(2x-3)} \quad \Rightarrow \quad 3(x+1) = 2(2x-3) \quad \Rightarrow \quad x = 9$

Do be careful to keep the brackets in, as a very common mistake would be to write $4^{3x+1} = 4^{4x-3}$.

Laws of logarithms

Definition: If $y = a^x$, $a > 0$, then $x = \log_a y$, i.e. x is the logarithm of y to the base a.

Laws

1 $\log_a y + \log_a x = \log_a(xy)$

2 $\log_a y - \log_a x = \log_a\left(\dfrac{y}{x}\right)$

3 $\log_a x^n = n \log_a x$

4 $\log_a a = 1$

5 $\log_a 1 = 0$

6 $\log_a x = \dfrac{\log_b x}{\log_b a}$, change of base formula.

Worked Example 7

(a) Simplify $4 \log_a 3 - 2 \log_a 2 + 3 \log_a 1$.

Working

$$4 \log_a 3 - 2 \log_a 2 + 3 \log_a 1 = \log_a 3^4 - \log_a 2^2 + 3 \cdot (0) \quad \text{using laws 3 and 5}$$
$$= \log_a \frac{3^4}{2^2} = \log_a \frac{81}{4} \quad \text{using law 2}$$

(b) Solve the equation $4^{2x+1} = 6^{1-x}$

Working

Equations such as this, where the bases of the indices are not the same and cannot be made so can be solved by taking logarithms of both sides and using $\log_a x^n = n \log_a x$. So

$4^{2x+1} = 6^{1-x} \quad \Rightarrow \quad \log 4^{2x+1} = \log 6^{1-x} \quad \Rightarrow \quad (2x+1)\log 4 = (1-x)\log 6$.

Using logarithms to the base 10 gives $1.9824x = 0.1761 \quad \Rightarrow \quad x \approx 0.0888$.

Polynomials

You must be able to add, subtract, multiply or divide simple polynomials.

Worked Example 8

(a) Multiply $2 - 3x + x^3$ by $2 - x + x^2$.

Working

Use the ordinary laws for algebraic multiplication, but leave spaces for missing terms

$$
\begin{array}{l}
\quad\quad\quad 2 - 3x \quad\quad\quad + x^3 \\
\quad\quad\quad\quad\quad 2 - x + x^2 \\
\hline
\times 2 \Rightarrow \quad 4 - 6x \quad\quad\quad + 2x^3 \\
\times (-x) \Rightarrow \quad -2x + 3x^2 \quad\quad\quad - x^4 \\
\times (x^2) \Rightarrow \quad\quad 2x^2 - 3x^3 \quad\quad + x^5 \\
\hline
4 - 8x + 5x^2 - x^3 - x^4 + x^5
\end{array}
$$

(b) Divide $x^5 - 2x^3 + x^2 + 3$ by $x^2 - 2x + 1$.

Working

$$
\begin{array}{r}
x^3 + 2x^2 + x + 1 \\
x^2 - 2x + 1 \overline{\smash{)}\, x^5 \quad\quad - 2x^3 + x^2 \quad\quad + 3} \\
\underline{x^5 - 2x^4 + x^3} \\
2x^4 - 3x^3 + x^2 \\
\underline{2x^4 - 4x^3 + 2x^2} \\
x^3 - x^2 \\
\underline{x^3 - 2x^2 + x} \\
x^2 - x + 3 \\
\underline{x^2 - 2x + 1} \\
x + 2
\end{array}
$$

Answer $\quad x^3 + 2x^2 + x + 1 + \dfrac{x + 2}{x^2 - 2x + 1}$

To help you to factorise polynomials you can use the remainder theorem/factor theorem.

The **remainder theorem** states that when a polynomial $f(x)$ is divided by $(x - a)$ the remainder is $f(a)$.

The **factor theorem** states that for a polynomial $f(x)$, if $f(a) = 0$ then $(x - a)$ is a factor of $f(x)$.

Worked Example 9

Given that $x + 2$ is a factor of $x^3 + px^2 + qx - 24$ and that division by $x - 5$ leaves a remainder of 56, find the value of the constants p and q. Solve the equation $x^3 + px^2 + qx - 24 = 0$.

Working

From the factor theorem, if $x + 2$ is a factor then

$(-2)^3 + p(-2)^2 + q(-2) - 24 = 0$

$\Rightarrow \quad\quad\quad\quad\quad\quad 4p - 2q = 32$

$\Rightarrow \quad\quad\quad\quad\quad\quad 2p - q = 16$ $\quad\quad\quad\quad\quad\quad\quad\quad\quad$ [1]

Using the remainder theorem for division by $x - 5$,

$5^3 + 5^2 p + 5q - 24 = 56$

$\Rightarrow \quad\quad\quad 5p + q = -9$ $\quad\quad\quad\quad\quad\quad\quad\quad\quad\quad\quad\quad$ [2]

Adding [1] and [2] $\quad 7p = 7 \quad \Rightarrow \quad p = 1$

Substituting in [2] $\quad\quad q = -14$

Hence $x^3 + x^2 - 14x - 24 = 0 \quad \Rightarrow \quad (x + 2)(x^2 - x - 12)$

The quadratic factor is obtained by first finding the x^2 and -12 terms and then fixing the x term. Then check the x^2 term (or the x term) in the cubic polynomial. Thus

$$x^3 + x^2 - 14x - 24 = (x+2)(x+3)(x-4) \quad \Rightarrow \quad x = -2, -3 \text{ or } 4$$

Partial fractions

Partial fractions are useful equivalent forms for more complicated fractions which you may need to differentiate, integrate or expand using the binomial theorem. You need to consider three forms which we will illustrate by examples. Note in each case the powers of the factors.

Worked Example 10

(a) Express as partial fractions $\dfrac{13}{(x-5)(2x+3)}$ (two linear factors)

Working

Let $\dfrac{13}{(x-5)(2x+3)} \equiv \dfrac{A}{x-5} + \dfrac{B}{2x+3}$

$\equiv \dfrac{A(2x+3) + B(x-5)}{(x-5)(2x+3)}$

We can now compare numerators

$13 \equiv A(2x+3) + B(x-5)$

Let $x = 5$, so $\quad 13 = 13A \quad \Rightarrow \quad A = 1$

Let $x = -1\frac{1}{2}$, so $\quad 13 = B\left(-1\frac{1}{2} - 5\right) \quad \Rightarrow \quad B = -2$

Hence $\dfrac{13}{(x-5)(2x+3)} \equiv \dfrac{1}{x-5} - \dfrac{2}{2x+3}$

(b) Express as partial fractions $\dfrac{2x^2 - 5x}{(x+2)(x-1)^2}$ (a repeated linear factor $(x-1)^2$)

Working

Let $\dfrac{2x^2 - 5x}{(x+2)(x-1)^2} \equiv \dfrac{A}{x+2} + \dfrac{B}{x-1} + \dfrac{C}{(x-1)^2}$

$\equiv \dfrac{A(x-1)^2 + B(x+2)(x-1) + C(x+2)}{(x+2)(x-1)^2}$

Comparing numerators

$2x^2 - 5x \equiv A(x-1)^2 + B(x+2)(x-1) + C(x+2)$

Let $x = 1$, so $\quad 2 - 5 = -3 = C(+1+2) \quad \Rightarrow \quad C = -1$

Let $x = -2$, so $\quad 2(-2)^2 - 5(-2) = 18 = 9A \quad \Rightarrow \quad A = 2$

Let $x = 0$, so $\quad 0 = A - 2B + 2C \quad \Rightarrow \quad 0 = 2 - 2B - 2 \quad \Rightarrow \quad B = 0$

Hence $\dfrac{2x^2 - 5x}{(x+2)(x-1)^2} \equiv \dfrac{2}{x+2} - \dfrac{1}{(x-1)^2}$

(c) Express as partial fractions $\dfrac{3x^2 - 7}{(x-2)(x^2+1)}$ (a quadratic factor (x^2+1))

Working

Let $\dfrac{3x^2 - 7}{(x-2)(x^2+1)} \equiv \dfrac{A}{x-2} + \dfrac{Bx+C}{x^2+1}$

$\equiv \dfrac{A(x^2+1) + (Bx+C)(x-2)}{(x-2)(x^2+1)}$

Comparing numerators

$$3x^2 - 7 \equiv A(x^2 + 1) + (Bx + C)(x - 2)$$

Let $x = 2$, so $12 - 7 = 5 = 5A \quad \Rightarrow \quad A = 1.$

Compare coefficients of x^2 terms $3 = A + B \quad \Rightarrow \quad 3 = 1 + B \quad \Rightarrow \quad B = 2$

Comparing constants $-7 = A - 2C = 1 - 2C \quad \Rightarrow \quad C = 4$

Hence $\dfrac{3x^2 - 7}{(x - 2)(x^2 + 1)} \equiv \dfrac{1}{x - 2} + \dfrac{2x + 4}{x^2 + 1}$

Note: In each of the above examples the degree of the numerator is less than the degree of the denominator. If this is not so then division must first be carried out.

PRACTICE QUESTIONS

1   Find the pairs of values (x, y) which satisfy the simultaneous equations

   $x - 2y = 1, \qquad 3xy - y^2 = 8$

2   Use the factor theorem to show that $3x - 2$ is a factor of $f(x)$, where
   $f(x) \equiv 6x^3 - 7x^2 - x + 2$. Hence, or otherwise, find
   (a) all the values of x for which $f(x) = 0$,
   (b) the roots of the equation $f(x + 2) = 0$.

3   Given $g(x) \equiv 3x^2 - 12x + 20$, find
   (a) the value, or values, of x for which $g(x) \leqslant 8$,
   (b) the set of values of x for which $g(x) < 56$.

4   Express in partial fractions: (a) $\dfrac{2}{x(x^2 + 2)}$ (b) $\dfrac{2}{x(x + 2)^2}$

5   The curve with equation $y = ax^2 + bx + c$, is shown, where $a > 0$. The curve touches the x-axis at the point A.

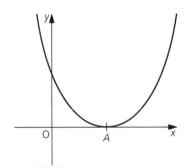

   (a) Write down an equation relating the constants a, b and c.
   (b) Find the coordinates of the point A in terms of b and a.

6   (a) Solve the equations (i) $2^x = 48$,   (ii) $2^{2y} - 2^y = -\frac{3}{16}$
   (b) Find the value of t for which

   $$\log_8\left(\frac{t}{2}\right) = \frac{\log_8 t}{\log_8 2}$$

   (Give answers to 3 s.f. where appropriate.)

7   (a) Giving your answers to 3 s.f., solve for x

   $$x(2x + 3) = 11$$

   (b) Given $f(x) \equiv x^3 - 28x - 48$
      (i) Express $f(x)$ as a product of three linear factors.

      (ii) Express $\dfrac{1}{f(x)}$ in partial fractions.

8 The variables x and y are related by the equation

$$y = kx^n$$

where k and n are constants. Given that $y = 25$ when $x = 2$ and $y = 0.5$ when $x = 7$, find values for k and n to 3 s.f.

9 Sketch the graphs of $y = |x + 2|$, $y = 6 - 2x$ and $y = \frac{1}{2}x + 2$. Hence, or otherwise, find the set of values of x for which
(a) $|x + 2| > 6 - 2x$,
(b) $|x + 2| \leqslant \frac{1}{2}x + 2$.

10 (a) Simplify $\dfrac{1}{3 - \sqrt{2}} + \dfrac{1}{3 + \sqrt{2}}$

(b) Given that $5 - \sqrt{3}$ is a root of the equation

$$x^2 - 10x + p = 0$$

find the value of p and the other root of the equation in surd form.

If you need further help on basic algebra techniques refer to Chapter 3 of the A/AS Longman Study Guide by the same authors

2 *Sequences and series*

✓ **TOPIC OUTLINE AND REVISION TIPS**

▶ A succession of terms

$$U_1, U_2, U_3, \ldots, U_n, \ldots$$

formed by a rule is called a **sequence**.
▶ U_n is called the nth term, or the **general term**.
▶ You need to recognise sequences which **converge**, **diverge**, **oscillate** or have **periodic** properties.

Examples of these different sequences are:

▶ **Convergent** The sequence $U_n = 2 - \left(\frac{1}{4}\right)^n$ has successive terms

$$\frac{7}{4}, \frac{31}{16}, \frac{127}{64}, \ldots$$

found by taking $n = 1, 2, 3, \ldots$, in turn.
As n increases, $\left(\frac{1}{4}\right)^n \to 0$ so that $U_n \to 2$ and we say the sequence is **convergent**.
▶ **Divergent** The sequence $U_n = n^2$ has successive terms

$$1, 4, 9, \ldots$$

As n increases, U_n gets larger without limit and we say the sequence is **divergent**.
▶ **Oscillate finitely** The sequence $U_n = (-1)^n$ has successive terms

$$-1, \ 1, \ -1, \ 1, \ldots$$

and is said to **oscillate finitely** between -1 and 1.
▶ **Oscillate infinitely** The sequence $U_n = (-2)^n$ has successive terms

$$-2, 4, -8, 16, \ldots$$

which increase as n increases without limit, but the signs of the terms alternate. This sequence **oscillates infinitely** between $-\infty$ and $+\infty$.
▶ **Periodic** The sequence $U_n = \sin \frac{n\pi}{2}$ has successive terms

$$1, 0, -1, 0, \ldots$$

▶ After 4 terms the sequence repeats the terms again in the same order. This sequence is **periodic** over 4 terms.

Recurrence relations
A relation may exist between two, or more, terms of a sequence whose initial terms are also given. This is called a **recurrence relation**.

Worked Example 1
Given that $U_{n+2} = U_{n+1} + U_n$ and $U_1 = 1, U_2 = 3$, find U_3 and U_4.

Working
By taking $n = 1$, $\quad U_3 = U_2 + U_1 = 3 + 1 = 4.$
By taking $n = 2$, $\quad U_4 = U_3 + U_2 = 4 + 3 = 7.$

$\sum$ notation and series

If the first N terms of a sequence are added together we have

$$U_1 + U_2 + U_3 + \ldots + U_N.$$

This is called a **finite series** and it can also be written as $\displaystyle\sum_{n=1}^{N} U_n$ which means

the sum of the terms $U_1, U_2, \ldots, U_N$, where U_n is the general term of the series.

For example $\displaystyle\sum_{n=1}^{17} 2n^2 = 2 + 2(2^2) + 2(3^2) + \ldots + 2(17^2)$, a series of 17 terms.

Arithmetic progressions

The sequence $U_n = a + (n-1)d$, where a and d are constants, has terms a, $a + d$, $a + 2d$, ..., and it is clear that $U_n - U_{n-1} = d$ because each successive term is d more than the one immediately before it. This sequence is called an **arithmetic progression** (AP), d is called the **common difference** and the series

$$a + (a + d) + (a + 2d) + \ldots + \{a + (n-1)d\}$$

is called an **arithmetic series** of n terms.

The sum of these terms is

$$S_n = \frac{n}{2}\{2a + (n-1)d\}$$

and the nth term is

$$T_n = a + (n-1)d.$$

Worked Example 2

An arithmetic series has 4th term 191 and the sum of the first 10 terms is 1 865. Find the first term, the common difference and the sum of the first 20 terms.

Working
Since the 4th term is 191,

$$a + 3d = 191 \tag{1}$$

Since the sum of 10 terms is 1 865,

$$\tfrac{10}{2}(2a + 9d) = 1\,865 \quad\Rightarrow\quad 2a + 9d = 373 \tag{2}$$

Solving [1] and [2] simultaneously $\quad 2a + 9d = 373$
$$3a + 9d = 573 \quad ([1] \times 3)$$

Subtracting $\quad\Rightarrow\quad a = 200$
From [1] $\quad\Rightarrow\quad d = -3$
$$S_{20} = \tfrac{20}{2}(2a + 19d) = 10(400 - 57) = 3\,430$$

Geometric progressions

The sequence $U_n = ar^{n-1}$, where a and r are constants, has successive terms

$$a, ar, ar^2, \ldots$$

It is clear that $U_n = rU_{n-1}$ because each successive term is r times the one immediately before it.

This sequence is called a **geometric progression** (GP), r is called the **common ratio** and the series

$$a + ar + ar^2 + \ldots + ar^{n-1}$$

is called a **geometric series** of n terms.

The sum of these terms is

$$S_n = \frac{a(1 - r^n)}{1 - r} \qquad (r \neq 1)$$

and the nth term is

$$T_n = ar^{n-1}.$$

Provided that $|r| < 1$, the infinite geometric series $a + ar + ar^2 + \ldots$ has a sum of $\frac{a}{1 - r}$.

Worked Example 3

A geometric series has first term 0.5 and common ratio -2.3. Find, to 3 sig. figs, the sum of the first 12 terms.

Working

We take $a = 0.5$, $r = -2.3$ and $n = 12$ in the formula to obtain

$$S_{12} = \frac{0.5\{1 - (-2.3)^{12}\}}{1 - (-2.3)} \approx 3\,320 \text{ (3 s.f.)}$$

Worked Example 4

A geometric series has first term 8 and second term 6. Find the sum to infinity of this series.

Working

We have $a = 8$, $ar = 6$, giving $r = \frac{6}{8} = \frac{3}{4}$. Hence

$$S_\infty = \frac{a}{1 - r} = \frac{8}{1 - \frac{3}{4}} = 32$$

Successive terms of APs and GPs

The terms a, b, c are successive terms of an AP if

$$b - a = c - b \quad \Rightarrow \quad 2b = a + c$$

The terms a, b, c are successive terms of a GP if

$$\frac{b}{a} = \frac{c}{b} \quad \Rightarrow \quad b^2 = ac$$

Binomial expansions

For a positive integer n,

$$(a + b)^n = a^n + \binom{n}{1}a^{n-1}b + \binom{n}{2}a^{n-2}b^2 + \ldots + \binom{n}{r}a^{n-r}b^r + \ldots + b^n,$$

$$(1 + x)^n = 1 + \binom{n}{1}x + \binom{n}{2}x^2 + \ldots + \binom{n}{r}x^r + \ldots + x^n,$$

where $\binom{n}{r} \equiv {}^nC_r = \frac{n!}{r!(n - r)!}$

When n is rational but not a positive integer, the binomial expansion is an infinite series

$$(1 + x)^n = 1 + nx + \frac{n(n - 1)}{2!}x^2 + \frac{n(n - 1)(n - 2)}{3!}x^3 + \ldots$$

This series is only valid when $|x| < 1$.

Worked Example 5

Expand $(3x - 2)^4$

Working

In the expansion of $(a + b)^n$, take $a = 3x$, $b = -2$ and $n = 4$ and we obtain

$$(3x - 2)^4 = (3x)^4 + \binom{4}{1}(3x)^3(-2) + \binom{4}{2}(3x)^2(-2)^2 + \binom{4}{3}(3x)(-2)^3 + (-2)^4$$

Now $\binom{4}{1} = 4$, $\binom{4}{2} = \dfrac{4!}{2!2!} = 6$, $\binom{4}{3} = \dfrac{4!}{3!1!} = 4$, so

$$(3x - 2)^4 = 81x^4 - 216x^3 + 216x^2 - 96x + 16$$

Worked Example 6

Find in ascending powers of x the first four terms in the series expansion of
(a) $(1 - 2x)^{-1}$, (b) $(3 + x)^{\frac{1}{2}}$. State, in each case, the set of values of x for which your series is valid.

Working

(a) Using the series for $(1 + x)^n$, for n rational, we have, replacing x by $(-2x)$ and n by -1,

$$(1 - 2x)^{-1} = 1 + (-1)(-2x) + \frac{(-1)(-1-1)}{2!}(-2x)^2$$
$$+ \frac{(-1)(-1-1)(-1-2)}{3!}(-2x)^3 + \dots$$
$$= 1 + 2x + 4x^2 + 8x^3 + \dots$$

The series is valid for $|2x| < 1 \implies |x| < \frac{1}{2}$, that is $-\frac{1}{2} < x < \frac{1}{2}$.

(b) Before the expansion of $(3 + x)^{\frac{1}{2}}$ can be found, we must rewrite $(3 + x)^{\frac{1}{2}}$ in a form similar to that of $(1 + x)^n$ like this:

$$(3 + x)^{\frac{1}{2}} = \left\{ 3\left(1 + \frac{x}{3}\right) \right\}^{\frac{1}{2}} = 3^{\frac{1}{2}}\left(1 + \frac{x}{3}\right)^{\frac{1}{2}}.$$

Now the series for $\left(1 + \dfrac{x}{3}\right)^{\frac{1}{2}}$ can be obtained by taking $n = \frac{1}{2}$ and by replacing x by $\dfrac{x}{3}$ in the series for $(1 + x)^n$.

$$(3 + x)^{\frac{1}{2}} = 3^{\frac{1}{2}}\left(1 + \frac{x}{3}\right)^{\frac{1}{2}}$$
$$= 3^{\frac{1}{2}}\left[1 + \left(\frac{1}{2}\right)\left(\frac{x}{3}\right) + \frac{\frac{1}{2}\left(\frac{1}{2} - 1\right)}{2!}\left(\frac{x}{3}\right)^2 + \frac{\frac{1}{2}\left(\frac{1}{2} - 1\right)\left(\frac{1}{2} - 2\right)}{3!}\left(\frac{x}{3}\right)^3 + \dots\right]$$
$$= 3^{\frac{1}{2}}\left(1 + \frac{1}{6}x - \frac{1}{72}x^2 + \frac{1}{432}x^3 + \dots\right)$$

The series is valid for $\left|\dfrac{x}{3}\right| < 1$, that is $|x| < 3$ or $-3 < x < 3$.

?

PRACTICE QUESTIONS

1. (a) Expand $(1 - x)^6$ in ascending powers of x, simplifying the coefficients.
   (b) Use your expansion to find $(0.997)^6$ correct to 8 d.p.
2. (a) Find the sum to n terms of the geometric series

$$\frac{1}{2} + \frac{1}{2^2} + \frac{1}{2^3} + \dots$$

(b) Write down the sum to infinity of the series.

(c) Find the least number of terms which need be taken so that their sum exceeds 0.9999.

3 Calculate the value of (a) $\displaystyle\sum_{n=1}^{80}(2n-1)$, (b) $\displaystyle\sum_{n=1}^{9}144(2^{-n})$, giving your answer to (b) to 1 d.p.

4 Given that U_n is the nth term of a sequence, state whether the sequence is convergent, divergent, oscillating or periodic, giving details of the behaviour in each case when U_n equals

(a) 3^{n-3},

(b) $2\cos n\pi$,

(c) $\cos^2\dfrac{n\pi}{4}$,

(d) $2+3^{3-n}$.

5 The value of a machine depreciates each year by an amount which is $r\%$ of its value at the beginning of the year. If the value of the machine is £3 000 now and $r=12$, find

(a) its value after 9 complete years, giving your answer to the nearest £,

(b) the number of years that have elapsed when the value of the machine is £375.

6 (a) Find in ascending powers of x the first 4 terms in the binomial expansion of $(1+x)^{\frac{1}{3}}$.

(b) Hence find the cube root of 1.02 to 6 decimal places.

7 (a) Express $\dfrac{2-3x}{1-3x+2x^2}$ in partial fractions.

(b) Hence expand $\dfrac{2-3x}{1-3x+2x^2}$ in ascending powers of x up to and including the term in x^3, stating the set of values of x for which the expansion is valid.

8 A sequence has nth term U_n, where

$$U_n = 4 - x^n$$

Explain whether or not the sequence is convergent when x equals

(a) $\frac{1}{3}$, (b) -1, (c) 2.

(d) When $x=\frac{1}{3}$, find $\displaystyle\sum_{n=1}^{N}U_n$.

If you need further help on sequences and series refer to Chapter 4 of the A/AS Longman Study Guide by the same authors

3 Coordinate geometry

TOPIC OUTLINE AND REVISION TIPS

You must be familiar with the various forms for the equation of a straight line, a circle, and the simple forms for the parabola, ellipse, and rectangular hyperbola. Questions will almost certainly be set involving tangents and normals to a curve whose equations may be given in either cartesian or parametric form.

Straight line

1 $ax + by + c = 0$, a, b, c constants,   general equation of straight line.
2 $y = mx + c$,   straight line gradient m, intercept on y-axis $(0, c)$.
3 $y - y_1 = m(x - x_1)$ straight line gradient m, passing through the point (x_1, y_1).
4 $\dfrac{y - y_1}{y_2 - y_1} = \dfrac{x - x_1}{x_2 - x_1}$ straight line passing through the points (x_1, y_1), (x_2, y_2).
5 Two lines are parallel if their gradients m_1 and m_2 are equal, i.e. if $m_1 = m_2$.
6 Two lines are perpendicular if their gradients m_1 and m_2 are such that $m_1 m_2 = -1$.

7 The gradient of the line joining the points (x_1, y_1) and (x_2, y_2) is $\dfrac{y_2 - y_1}{x_2 - x_1}$.

8 The distance between two points $(x_1, y_1)(x_2, y_2)$ is $\sqrt{\{(x_2 - x_1)^2 + (y_2 - y_1)^2\}}$.

9 The midpoint of the straight line joining the two points (x_1, y_1) and (x_2, y_2) has coordinates $\{\frac{1}{2}(x_1 + x_2), \frac{1}{2}(y_1 + y_2)\}$. Do not make the common mistake of using minus signs here.

You should be able to recognise and sketch curves such as those shown below.

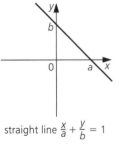

straight line $\frac{x}{a} + \frac{y}{b} = 1$

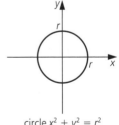

circle $x^2 + y^2 = r^2$

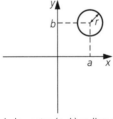

circle centre (a, b) radius r
$(x - a)^2 + (y - b)^2 = r^2$

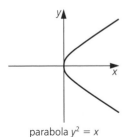

parabola $y^2 = x$

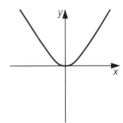

parabola $y = x^2$

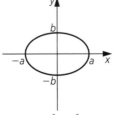

ellipse $\frac{x^2}{a^2} + \frac{y^2}{b^2} = 1$

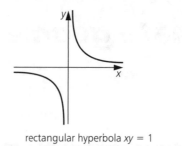

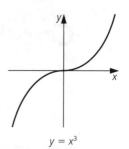

rectangular hyperbola $xy = 1$ $y = x^3$

Worked Example 1

Find the equation of the straight line joining the points $A(1, -2)$ and $B\left(3, 1\frac{1}{2}\right)$. Show that the line passes through the point $C\left(-1, -5\frac{1}{2}\right)$ and find the distance AC.

Working

$A \equiv (1, -2), \quad B \equiv \left(3, 1\frac{1}{2}\right)$.

You are given two points on the line so it is necessary to use the equation

$$\frac{y - y_1}{y_2 - y_1} = \frac{x - x_1}{x_2 - x_1}$$

$$\Rightarrow \quad \frac{y - (-2)}{1\frac{1}{2} - (-2)} = \frac{x - 1}{3 - 1} \quad \Rightarrow \quad \frac{y + 2}{3\frac{1}{2}} = \frac{x - 1}{2}$$

$$\Rightarrow \quad 2y = 3\frac{1}{2}x - 7\frac{1}{2} \quad \text{or} \quad 4y = 7x - 15$$

If this line passes through the point C then the coordinates of C satisfy the equation

$$\text{LHS} = 4y = 4 \times \left(-5\frac{1}{2}\right) = -22$$
$$\text{RHS} = 7x - 15 = 7 \times (-1) - 15 = -22 = \text{LHS}$$

$$AC^2 = \sqrt{\left\{(1 - (-1))^2 + \left(-2 - \left(-5\frac{1}{2}\right)\right)^2\right\}} = \sqrt{\left(4 + \frac{49}{4}\right)} = \sqrt{\frac{65}{4}} = \frac{1}{2}\sqrt{65}$$

Worked Example 2

The straight line joining points A and B has midpoint M. Given that $A \equiv (2, -3)$ and $M \equiv (5, 1)$ calculate the coordinates of B.

Working

Let the coordinates of B be (x, y). Then if M is the midpoint of AB

$$\frac{2 + x}{2} = 5 \quad \Rightarrow \quad x = 8 \quad \text{and} \quad \frac{-3 + y}{2} = 1 \quad \Rightarrow \quad y = 5$$

Worked Example 3

Find an equation of the perpendicular bisector of the line joining the points $A(3, -5)$ and $B(-1, -3)$.

Working

To find an equation we need the gradient of the line and the coordinates of the midpoint of AB.

The gradient of AB is $\dfrac{y_2 - y_1}{x_2 - x_1} = \dfrac{-3 - (-5)}{-1 - 3} = \dfrac{2}{-4} = -\dfrac{1}{2}$. Hence the line perpendicular to AB has gradient m where $\left(-\frac{1}{2}\right)m = -1$, i.e. $m = 2$.

The midpoint of AB is $\left\{\frac{1}{2}(3 + (-1)), \frac{1}{2}(-5 - 3)\right\} = (1, -4)$.

Using $y - y_1 = m(x - x_1)$ where $(x_1, y_1) \equiv (1, -4)$ and $m = 2$, we get

$$y - (-4) = 2(x - 1) \quad \Rightarrow \quad y = 2x - 6$$

Three dimensions

The distance between two points in two-dimensional space can be extended to three-dimensional space:

$$ON^2 = x_1^2 + y_1^2, \quad \triangle OMN \text{ right-angled at } M$$

$$OP^2 = ON^2 + NP^2 = \left(x_1^2 + y_1^2\right) + z_1^2, \triangle ONP \text{ right-angled at } N$$

$\Rightarrow \quad OP = \sqrt{\left(x_1^2 + y_1^2 + z_1^2\right)}$

$\Rightarrow \quad$ If $P \equiv (x_1, y_1, z_1), Q \equiv (x_2, y_2, z_2)$ then

$$PQ = \sqrt{\left\{(x_2 - x_1)^2 + (y_2 - y_1)^2 + (z_2 - z_1)^2\right\}}$$

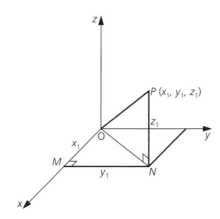

Worked Example 4

Find the distance between the points $A(3, 1, -2)$ and $B(1, -2, 4)$.

Working
$AB^2 = (1 - 3)^2 + (-2 - 1)^2 + \left(4 - (-2)\right)^2 = 4 + 9 + 36 = 49$

$\Rightarrow \quad AB = \sqrt{49} = 7$

Parametric coordinates

It is sometimes more convenient to express a relation between two variables x and y, say, by introducing a third variable t, say. For example the cartesian equation $y^2 = 4x$ can be replaced by the equations $x = t^2, y = 2t$ since whatever the value of t the equations $x = t^2, y = 2t$ satisfy the relationship $y^2 = 4x$. The new variable t is called a parameter and $x = t^2, y = 2t$ are called parametric equations.

Curves whose equation is given in parametric coordinates can be sketched either by finding corresponding values of x and y for various values of t or, if the equations are adaptable, by eliminating t between the parametric equations, to obtain the cartesian equation.

Worked Example 5

Sketch the curve given by the parametric equations $x = 2 - t, y = t^2$.

Working
Eliminate t between the equations:

$x = 2 - t \Rightarrow t = 2 - x$

$y = t^2$

$\Rightarrow y = (2 - x)^2$

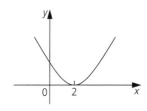

Alternatively, plot the points

t	-3	-2	-1	0	1	2	3
x	5	4	3	2	1	0	-1
y	9	4	1	0	1	4	9

This method should be employed only when it is difficult or impossible to eliminate the parameter t.

Curve sketching

If you do not have a graphical calculator to help you sketch a curve, then ask yourself the following questions when the equation of the curve is given in cartesian form.

1 Where does the curve cut the axes?
2 Is the curve symmetrical about the x-axis, i.e. does its equation contain even powers of y only?
3 Is the curve symmetrical about the y-axis, i.e. does its equation contain even powers of x only?
4 What happens to y if x is made large, i.e. $x \rightarrow \pm \infty$?
5 What happens to x if y is made large, i.e. $y \rightarrow \pm \infty$?
6 Are there any values (a) of x which make y infinite? (b) of y which make x infinite?
7 Are there any points for which the curve is undefined?
8 Finally, if all this fails, where do the stationary points occur?

Worked Example 6

(a) Sketch the curve $y = (x-1)^3$.

If $x = 1$, $y = 0$
If $x = 0$, $y = -1$
The curve does not have any symmetry.
If x is made large, y gets even larger
i.e. if $x \rightarrow +\infty$, $y \rightarrow +\infty$
if $x \rightarrow -\infty$, $y \rightarrow -\infty$
The curve is defined for all values of x and y.

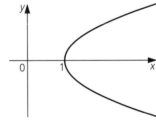

(b) Sketch the curve $y^2 = 4(x-1)$.

If $x = 1$, $y = 0$
The curve contains even powers of y only, so is symmetrical about x-axis
If $x < 1$ then $y^2 < 0$ which is impossible, hence curve exists only for $x \geqslant 1$
If $x \rightarrow +\infty$, $y^2 \rightarrow \infty$, $y \rightarrow \pm \infty$.

(c) Sketch the curve
$y = (x+2)(x-1)(x-3)$.
$y = 0$ when $x = -2$, 1 or 3
$x = 0$, $y = 6$
If $x \rightarrow \infty$, $y \rightarrow \infty$
If $x \rightarrow -\infty$, $y \rightarrow -\infty$
If $x > 3$, $y > 0$
If $1 < x < 3$, $y < 0$ (Try $x = 2$)
If $-2 < x < 1$, $y > 0$ (Try $x = -1$)
If $x < -2$, $y < 0$.

If you were asked for more specific information concerning the turning points then you would have to resort to differentiation.

Reduction to linear form

Many equations which would normally produce curves (i.e. not straight lines) when values of y are plotted against x can be rearranged and new variables chosen so that a straight line graph can be obtained. This exercise is particularly useful when it is required to check an experimental law in science and economics.

Consider the equation $y = ax + bx^2$, where a and b are constants. This is the equation of a parabolic curve. However, rearranging the equation in the form $\dfrac{y}{x} = a + bx$, and making the substitution $\dfrac{y}{x} = Y \Rightarrow Y = a + bx$, results in a straight line graph when x is plotted against Y.

Comparing with the equation $y = mx + c$ we now see that a is given by the intercept on the Y-axis and b is the gradient of the straight line.

Worked Example 7

Corresponding values of the variables x and y are given in the table below. It is believed that x and y are related by an equation of the form $y = Ax + Bx^2$ where A and B are constants. By rearranging the equation in the form $\dfrac{y}{x} = A + Bx$ and drawing a graph of $\dfrac{y}{x}$ against x, verify that this is so and determine approximate values of the constants A and B.

x	1	$1\frac{1}{2}$	2	$2\frac{1}{2}$	3	$3\frac{1}{2}$	4
y	−0.5	0.37	2	4.38	7.5	11.37	16

x	1.0	1.5	2	2.5	3.0	3.5	4.0
$\dfrac{y}{x}$	−0.5	0.247	1.0	1.75	2.5	3.25	4

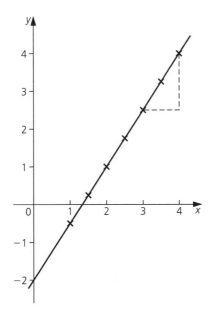

$\dfrac{y}{x} = A + Bx$ is a straight-line graph

$\Rightarrow \quad A = \text{intercept on } \dfrac{y}{x}\text{-axis} \approx -1.95$

$\qquad B = \text{gradient} \approx \dfrac{1.5}{1} \approx 1.5$

$\Rightarrow \quad y = -1.95x + 1.5x^2$

Examples of other given equations and rearranged equations are

Given equation	Rearranged equation	Axes	
		Y axis	X axis
$y = ax + \dfrac{b}{x}$	$xy = ax^2 + b$	$Y = xy$	$X = x^2$
$y = \dfrac{1}{ax + b}$	$\dfrac{1}{y} = ax + b$	$Y = \dfrac{1}{y}$	$X = x$
$y = ax^b$	$\log y = \log a + b \log x$	$Y = \log y$	$X = \log x$
$y = ae^{bx}$	$\ln y = \ln a + bx$	$Y = \ln y$	$X = x$
$\dfrac{a}{x} + \dfrac{b}{y} = 1$	$a\left(\dfrac{1}{x}\right) + b\left(\dfrac{1}{y}\right) = 1$	$Y = \dfrac{1}{y}$	$X = \dfrac{1}{x}$

PRACTICE QUESTIONS

1 The points P, Q and R are at $(1, 2)$, $(9, 6)$ and $(3, 8)$ respectively.
   (a) Find the coordinates of M, the midpoint of PQ.
   (b) Show that the line RM is perpendicular to PQ.
   (c) Find the area of $\triangle PQR$.

2 Sketch the line $2x + y = 1$ and the ellipse with equation $4x^2 + y^2 = 13$. Calculate the coordinates of their points of intersection.

3 Sketch the line $y = 3 - x$ and the parabola with equation $y = (x - 1)^2$. The curve and line meet in the points A and B, where the x-coordinate of A is positive.
   Find the coordinates of A and B and an equation of the tangent to the curve at A.

4 The origin is O and A and B are the points $(3, 2)$ and $(2, 1)$ respectively. Find the equation of the circle
   (a) which passes through O, A and B,
   (b) which has AO as a diameter.

5 (a) Find the equations of the lines l_1 and l_2 which are parallel to the lines $y = 3x$ and $y = 2x$ and pass through the point $A(4, 3)$.
   (b) The points A and the origin O are opposite vertices of a parallelogram whose sides are l_1, l_2, $y = 3x$ and $y = 2x$. Find for this parallelogram (i) the area, (ii) the lengths of its diagonals.

6 The isosceles triangle ABC has $\angle BAC = 90°$. The coordinates of A are $(0, -2)$ and the line BC has equation $4x - y - 19 = 0$ and B is in the first quadrant.
   (a) Find equations for the lines AB and AC.
   (b) Find the coordinates of B and show that C has coordinates $(3, -7)$.
   (c) Find the area of $\triangle ABC$.

4 Functions

✓ ◎ **TOPIC OUTLINE AND REVISION TIPS**

▶ **Function**   A **function** is a mapping between two variables, x and y, in which x is called the **independent variable** and y is called the **dependent variable**. The function f is then written as

$$f : x \mapsto y \quad \text{or} \quad y = f(x)$$

▶ **Domain**   The set of values taken by x is called the **domain** of f and the corresponding set taken by y is called the **range** of the function f.

▶ **Rule**   When you describe a function you must state both the **rule** for getting from x to y and the **domain**.

Worked Example 1

State the rule, domain and range, and draw the graph of the function f given by

$$f : x \mapsto 3x^2 - 2 \qquad x \in \mathbb{R}$$

Working

The **rule** is '3 times the square of x then take away 2' and the **domain** is 'all real values of x'.

Since for all $x \in \mathbb{R}$, $3x^2 \geqslant 0$, then $3x^2 - 2 \geqslant -2$ and so the **range** of f is y where $y \in \mathbb{R}$ and $y \geqslant -2$.

The graph of f is shown below.

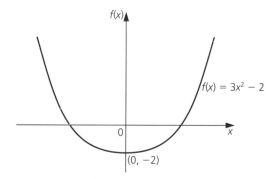

Composite function

For two functions f and g the composite function fg (sometimes written $f \circ g$) is formed by applying the rule of f to $g(x)$, that is

$$fg : x \mapsto f[g(x)] = fg(x)$$

Similarly, the composite function gf is formed by applying the rule of g to $f(x)$: that is

$$gf : x \mapsto g[f(x)] = gf(x)$$

Worked Example 2

Given that $f(x) = 3x^2 - 2$, $x \in \mathbb{R}$ and $g(x) = e^{2x}$, $x \in \mathbb{R}$, form the composite functions fg and gf.

Working

$$fg(x) = f[g(x)] = f\left(e^{2x}\right) = 3\left(e^{2x}\right)^2 - 2$$
$$\therefore \quad fg(x) = 3e^{4x} - 2 \qquad x \in \mathbb{R}$$
$$gf(x) = g[f(x)] = g\left[3x^2 - 2\right] = e^{2(3x^2 - 2)}$$
$$\therefore \quad gf(x) = e^{6x^2 - 4} \qquad x \in \mathbb{R}$$

A one–one function

This is such that each member of the domain corresponds to one, and only one, member of the range.

Inverse functions

For a one–one function f, an **inverse function** f^{-1} exists and $ff^{-1}(x) = f^{-1}f(x) = x$. The line $y = x$ is an axis of symmetry for the graphs of $y = f(x)$ and $y = f^{-1}(x)$

Worked Example 3

The exponential function $e^x, x \in \mathbb{R}$, and the logarithmic function $\ln x, x > 0, x \in \mathbb{R}$, are inverse functions. Note that the range of each is the domain of the other and their graphs are shown below.

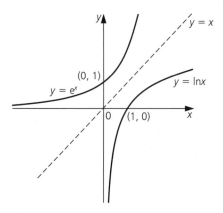

Worked Example 4

The function f is defined by

$$f : x \mapsto \frac{2x - 1}{x + 2} \qquad x \neq -2, x \in \mathbb{R}$$

Find, in a similar form, the inverse function f^{-1}.

Working

We write $y = \dfrac{2x - 1}{x + 2}$ and express x in terms of y.

$$y(x + 2) = 2x - 1 \quad \Rightarrow \quad xy + 2y = 2x - 1$$
$$\Rightarrow \quad 2y + 1 = 2x - xy$$
$$\therefore \quad x(2 - y) = 2y + 1$$
$$x = \frac{2y + 1}{2 - y}$$

Interchanging x and $y \equiv$ reflecting in line $y = x$.

Therefore the inverse curve has equation $y = \dfrac{2x + 1}{2 - x}$ and

$$f^{-1} : x \mapsto \frac{2x + 1}{2 - x} \qquad x \in \mathbb{R}, x \neq 2$$

Simple transformations of the curve with equation $y = f(x)$

1 $y = af(x)$

All points on x-axis remain the same.

The point $[t, f(t)]$ on $y = f(x)$ goes to $[t, af(t)]$ on $y = af(x)$.

The transformation stretches the curve out in the y direction

2 $y = f(x) + a$

Translation of curve through a distance a in y^+ direction for $a > 0$ and in the y^- direction for $a < 0$.

3 $y = f(x + a)$

Translation of curve in x^+ direction for $a < 0$ and in x^- direction for $a > 0$.

4 $y = f(ax)$

All points on y-axis remain the same.

The point $[t, f(t)]$ on $y = f(x)$ goes to $[at, f(at)]$ on $y = f(ax)$.

Worked Example 5

Sketch the curve $y = 2x - x^2$. Apply, in turn, the four transformations listed above to the curve $y = 2x - x^2$ showing the transformed curve in each case, for $a = 3$.

Working

$y = 2x - x^2$

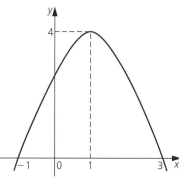

1 $y = 3(2x - x^2) \quad \equiv \quad y = af(x)$

Stretches curve out in y-direction

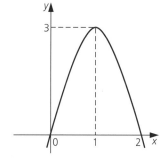

2 $y = (2x - x^2) + 3$
$\equiv f(x) + a$

Translates curve through distance 3 in positive y direction

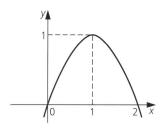

3 $y = 2(x + 3) - (x + 3)^2$
$\equiv f(x + a)$

Translates curve through distance 3 in negative x direction.

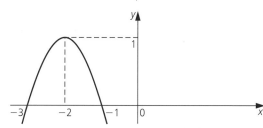

4 $y = 2(3x) - (3x)^2$
     $\equiv f(ax)$

Squeezes curve up in the
positive x direction

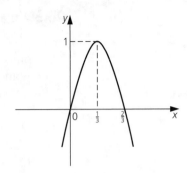

PRACTICE QUESTIONS

1 The function f is defined by

$$f : x \mapsto \frac{5}{1+x^2} \qquad x \in \mathbb{R}, x \geqslant 0$$

(a) Find the range of f.
(b) Define the inverse function f^{-1}.
(c) Sketch the curves $y = f(x)$ and $y = f^{-1}(x)$ on the same diagram.

2 The functions f and g are defined by

$$f : x \mapsto x^2 + 2 \qquad x \in \mathbb{R}$$

$$g : x \mapsto x - 3 \qquad x \in \mathbb{R}$$

(a) Find in terms of x: (i) $fg(x)$, (ii) $gf(x)$, (iii) $ff(x)$.
(b) Find the set of values of x for which $fg^{-1}(x) \leqslant 6$.

3 Show by means of sketches how the curve $y = 3 - \cos 2x$ can be built up by a series of simple transformations from the graph of the curve $y = \cos x$ for $-\pi \leqslant x \leqslant \pi$.

4 The curve $y = f(x)$ is shown and is symmetrical about the line $x = 2$, meeting the x-axis at $(4, 0)$ and the origin. The range of $f(x)$ is y, where $y \leqslant 7$, and the curve has just one turning point.

Sketch, in separate diagrams, the curves with equations
(a) $y = f(x + 4)$,
(b) $y = f(x) - 4$, (c) $y = -f(2x)$, (d) $y^2 = f(x)$.

5 (a) Sketch the curve with equation $y = x^2(2 - x)$, where the coordinates of intersections with the axes and turning points should be given.
(b) Hence, or otherwise, sketch the curves with equations

(i) $y^2 = x^2(2 - x)$

(ii) $y = \dfrac{1}{x^2(2 - x)}$.

Trigonometry

TOPIC OUTLINE AND REVISION TIPS

Degrees and radians

All angles are measured in either degrees or radians. Do make sure that you know which unit you are working in and give your answers in the units that the question requires.

One complete revolution $= 2\pi$ radians $= 360°$ so,

Degrees	$0°$	$30°$	$45°$	$60°$	$90°$	$180°$	$360°$
Radians	0	$\dfrac{\pi}{6}$	$\dfrac{\pi}{4}$	$\dfrac{\pi}{3}$	$\dfrac{\pi}{2}$	π	2π

Mensuration of circle

For a circle radius r, θ measured in radians

Arc length of $AB = r\theta$,

Area of sector $ACB = \frac{1}{2}r^2\theta$

Area of segment (minor) $ABD = \frac{1}{2}r^2(\theta - \sin\theta)$

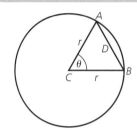

Right-angled triangle

Remember, for any right-angled triangle OAB

$$\sin\theta = \frac{\text{Opposite}}{\text{Hypotenuse}} = \frac{AB}{OB} = \frac{y}{r}$$

$$\cos\theta = \frac{\text{Adjacent}}{\text{Hypotenuse}} = \frac{OA}{OB} = \frac{x}{r}$$

$$\tan\theta = \frac{\text{Opposite}}{\text{Adjacent}} = \frac{AB}{OA} = \frac{y}{x}$$

Further, $\operatorname{cosec}\theta = \dfrac{1}{\sin\theta}$, $\sec\theta = \dfrac{1}{\cos\theta}$, $\cot\theta = \dfrac{1}{\tan\theta}$

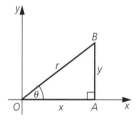

Angles over 90°

Remember, also, that for angles over $90°$ we can still use the above definitions in terms of x, y and r, but that whilst r is always positive the signs of x and y must be taken into account. A useful aid in remembering which trigonometric ratios are positive is the CAST diagram

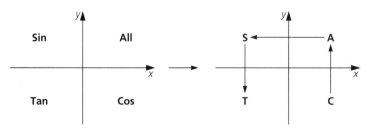

Worked Example 1

Find the values of (a) $\sin 210°$, (b) $\tan 120°$, (c) $\cos 315°$.

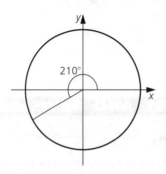

Working

(a) $210°$ is in the 3rd quadrant, so
$$\sin 210° = -\sin 30° = -\tfrac{1}{2},$$

(b) $120°$ is in the 2nd quadrant, so
$$\tan 120° = -\tan 60° = -\sqrt{3},$$

(c) $315°$ is in the 4th quadrant, so
$$\cos 315° = \cos 45° = \frac{1}{\sqrt{2}} = \frac{\sqrt{2}}{2}.$$

Always check your answer on your calculator.

Worked Example 2

In the diagram below, $OA = OB = 15$ cm and $AC = CB = 12$ cm,
AMB is the arc of a circle centre C radius AC,
ANB is the arc of a circle centre O radius OA.
Calculate to 2 decimal places: (a) $A\widehat{O}B$ in radians, (b) area $\triangle OAB$ (c) area of the shaded region R.

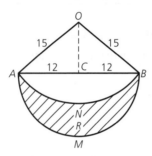

Working

(a) From $\triangle AOC$

$\sin A\widehat{O}C = \frac{12}{15} = 0.8 \quad \Rightarrow \quad A\widehat{O}C = 0.927$ radians ≈ 0.93

$\Rightarrow A\widehat{O}C = 2A\widehat{O}C \approx 1.85$ radians

(b) Using Pythagoras

Area $\triangle AOB = 12 \times \sqrt{(15^2 - 12^2)} = 108 \text{ cm}^2$

(c)   Area $OANB = \frac{1}{2} \times 15^2 \times 1.854 = 208.575$

$\Rightarrow$ Area of $ANBC = 208.575 - 108 = 100.575$

$\Rightarrow$ Area of $AMBC = \frac{1}{2}\pi \times 12^2 = 226.194$ (Area of semicircle)

$\Rightarrow$ Area of region $R = 226.194 - 100.575 = 125.62 \text{ cm}^2$

Do be careful to give your final answer to 2 d.p.

Sine and cosine rules

You must be able to solve problems in 2 and 3 dimensions which may involve the sine and cosine rules.

Sine rule $\dfrac{a}{\sin A} = \dfrac{b}{\sin B} = \dfrac{c}{\sin C}$

Cosine rule $a^2 = b^2 + c^2 - 2bc \cos A$

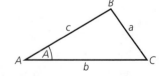

Always try to draw a decent three-dimensional diagram if the question requires it. Do not draw a series of two-dimensional diagrams if you can avoid it as experience shows that candidates who do so invariably fail to answer the question correctly. Mark all known right angles on your diagram and be careful when using the sine rule to find the smallest angles first, as there are two angles between $0°$ and $180°$ having the same sine.

Worked Example 3

In triangle ABC, $AB = 13\,\text{cm}$, $BC = 15\,\text{cm}$ and angle $ACB = 60°$. Given that $AC = x\,\text{cm}$ find possible values of x.

Working

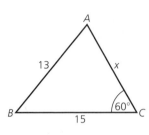

Draw a diagram and mark on it the given information. This way you will not make any errors when applying the sine or cosine rule.

Using the cosine rule with angle C

$$c^2 = a^2 + b^2 - 2ab\cos C$$
$$\Rightarrow \quad 13^2 = 15^2 + x^2 - 2 \times 15 \times x \cos 60°$$
$$\Rightarrow \quad x^2 - 15x + 56 = 0$$
$$(x - 7)(x - 8) = 0$$
$$\Rightarrow \quad x = 7 \text{ or } 8$$

Three-dimensional problems

When dealing with problems in three dimensions do remember the following.

1 A line L perpendicular to a plane is perpendicular to every line in that plane which intersects L.
2 The angle between two planes is the angle between two lines, one in each plane and both perpendicular to the common line.
3 The angle between a line and a plane is the angle between the line and its projection on the plane.
4 The line of greatest slope in a plane is a line perpendicular to the line of intersection of the plane and a horizontal plane.

Worked Example 4

Points A, B and C lie on horizontal ground such that $AB = 17\,\text{m}$, $BC = 14\,\text{m}$ and $CA = 19\,\text{m}$ and a vertical mast AH of height $8\,\text{m}$ is erected at A. Calculate (a) $A\widehat{B}C$, (b) the acute angle between the planes HBC and ABC correct to $0.1°$.

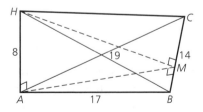

Working
First draw a clear 'three-dimensional' diagram of the situation and mark on it known distances and angles.
Remember HA is perpendicular to all lines in the plane of ABC passing through A.

To find angle ABC we need to apply the cosine rule to $\triangle ABC$:

$$19^2 = 17^2 + 14^2 - 2 \times 17 \times 14 \cos ABC$$
$$\Rightarrow \quad \cos ABC = \frac{17^2 + 14^2 - 19^2}{2 \times 17 \times 14}$$
$$\Rightarrow \quad A\widehat{B}C = 74.9°$$

BC is the line of intersection of the two planes so we need to take a point M on BC such that HM is perpendicular to BC. AM is then the projection of HM on plane ABC and angle HMA is the required angle between the planes HBC and ABC.

From $\triangle ABM$ right-angled at M,

$$AM = AB \sin A\widehat{B}M = 17 \sin 74.9°$$

From $\triangle HAM$ right-angled at A,

$$\tan H\widehat{M}A = \frac{AH}{AM} = \frac{8}{17 \sin 74.9°}$$

$\Rightarrow \quad H\widehat{M}A = 25.99° = 26.0° \qquad$ (to 1 d.p.)

Graphs of the trigonometric functions

You must be able to sketch the graphs of the trigonometric functions and derive curves associated with them.

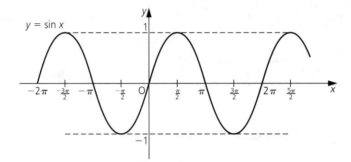

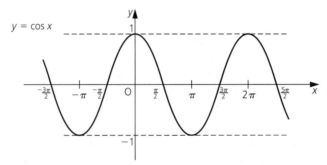

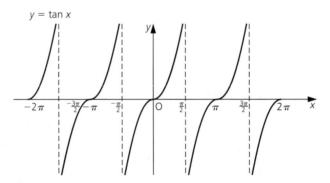

The curves are periodic, thus showing that there are many solutions to trigonometric equations and whilst you will only get one solution – the principal value – from your calculator, you will be required to find all solutions within a specified interval.

Worked Example 5

Solve the equations (a) $\sin \theta = -0.842$, (b) $\tan 3\theta = 1$ for $0 < \theta < 2\pi$, (c) $\sec (2x - 10)° = 2$ for $-180° < x < 180°$.

Working

(a) $\sin \theta = -0.842 \quad \Rightarrow \quad$ the sine is negative so the angles are in the 3rd and 4th quadrants

$\Rightarrow \quad \theta = 5.28$ radians or 4.14 radians.

(b) Since the equation involves $\tan 3\theta$ it is necessary, in the first instance, to solve 3θ for $0 < 3\theta < 6\pi$:

$$\tan 3\theta = 1 \quad \Rightarrow \quad 3\theta = \frac{\pi}{4}, \frac{5\pi}{4}, \frac{9\pi}{4}, \frac{13\pi}{4}, \frac{17\pi}{4}, \frac{21\pi}{4}$$

$$\Rightarrow \quad \theta = \frac{\pi}{12}, \frac{5\pi}{12}, \frac{9\pi}{12}, \frac{13\pi}{12}, \frac{17\pi}{12}, \frac{21\pi}{12}$$

(c) Since the equation involves $(2x - 10)°$ it is necessary, in the first instance, to solve the equation for $-360° < (2x - 10)° < 360°$:

$$\sec(2x - 10)° = 2 \quad \Rightarrow \quad \cos(2x - 10)° = \tfrac{1}{2}$$
$$\Rightarrow \quad (2x - 10)° = \pm 60°, \pm 300°, \quad \text{i.e. } 2x = 10° \pm 60°, 10° \pm 300°$$
$$\Rightarrow \quad x = -25°, 35°, -145°, 155°$$

Identities

Remember, $\cos^2 \theta + \sin^2 \theta \equiv 1$ from which you can deduce $\sec^2 \theta = 1 + \tan^2 \theta$ and $\operatorname{cosec}^2 \theta = 1 + \cot^2 \theta$. Further

$$\sin(A \pm B) \equiv \sin A \cos B \pm \cos A \sin B$$
$$\cos(A \pm B) \equiv \cos A \cos B \mp \sin A \cos B \qquad \text{(note } \mp \text{ on RHS)}$$
$$\tan(A \pm B) \equiv \frac{\tan A \pm \tan B}{1 \mp \tan A \tan B}$$

From which can be deduced

$$\sin 2A \equiv 2 \sin A \cos A$$

$$\cos 2A \equiv \cos^2 A - \sin^2 A = 2\cos^2 A - 1 = 1 - 2\sin^2 A$$

$$\tan 2A \equiv \frac{2 \tan A}{1 - \tan^2 A}, \quad \sin 2A \equiv \frac{2 \tan A}{1 + \tan^2 A}, \quad \cos 2A \equiv \frac{1 - \tan^2 A}{1 + \tan^2 A}$$

Worked Example 6

Solve the equation $\cos 2x + \sin x = 0$, for $0 < x < 2\pi$.

Working

To solve an equation such as this it is necessary to reduce the equation to one containing only sines or cosines of x. We can do this using the identity $\cos 2x = 1 - 2\sin^2 x$. Thus

$$\cos 2x + \sin x = 0 \quad \Rightarrow \quad 1 - 2\sin^2 x + \sin x = 0,$$

a quadratic equation in $\sin x$. Multiplying through by -1 gives

$$2\sin^2 x - \sin x - 1 = 0 \quad \Rightarrow \quad (2\sin x + 1)(\sin x - 1) = 0$$
$$\Rightarrow \quad \sin x = -\tfrac{1}{2} \text{ or } 1$$

$$\sin x = -\tfrac{1}{2} \quad \Rightarrow \quad x = \frac{7\pi}{6} \text{ or } \frac{11\pi}{6}$$
$$\sin x = 1 \quad \Rightarrow \quad x = \frac{\pi}{2}$$
$$\Rightarrow \quad x = \frac{\pi}{2}, \frac{7\pi}{6} \text{ or } \frac{11\pi}{6}$$

Do remember that $0 < x < 2\pi$ implies that you are working in radians so do not give your answer as $90°, 210°, 330°$. This is a very common error that students make in the heat of the examination. An alternative way of answering this question is shown later.

Worked Example 7

Solve the equation $3\cos\theta + \cot\theta = 0$ for $0° < \theta < 360°$.

Working

Again we must think of expressing everything in terms of the same trigonometric function or at least rearranging the equation so that a common factor can be taken out.

$$3\cos\theta + \cot\theta = 0 \quad \Rightarrow \quad 3\cos\theta + \frac{\cos\theta}{\sin\theta} = 0 (*)$$

$$\Rightarrow \quad \cos\theta\left(3 + \frac{1}{\sin\theta}\right) = 0 \quad \Rightarrow \quad \cos\theta = 0 \text{ or } \sin\theta = -\tfrac{1}{3}$$

$$\cos\theta = 0 \quad \Rightarrow \quad \theta = 90° \text{ or } 270°$$
$$\sin\theta = -\tfrac{1}{3} \quad \Rightarrow \quad \theta = 199.47° \text{ or } 340.53°$$

Warning: Do not make the common mistake at the point $*$ of cancelling out the $\cos\theta$'s to obtain $3 + \dfrac{1}{\sin\theta} = 0$ as this would mean that you have 'wiped out' half of the solution with the consequence that you would lose the corresponding marks. Unfortunately, many candidates do this in the examination.

General values of trigonometric equations

As the trigonometric functions are periodic there are many solutions to an equation of the form $\sin x = \frac{1}{2}$, i.e. there are many angles whose sine is $\frac{1}{2}$. Reference to the graphs will show that the general solution of such equations can be summarised in the following formulae.

$$\sin x = a \quad \Rightarrow \quad x = n\pi + (-1)^n\alpha \qquad n \in \mathbb{Z} \text{ and } \sin\alpha = a$$
$$\cos x = a \quad \Rightarrow \quad x = 2n\pi \pm \alpha \qquad n \in \mathbb{Z} \text{ and } \cos\alpha = a$$
$$\tan x = a \quad \Rightarrow \quad x = n\pi + \alpha \qquad n \in \mathbb{Z} \text{ and } \tan\alpha = a$$

Use of these formulae can often simplify the solution of a trigonometric equation.

Worked Example 8

Earlier we solved the equation $\cos 2x + \sin x = 0$ by using $\cos 2x = 1 - 2\sin^2 x$ and then factorising the resultant quadratic in $\sin x$.

Instead of using this approach we could have said

$$\sin x = -\cos\left(\frac{\pi}{2} + x\right)$$

$$\Rightarrow \quad \cos 2x + \sin x = \cos 2x - \cos\left(\frac{\pi}{2} + x\right) = 0$$

$$\Rightarrow \quad \cos 2x = \cos\left(\frac{\pi}{2} + x\right) \quad \Rightarrow \quad 2x = 2n\pi \pm \left(\frac{\pi}{2} + x\right)$$

Using the $+$ sign $\Rightarrow \quad x = 2n\pi + \dfrac{\pi}{2}$, for which $n = 0 \quad \Rightarrow \quad x = \dfrac{\pi}{2}$.

Using the $-$ sign $\Rightarrow \quad 3x = 2n\pi - \dfrac{\pi}{2}$, for which $n = 1 \quad \Rightarrow \quad x = \dfrac{\pi}{2}$,

$$n = 2 \quad \Rightarrow \quad x = \dfrac{7\pi}{6},$$

$$n = 3 \quad \Rightarrow \quad x = \dfrac{11\pi}{6}.$$

? PRACTICE QUESTIONS

1. Find the values of x in $[0, 360°]$ for which
   (a) $(2\cos x - 1)(2\sin x + 1) = 0$,
   (b) $2\cos^2 x = 5\sin x - 1$,
   (c) $\tan^2 x = 5 - \sec x$,
   (d) $\operatorname{cosec} x = 4\cos x$

2. The $\triangle ABC$ has $AB = 6\,\text{cm}$, $AC = \frac{1}{2}BC = x\,\text{cm}$ and $\angle CAB = 120°$. Find
   (a) the value of x to 2 d.p.,   (b) $\angle ABC$ to the nearest degree.

3. Two ships A and B set out from a port P. A moves at $25\,\text{km h}^{-1}$ in the direction $128°$ and B moves at $17\,\text{km h}^{-1}$ in the direction $324°$.
   (a) Find the distance between A and B after 2 hours.
   (b) Find the bearing of A from B at this time, to the nearest degree.

4. (a) Prove that
   (i) $\sin 3x \equiv 3\sin x - 4\sin^3 x$
   (ii) $\cos 2y - \cos 4y \equiv 2\cos^2 y - 2\cos^2 2y$
   (b) Given that $-180° \leqslant x \leqslant 180°$, find the values of x for which
   $$\sin(x + 60°) = 2\cos x$$

5. Show that $\sin 2x \equiv \dfrac{2\tan x}{1 + \tan^2 x}$ and $\cos 2x \equiv \dfrac{1 - \tan^2 x}{1 + \tan^2 x}$.
   Hence solve the equation $\sin 2x = 2 - 3\cos 2x$ for $0 \leqslant x \leqslant 2\pi$, giving your answer in radians to 2 decimal places.

6.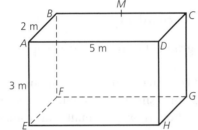

   The cuboid $ABCDEFGH$ which is shown has $AB = 2\,\text{m}$, $AD = 5\,\text{m}$ and $AE = 3\,\text{m}$. Calculate, to $0.1°$, (a) $\angle CGA$,   (b) $\angle HEC$,   (c) $\angle EMH$, where M is the midpoint of BC,   (d) the obtuse angle between BH and CE.

7. A circle of radius 12 cm has a chord PQ as shown. $\angle POQ = \dfrac{\pi}{3}$ radians, where O is the centre. Find
   (a) the length of the arc PSQ,
   (b) the area of the shaded region,

   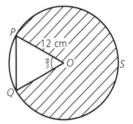

   (c) the area of the shaded region shown in the second diagram.

   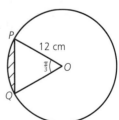

8. Given that $\sin x = \frac{4}{5}$ and $90° < x < 180°$, and $\cos y = \frac{3}{5}$ and $0 < y < 90°$, find **exact** values for: (a) $\sin 2x$, (b) $\sin(x + y)$, (c) $\cos 2y$, (d) $\tan(x + y)$, (e) $\cos(2y - x)$.

Differentiation

TOPIC OUTLINE AND REVISION TIPS

Differential coefficient

Consider points $P(x_1, y_1)$ $Q(x_2, y_2)$ on the curve $y = f(x)$.

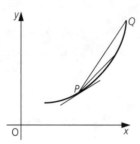

The gradient of chord PQ is $\dfrac{y_2 - y_1}{x_2 - x_1}$. As Q moves on the curve $y = f(x)$ towards P, the gradient of the chord PQ approaches that of the tangent to the curve at P.

We write the coordinates of P as (x, y) and those of Q as $(x + \delta x, y + \delta y)$ where δx stands for a small increment in x and δy the corresponding small increment in y. Then as δx gets smaller and smaller and ultimately approaches zero we obtain the gradient of the tangent to the curve at P, i.e. the rate of change of y with respect to x at the point P. It is written as

$$\frac{dy}{dx} = \lim_{\delta x \to 0} \frac{\delta y}{\delta x}$$

and is called the **differential coefficient** of y with respect to x (or the derivative of y with respect to x).

When $y = f(x)$ we often write $\dfrac{dy}{dx}$ as $f'(x)$, called the **derived function** of f.

Normally you will not be required to find the differential coefficients of functions by actually taking the limit of $\dfrac{\delta y}{\delta x}$, but you will be required to know the standard results for certain functions. You will build up a list of standard results which you should *definitely* learn. The basic results include

$y = f(x)$	$\dfrac{dy}{dx} = f'(x)$
C, a constant	0
$x^n, n \neq 0$	nx^{n-1}
$\sin x$	$\cos x$
$\cos x$	$-\sin x$
$\tan x$	$\sec^2 x$
$\ln x$	$\dfrac{1}{x}$
e^x	e^x

Other basic rules which you must learn and be able to use automatically include the following, where u and v are functions of x

1 $y = u \pm v \quad \Rightarrow \quad \dfrac{dy}{dx} = \dfrac{du}{dx} \pm \dfrac{dv}{dx}$

2 $y = u \cdot v \quad \Rightarrow \quad \dfrac{dy}{dx} = u \dfrac{dv}{dx} \pm v \dfrac{du}{dx}$ \quad the **product rule**

3 $y = \dfrac{u}{v} \quad \Rightarrow \quad \dfrac{dy}{dx} = \dfrac{v \dfrac{du}{dx} - u \dfrac{dv}{dx}}{v^2}$ \quad the **quotient rule**

4 $y = f(u)$ where $u = F(x) \quad \Rightarrow \quad \dfrac{dy}{dx} = \dfrac{dy}{du} \times \dfrac{du}{dx}$, the **chain rule**; sometimes referred to as the *differentiation of a function of a function*. Note that although $\dfrac{dy}{du}$ and $\dfrac{du}{dx}$ are not fractions, they can, for the purpose of the chain rule, be treated in the same way as fractions. The rule can be extended to $\dfrac{dy}{dx} = \dfrac{dy}{du} \dfrac{du}{dv} \dfrac{dv}{dx}$ if necessary.

5 $\dfrac{dy}{dx} = \dfrac{1}{\left(\dfrac{dx}{dy}\right)}$

Chain rule

The chain rule can be used to advantage to express your list of basic results in a slightly more generalised form. Given that a and b are constants we can write

$y = f(x)$	$\dfrac{dy}{dx} = f'(x)$
$(ax + b)^n, \quad n \neq 0$	$n(ax + b)^{n-1}$
$\sin ax$	$a \cos ax$
$\cos ax$	$-a \sin ax$
$\tan ax$	$a \sec^2 ax$
e^{ax}	ae^{ax}
$\ln(ax + b)$	$\dfrac{a}{ax + b}$

Useful alternative forms for the last two results are

$$y = e^{f(x)} \quad \Rightarrow \quad \frac{dy}{dx} = e^{f(x)} \times f'(x)$$

$$y = \ln f(x) \quad \Rightarrow \quad \frac{dy}{dx} = \frac{1}{f(x)} \times f'(x)$$

Examine the following worked examples and then try as many similar examples as you can. You will find many such examples in Chapters 6 and 7 of the A/AS Longman Mathematics Study Guides.

Worked Example 1

(a) $y = 7x^4, \quad \dfrac{dy}{dx} = 7 \times 4x^3 = 28x^3$

(b) $y = x^{\frac{3}{2}} + 3x^{-\frac{1}{2}}, \quad \dfrac{dy}{dx} = \dfrac{3}{2}x^{\frac{1}{2}} + 3\left(-\dfrac{1}{2}\right)x^{-\frac{3}{2}} = \dfrac{3}{2}\left(x^{\frac{1}{2}} - x^{-\frac{3}{2}}\right)$

(c) $y = \tan 2x, \quad \dfrac{dy}{dx} = \left(\sec^2 2x\right)(2) = 2\sec^2 2x$

(d) $y = \sin x \cos x$, $\quad \dfrac{dy}{dx} = (\cos x)(\cos x) + (\sin x)(-\sin x)$

$$= \cos^2 x - \sin^2 x = \cos 2x$$

(e) $y = \dfrac{1}{\sqrt{(x+2)}} \quad \Rightarrow \quad y = (x+2)^{-\frac{1}{2}}, \quad \dfrac{dy}{dx} = \left(-\tfrac{1}{2}\right)(x+2)^{-\frac{3}{2}} = \dfrac{-1}{2(x+2)^{\frac{3}{2}}}$

(f) $y = e^{-2x}$, $\quad \dfrac{dy}{dx} = -2e^{-2x}$

(g) $y = \ln(1 - 3x)$, $\quad \dfrac{dy}{dx} = \left(\dfrac{1}{1-3x}\right)(-3) = \dfrac{-3}{1-3x}$

(h) $y = \dfrac{\sin 2x}{x^2}$, $\quad \dfrac{dy}{dx} = \dfrac{(x^2)(2\cos 2x) - (\sin 2x)(2x)}{(x^2)^2}$

$$= \dfrac{2x\cos 2x - 2\sin 2x}{x^3}$$

(i) $y = \tan^2 3x$, $\quad \dfrac{dy}{dx} = (2\tan 3x)(\sec^2 3x)(3)$

$$= (6\tan 3x)(\sec^2 3x)$$

Students often lose marks because

▶ the standard results have not been learnt thoroughly,
▶ sufficient care has not been taken in 'talking oneself through' the necessary operations.

Worked Example 2

(a) Differentiate $y = \sqrt{(2 - x^3)}$ with respect to x.

Working
You should recognise y as a function of x raised to the power $\frac{1}{2}$, i.e. $(2 - x^3)^{\frac{1}{2}}$. Differentiation therefore involves multiplying by the power $\frac{1}{2}$, reducing the power by 1, i.e. $(2 - x^3)^{-\frac{1}{2}}$ and finally multiplying by the derivative of the expression inside the bracket $(-3x^2)$, to give

$$\dfrac{dy}{dx} = \dfrac{1}{2}(2 - x^3)^{-\frac{1}{2}}(-3x^2) = -\dfrac{3}{2} \times \dfrac{x^2}{\sqrt{(2 - x^3)}}$$

(b) Differentiate $y = \cos(3x)$ with respect to x.

Working
You have been asked to find the derivative of the cosine of a function of x. Thus you need the derivative of a cosine which is $(-\sin 3x)$. This must then be multiplied by the derivative of the angle, i.e. $\dfrac{d}{dx}(3x) = 3$, giving

$$\dfrac{dy}{dx} = (-\sin 3x)(3) = -3\sin 3x$$

(c) Differentiate $y = \ln\sqrt{\left(\dfrac{1-x}{1+x}\right)}$ with respect to x.

Working
This time you must find the derivative of a complicated logarithmic function. Can the function be simplified before differentiating? Yes it can, by using the laws of logarithms

$$\ln\sqrt{\left(\dfrac{1-x}{1+x}\right)} = \ln\left(\dfrac{1-x}{1+x}\right)^{\frac{1}{2}} = \dfrac{1}{2}\ln\left(\dfrac{1-x}{1+x}\right)$$

$$= \dfrac{1}{2}\{\ln(1-x) - \ln(1+x)\}$$

The derivative of a logarithmic function is 1 divided by the function and multiplied by the derivative of the function. This gives

$$y = \frac{1}{2}\left\{\left(\frac{1}{1-x}\right)(-1) - \left(\frac{1}{1+x}\right)(1)\right\} = \frac{-1}{2}\left\{\frac{1}{1-x} + \frac{1}{1+x}\right\}$$

$$= -\frac{1}{1-x^2}$$

Parametric equations

For parametric equations, the chain rule is required.

Worked Example 3

Given $y = 2\cos\theta$, $x = 3\sin\theta$, find $\dfrac{dy}{d\theta}$.

Working

$$\frac{dy}{d\theta} = -2\sin\theta, \quad \frac{dx}{d\theta} = 3\cos\theta$$

$$\Rightarrow \quad \frac{dy}{dx} = \frac{dy}{d\theta} \times \frac{d\theta}{dx} = -2\sin\theta \times \frac{1}{3\cos\theta} \quad \text{since } \frac{d\theta}{dx} = \frac{1}{\dfrac{dx}{d\theta}}$$

$$\Rightarrow \quad \frac{dy}{dx} = -\frac{2}{3}\tan\theta$$

Implicit functions

The chain rule is again required in order to differentiate a function of y with respect to x.

Consider $\dfrac{d}{dx}(y^n)$. Now y^n can only be differentiated with respect to y, but using the chain rule we can write

$$\frac{d}{dx}(y^n) = \frac{dy}{dx}\frac{d}{dy}(y^n) = \frac{dy}{dx} \times ny^{n-1} = ny^{n-1}\frac{dy}{dx}$$

Worked Example 4

Find $\dfrac{dy}{dx}$ given that $y^3 + x^2 + 3xy - 4 = 0$.

Working
All that is required is careful use of the chain rule. First write

$$\frac{d}{dx}(y^3) + \frac{d}{dx}(x^2) + \frac{d}{dx}(3xy) - \frac{d}{dx}(4) = 0$$

Now use the chain rule where necessary

$$\frac{dy}{dx}\frac{d}{dy}(y^3) + \frac{d}{dx}(x^2) + \left\{3y\frac{d}{dx}(x) + 3x\frac{dy}{dx}\frac{d}{dy}(y)\right\} - \frac{d}{dx}(4) = 0$$

$$\Rightarrow 3y^2\frac{dy}{dx} + 2x + \left\{(3y)(1) + 3x\frac{dy}{dx}\right\} - 0 = 0$$

$$\Rightarrow \frac{dy}{dx} = \frac{-2x - 3y}{3y^2 + 3x}$$

Many students think that they must always start with a $\dfrac{dy}{dx}$ and write

$$\frac{dy}{dx} = \frac{d}{dx}(y^3) + \frac{d}{dx}(x^2) + \ldots,$$

and consequently end up with an extra term which they accept by ignoring the $= 0$ on the right-hand side.

Logarithmic differentiation

Functions such as 2^x can only be differentiated by first using logarithms. We write

$$y = 2^x \quad \Rightarrow \quad \ln y = \ln 2^x = x \ln 2$$

$$\Rightarrow \quad \frac{d}{dx}(\ln y) = \frac{d}{dx}(x \ln 2) \quad \Rightarrow \quad \frac{dy}{dx}\frac{d}{dy}(\ln y) = \frac{d}{dx}(x \ln 2)$$

$$\Rightarrow \quad \frac{dy}{dx}\frac{1}{y} = 1(\ln 2) \quad \Rightarrow \quad \frac{dy}{dx} = y \ln 2 = 2^x \ln 2$$

Higher derivatives

You must be familiar with higher derivatives. If $\dfrac{dy}{dx}$ is a function of x then it can be differentiated again with respect to x to give a second derivative, written as $\dfrac{d}{dx}\left(\dfrac{dy}{dx}\right) = \dfrac{d^2y}{dx^2}$ or alternatively $\dfrac{d}{dx}(f'(x)) = f''(x)$.

Likewise, $\dfrac{d}{dx}\left(\dfrac{d^2y}{dx^2}\right) = \dfrac{d^3y}{dx^3}$ is the third derivative.

Worked Example 5

If $y = \ln(1 + x)$, find the value of $\dfrac{d^2y}{dx^2}$ when $x = 3$.

Working

$$y = \ln(1 + x) \quad \Rightarrow \quad \frac{dy}{dx} = \frac{1}{1+x} = (1+x)^{-1}$$

$$\frac{d^2y}{dx^2} = (-1)(1+x)^{-2} = \frac{-1}{(1+x)^2} = -\frac{1}{4^2} \quad \text{when } x = 3$$

Worked Example 6

Given that $y = (A + x)\cos x$ where A is a constant, show that $\dfrac{d^2y}{dx^2} + y = 0$.

Working

$$\frac{dy}{dx} = (A + x)(-\sin x) + \cos x \qquad \text{(using the product rule)}$$

$$\Rightarrow \quad \frac{d^2y}{dx^2} = (A + x)(-\cos x) - 1(\sin x - \sin x)$$

$$= -(A + x)\cos x = -y$$

$$\Rightarrow \quad \frac{d^2y}{dx^2} + y = 0$$

Applications of differentiation

You must be familiar with the applications of differentiation to gradients, equations of tangents and normals, maxima, minima, stationary points, increasing and decreasing functions, rates of change and the formation of simple differential equations. We illustrate these applications by worked examples.

Tangents and normals

Worked Example 7

Find the equations of the tangent and normal to the curve $y = \dfrac{x}{(x-1)^{\frac{1}{2}}}$ at the point $(5, 2\frac{1}{2})$.

Working

We first need to find $\dfrac{dy}{dx}$ using the quotient rule for $y = \dfrac{u}{v}$ where $u = x$ and $v = (x-1)^{\frac{1}{2}}$

$$\frac{dy}{dx} = \frac{v\dfrac{du}{dx} - u\dfrac{dv}{dx}}{v^2} = \frac{(x-1)^{\frac{1}{2}}(1) - x \times \frac{1}{2}(x-1)^{-\frac{1}{2}}}{(x-1)}$$

$$= \frac{(x-1) - \frac{1}{2}x}{(x-1)^{\frac{3}{2}}}$$

At $x = 5$, $\dfrac{dy}{dx} = \dfrac{4 - \frac{5}{2}}{4^{\frac{3}{2}}} = \dfrac{1\frac{1}{2}}{8} = \dfrac{3}{16}$

Hence the equation of the tangent at $\left(5, 2\frac{1}{2}\right)$ is $y - 2\frac{1}{2} = \frac{3}{16}(x-5)$, or

$16y = 3x + 25$

The gradient of the normal at $\left(5, 2\frac{1}{2}\right)$ is m, where $\frac{3}{16}m = -1$, i.e. $m = -\frac{16}{3}$.

Hence the equation of the normal at $\left(5, 2\frac{1}{2}\right)$ is $y - 2\frac{1}{2} = -\frac{16}{3}(x-5)$, or

$3y = 87\frac{1}{2} - 16x \quad \Rightarrow \quad 6y + 32x = 175$

Maxima and minima

Worked Example 8

Find the coordinates of the stationary points on the curve $y = x^3 - 3x - 2$. State whether they are maxima, minima or points of inflexion. Sketch the curve.

Stationary points are points where the function is neither increasing nor decreasing, i.e. where $\dfrac{dy}{dx} = 0$.

Working

$\dfrac{dy}{dx} = 3x^2 - 3 \quad \Rightarrow \quad \dfrac{dy}{dx} = 0 \quad \text{when} \quad 3x^2 - 3 = 0 \quad \Rightarrow \quad x = \pm 1$

Hence stationary points occur at $x = 1, y = -4$ and $x = -1, y = 0$. To test the nature of the stationary points it is necessary to consider the sign of the second derivative at those points:

$$\frac{d^2y}{dx^2} = 6x$$

At $(1, -4)$ $\dfrac{d^2y}{dx^2} = 6$, a positive, so there is a minimum at $(1, -4)$,

At $(-1, 0)$ $\dfrac{d^2y}{dx^2} = -6$, a negative, so there is a maximum at $(-1, 0)$.

$y = x^3 - 3x - 2 = (x+1)(x^2 - x - 2) = (x+1)^2(x-2)$

When $y = 0$ $x = -1$ or 2,
When $x = 0$ $y = -2$.
As $x \to +\infty$, $y \to +\infty$
As $x \to -\infty$, $y \to -\infty$

Questions involving maxima or minima may also be set in practical problem form for which $f(x)$ has to be determined.

Worked Example 9

A rectangular garden consists of a rectangular lawn of area $72\,\text{m}^2$ surrounded by concrete path. The path is 2 m wide at two opposite edges of the garden and 1 m wide along each of the other two edges. Find the dimensions of the garden of smallest area satisfying these requirements.

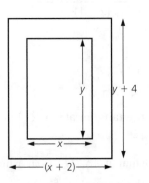

Working

Let the dimensions be as shown in the diagram. The area of the garden $A = (x+2)(y+4)$. This equation unfortunately contains two variables, x and y, so there is little we can do with it until we have eliminated one of the variables. Fortunately, we can do this since we are told that the area xy of the lawn is $72\,\text{m}^2$, i.e. $xy = 72$, giving $y = \dfrac{72}{x}$.

Substituting this in A gives

$$A = (x+2)\left(\frac{72}{x} + 4\right)$$

$$= 4x + \frac{144}{x} + 80$$

Hence $\dfrac{\mathrm{d}A}{\mathrm{d}x} = 4 - \dfrac{144}{x^2}$ and $\dfrac{\mathrm{d}A}{\mathrm{d}x} = 0 \quad \Rightarrow \quad 4 - \dfrac{144}{x^2} = 0,\, x^2 = 36 \quad \Rightarrow \quad x = 6.$

To test that $x = 6$ gives a minimum value for A we consider $\dfrac{\mathrm{d}^2 A}{\mathrm{d}x^2}$

$\dfrac{\mathrm{d}^2 A}{\mathrm{d}x^2} = 0 + 2\left(\dfrac{144}{x^3}\right)$, which is positive when $x = 6$

Hence $y = \frac{72}{6} = 12.$

The dimensions of the smallest garden are therefore $8\,\text{m} \times 16\,\text{m} = 128\,\text{m}^2$ (Do not fail to give this last line.)

Rates of change

Worked Example 10

A straight metal bar of square cross-section has dimensions $x\,\text{cm} \times x\,\text{cm} \times 100x\,\text{cm}$. The bar is expanding due to heating. Given that when $x = 5$ the area of the cross-section is increasing at $0.025\,\text{cm}^2\,\text{s}^{-1}$ find the rate of increase of the side of the cross-section at that instant.

Find also the rate of increase of the volume of the bar at that instant.

Working

First write down the information given in the question in mathematical form:

Volume V of bar $= x \times x \times 100x = 100x^3$,

Area of cross-section $= A = x \times x$,

When $x = 5$, $\dfrac{\mathrm{d}A}{\mathrm{d}t} = 0.025.$

Next write down what is required:

First, $\dfrac{\mathrm{d}x}{\mathrm{d}t}$ when $x = 5$.

Second, $\dfrac{\mathrm{d}V}{\mathrm{d}t}$ when $x = 5$.

Now write down the connection using the chain rule.

First, $\dfrac{dx}{dt} = \dfrac{dx}{dA} \times \dfrac{dA}{dt}$

Now, $A = x^2 \Rightarrow \dfrac{dA}{dx} = 2x$, and $\dfrac{dA}{dt} = 0.025$ when $x = 5$.

Hence

$$\dfrac{dx}{dt} = \dfrac{1}{2x} \times 0.025 = \dfrac{1}{10} \times 0.025 = 0.0025 \, \text{cm s}^{-1}$$

Second, $\dfrac{dV}{dt} = \dfrac{dV}{dx} \times \dfrac{dx}{dt}$

$V = 100x^3 \Rightarrow \dfrac{dV}{dx} = 300x^2;\ x = 5$ and $\dfrac{dx}{dt} = 0.0025$ (just found), hence

$$\dfrac{dV}{dt} = 300x^2 \times 0.0025 = 7500 \times 0.0025 = 18.75 \, \text{cm}^3\, \text{s}^{-1}$$

PRACTICE QUESTIONS

1 Differentiate with respect to x: (a) $(2x + 1)^3$, (b) $\dfrac{\sin x}{x}$, (c) $e^{2x} \ln x$,
   (d) $\sin^3 2x$, (e) $\dfrac{\ln x}{\cos x}$.

2 Given that $y = x - \dfrac{3 \sin x}{2 + \cos x}$, show that

$$\dfrac{dy}{dx} = \left(\dfrac{1 - \cos x}{2 + \cos x} \right)^2$$

3 (a) Find the stationary points of the function $y = 3x - x^3$ and determine their nature.
   (b) Hence sketch the curve $y = 3x - x^3$ showing where it cuts the x-axis and where it has turning points.

4 Given $y = 3e^{3x} - 9e^{2x} + 8e^x$ show that $\dfrac{dy}{dx} = 9e^{2x} - 18e^x + 8$. Hence or otherwise find the stationary values of y and determine their nature.

5 Differentiate the equation $3x^2 + 5xy - 2y^2 = 8$ with respect to x. Hence find $\dfrac{dy}{dx}$ in terms of x and y.

6 (a) Find an equation of the tangent to the curve $y = x^2(x + 1)$ at the point $(-1, 0)$.
   (b) Prove that there is a parallel tangent to the curve and obtain its equation.
   (c) Find also the maximum and minimum ordinates of the curve.

7 The volume of a sphere is increasing at the rate of $4 \, \text{cm}^3 \, \text{s}^{-1}$. Find the rate of increase of its surface area when the radius of the sphere is 3 cm.

8 The function f is defined by $f(x) = x^3 - 7x^2 + 8x - 5, x \in \mathbb{R}$. Find the set of values of x for which f is (a) increasing, (b) decreasing.

9 A quadratic function $y = ax^2 + bx + c$ has a maximum value 20 at $x = 2$. Also $y = 8$ when $x = 0$.
   (a) Find the values of a, b, c.
   (b) State the set of values of x for which y is decreasing.

10 A rectangular box with no lid has a square base of side x cm and a height y cm. The box is made from $108 \, \text{cm}^2$ of cardboard of negligible thickness.
   Prove that $y \equiv \dfrac{108 - x^2}{4x}$ and show that the volume $V \, \text{cm}^3$ is given by
   $V = 27 - \frac{1}{4} x^3$. Using differentiation find the maximum volume of the box as x and y vary.

7

Integration

Integrals

As with differentiation, it is essential that you know the list of standard results for integrals and are able to apply them without difficulty. Again, do not become dependent upon the table of results given by some examination boards in their formulae booklets.

Integrand $f(x)$	$\int f(x)\,dx$
x^n	$\dfrac{x^{n+1}}{n+1}$, $\quad n \neq -1$
$\dfrac{1}{x}$	$\ln|x|$
e^x	e^x
$\sin x$	$-\cos x$
$\cos x$	$\sin x$
$\sec^2 x$	$\tan x$
$\csc^2 x$	$-\cot x$

Remember that each of the above results is not unique, but that each should be associated with an arbitrary constant C, the constant of integration. For convenience we shall drop the constant of integration, introducing it only when it is essential to the problem.

Other basic results include

1 $\displaystyle\int cf(x)\,dx = c\int f(x)\,dx$ e.g. $\displaystyle\int 7x^3\,dx = \frac{7x^4}{4}$,

2 $\displaystyle\int \{f(x) + g(x)\}\,dx = \int f(x)\,dx + \int g(x)\,dx$ e.g. $\displaystyle\int (\sin x + e^x)\,dx = -\cos x + e^x$,

3 If $\displaystyle\int f(x)\,dx = F(x)$ then $\displaystyle\int f(x+a)\,dx = F(x+a)$ where a is any constant, e.g.

$\displaystyle\int 3x^4\,dx = \frac{3x^5}{5}$ and $\displaystyle\int 3(x+2)^4\,dx = \frac{3(x+2)^5}{5}$,

i.e. the addition of a constant to the variable makes no difference to the form of the integral.

However, you must exercise care when using this rule. It only applies when x is replaced by $(x + a)$ and does not cover the case when the expression inside the brackets is not linear i.e. first degree in x. Thus

$\displaystyle\int (x^2 + 3)^2\,dx \neq \frac{(x^2 + 3)^3}{3}$. To integrate $(x^2 + 3)^2$ you would have to use

$(x^2 + 3)^2 = x^4 + 6x + 9$.

4 If $\displaystyle\int f(x)\,dx = F(x)$ then $\displaystyle\int f(bx + a)\,dx = \frac{1}{b}F(bx + a)$ where a and b are

constants. In other words if x is replaced by $(bx + a)$ then the form of the integral remains the same but the answer must be divided by b, the coefficient of x. Again you are reminded that the expression in the bracket must be linear. For example,

$$\int \frac{2}{3x+1}\,dx \quad\Rightarrow\quad \int \frac{1}{x}\,dx = \ln|x| \quad\text{so}\quad \int \frac{2}{3x+1}\,dx = \frac{2}{3}\ln|3x+1|$$

Similarly $\int \cos 2x\,dx = \frac{1}{2}\sin 2x$ and $\int \sin 4x\,dx = -\frac{1}{4}\cos 4x$.

Hence you can replace the table of standard integrals by a slightly more advanced and useful table.

$f(x)$	$\int f(x)\,dx$
$(bx+a)^n$	$\left(\frac{1}{n+1}\right)\left(\frac{1}{b}\right)(bx+a)^{n+1}, n \neq -1$
$\dfrac{1}{bx+a}$	$\dfrac{1}{b}\ln(bx+a)$
e^{ax}	$\dfrac{1}{a}e^{ax}$
$\sin ax$	$-\dfrac{1}{a}\cos ax$
$\cos ax$	$\dfrac{1}{a}\sin ax$
$\sec^2 ax$	$\dfrac{1}{a}\tan ax$
$\csc^2 ax$	$-\dfrac{1}{a}\cot ax$

It is sometimes necessary to reduce the integrand to one of the above forms in order to integrate. Do not forget that the trigonometric identities can help in this. For example,

$$\int \cos^2 x\,dx = \int \frac{1}{2}(\cos 2x + 1)\,dx \quad\text{since}\quad \cos 2x = 2\cos^2 x - 1$$

$$= \frac{1}{2}\left(\frac{1}{2}\sin 2x + x\right)$$

$$\int \tan^2 3x\,dx = \int (\sec^2 3x - 1)\,dx \quad\text{since}\quad \sec^2 3x = 1 + \tan^2 3x$$

$$= \frac{1}{3}\tan 3x - x$$

Using the substitution

For more difficult integrals the examiners will normally give you the substitution.

Worked Example 1

(a) Use the substitution $x = t^2$ to find $\int \dfrac{1}{2x+\sqrt{x}}\,dx$.

Working
$$x = t^2 \quad\Rightarrow\quad dx \equiv 2t\,dt$$

$$\int \frac{1}{2x+\sqrt{x}}\,dx = \int \frac{1}{2t^2+t} \times 2t\,dt = \int \frac{2}{2t+1}\,dt$$

$$= \ln|2t+1|$$

$$= \ln|2\sqrt{x}+1| + c$$

(b) Use the substitution $t = \sin x$ to find $\int \cos^3 x\,dx$.

Working

$$t = \sin x \quad \Rightarrow \quad dt \equiv \cos x \, dx$$

$$\int \cos^3 x \, dx = \int \cos^2 x \cos x \, dx = \int (1 - \sin^2 x) \cos x \, dx \quad \text{since} \quad \cos^2 x = 1 - \sin^2 x$$

$$\Rightarrow \quad \int (1 - t^2) \, dt = t - \frac{1}{3} t^3 = \sin x - \frac{1}{3} \sin^3 x + C$$

(c) Use the substitution $t = 3x + 1$ to find $\int \dfrac{6x^2}{3x + 1} \, dx$.

Working

$$3x + 1 = t \quad \Rightarrow \quad 3 \, dx \equiv dt \quad \text{and} \quad x = \frac{(t - 1)}{3}$$

$$\int \frac{6x^2}{3x + 1} \, dx = \int \frac{6}{t} \times \left(\frac{t - 1}{3} \right)^2 dt = \int \frac{2}{3} \frac{(t^2 - 2t + 1)}{t} \, dt$$

$$= \frac{2}{3} \int \left(t - 2 + \frac{1}{t} \right) dt = \frac{2}{3} \left(\frac{1}{2} t^2 - 2t + \ln t \right)$$

$$= \frac{2}{3} \left\{ \frac{1}{2} (3x + 1)^2 - 2(3x + 1) + \ln(3x + 1) \right\} + C$$

You may sometimes be led into the simplified form of the integrand by the wording of the question.

Worked Example 2

Express $\dfrac{2x + 1}{x^2 - 3x + 2}$ in partial fractions and hence or otherwise evaluate

$$\int_3^4 \frac{2x + 1}{x^2 - 3x + 2} \, dx.$$

Working

$$\frac{2x + 1}{x^2 - 3x + 2} \equiv \frac{2x + 1}{(x - 1)(x - 2)} \equiv \frac{A}{x - 1} + \frac{B}{x - 2} = \frac{A(x - 2) + B(x - 1)}{(x - 1)(x - 2)}$$

$$\Rightarrow \quad 2x + 1 \equiv A(x - 2) + B(x - 1)$$

Let $x = 1$, then $\quad 3 = -A \quad \Rightarrow \quad A = -3$

Let $x = 2$, then $\quad 5 = B$

$$\Rightarrow \qquad \frac{2x + 1}{x^2 - 3x + 2} \equiv -\frac{3}{x - 1} + \frac{5}{x - 2}$$

$$\Rightarrow \quad \int \frac{2x + 1}{x^2 - 3x + 2} \, dx = \int \frac{-3}{x - 1} \, dx + \int \frac{5}{x - 2} \, dx = -3 \ln(x - 1) + 5 \ln(x - 2)$$

The integral is a definite integral so that all that is required is to substitute the limits in turn and find the numerical value, thus

$$\int_3^4 \frac{2x + 1}{(x^2 - 3x + 2)} \, dx = \left[-3 \ln(x - 1) + 5 \ln(x - 2) \right]_3^4$$

$$= -3 \ln(4 - 1) + 5 \ln(4 - 2) - \{ -3 \ln(3 - 1) + 5 \ln(3 - 2) \}$$

(Do remember to use brackets, otherwise it is very easy to make a sign error.)

$$\Rightarrow \quad -3 \ln 3 + 5 \ln 2 + 3 \ln 2 - 5 \ln 1 = -\ln 3^3 + \ln 2^5 + \ln 2^3 - 0$$

$$= \ln \left(\frac{2^8}{3^3} \right) \quad \text{using the properties of logarithms}$$

Integration by parts

This is derived from the product rule for differentiation

$$\frac{d}{dx}(uv) = u\frac{dv}{dx} + v\frac{du}{dx}$$

$$\Rightarrow \quad u\frac{dv}{dx} = \frac{d}{dx}(uv) - v\frac{du}{dx}$$

and integrating with respect to x gives

$$\int\left(u\frac{dv}{dx}\right)dx = uv - \int\left(v\frac{du}{dx}\right)dx$$

Note that one of the terms in the integrand on the left-hand side has to be integrated, namely $\frac{dv}{dx}$, and one has to be differentiated. If the integrand involves an x or power of x then this is usually the one to differentiate, i.e. u.

Worked Example 3

(a) Find $\int xe^{2x}dx$.

Working

Let $x \equiv u$, $e^{2x} \equiv \frac{dv}{dx}$. Then

$$\int xe^{2x}\,dx = x\left(\frac{1}{2}e^{2x}\right) - \int\left(\frac{1}{2}e^{2x}\right) \times 1\,dx$$

$$= \frac{1}{2}xe^{2x} - \frac{1}{4}e^{2x}$$

(b) Find $\int x^2 \ln x\,dx$.

Normally we would think of differentiating the x^2 term, but this is one case where we do not since this would require $\int \ln x\,dx$ which is difficult to find. Hence choose $u = \ln x$ and $\frac{dv}{dx} = x^2$. Then

$$\int x^2 \ln dx = \frac{x^3}{3}\ln x - \int\frac{x^3}{3} \times \frac{1}{x}\,dx = \frac{x^3}{3}\ln x - \int\frac{x^2}{3}\,dx$$

$$= \frac{x^3}{3}\ln x - \frac{x^3}{9}$$

Integration by parts normally involves the integral of a product. We said $\int \ln x\,dx$ was difficult, but we can in fact integrate by turning $\ln x$ into a product of $1 \times \ln x$ and choosing $1 \equiv u$ and $\ln x \equiv \frac{dv}{dx}$:

$$\int \ln x\,dx = \int 1\ln x\,dx$$

$$= x \times \ln x - \int x \times \frac{1}{x}\,dx = x\ln x - x$$

Applications of integration

Two important applications of integration involve the calculation of areas of regions and volumes of revolution. It is necessary to commit to memory the appropriate integrals or alternatively to build them up by considering an appropriate elementary strip and regarding the integral sign as standing for the summation of the areas or volumes of revolution as designated by the limits of the integral.

Areas

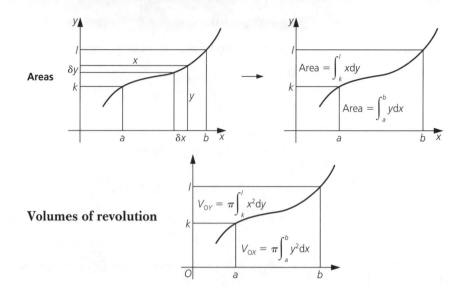

Volumes of revolution

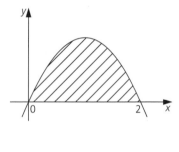

Worked Example 4

(a) Find the area of the finite region contained between the curve $y = 2x - x^2$ and the x-axis. Find the volume when this region is revolved completely about the x-axis.

Working
First it is necessary to sketch the
curve in order to determine the
limits of integration

$y = 0 \quad \Rightarrow \quad 2x - x^2 = 0 = x(2 - x)$

$\qquad \Rightarrow \quad x = 0, x = 2$

Required area $= \displaystyle\int_0^2 y\,dx = \int_0^2 (2x - x^2)\,dx$

$\qquad = \left[x^2 - \dfrac{1}{3}x^3 \right]_0^2 = 2^2 - \dfrac{1}{3} \times 2^3 = \dfrac{4}{3}$

$V_{OX} = \pi \displaystyle\int_0^2 y^2\,dx = \pi \int_0^2 (2x - x^2)^2\,dx = \pi \int_0^2 (4x^2 - 4x^3 + x^4)\,dx$

$\qquad = \pi \left[4\dfrac{x^3}{3} - 4\dfrac{x^4}{4} + \dfrac{x^5}{5} \right]_0^2 = \pi \left[4\dfrac{2^3}{3} - 2^4 + \dfrac{2^5}{5} \right] = \dfrac{16\pi}{15}$

(b) Find the area of the finite region bounded by the curves with equation $y = x^2, y^2 = 8x$.

Working
It is essential to sketch the curves.
   The curves meet where

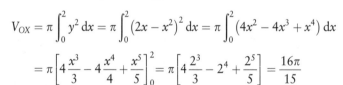

$y^2 = 8x = (x^2)^2$

$\Rightarrow \quad x(x^3 - 8) = 0$

$\Rightarrow \quad x = 0 \text{ or } 2$

Required area = area of shaded
region, which is

$\displaystyle\int_0^2 y_1\,dx - \int_0^2 y_2\,dx \quad \text{where} \quad y_1 = \sqrt{(8x)} \quad \text{and} \quad y_2 = x^2$

$\Rightarrow \quad \text{Area} = \displaystyle\int_0^2 (\sqrt{(8x)} - x^2)\,dx = \left[\dfrac{2\sqrt{8}}{3}x^{\frac{3}{2}} - \dfrac{x^3}{3} \right]_0^2 = \left(\dfrac{2\sqrt{8}}{3} \right)(\sqrt{8}) - \dfrac{8}{3} = \dfrac{8}{3} = 2\dfrac{2}{3}$

Formation and solution of first-order differential equations

You may be asked to form and solve a first-order differential equation, although it is possible that you may be given the equation. The equation will be one where the variables can be separated, i.e. you can collect the x s, say, with the dx and the y s with the dy. The question then becomes one of solving two integrals.

Worked Example 5

(a) Solve the differential equation $2\dfrac{\mathrm{d}y}{\mathrm{d}x} = 2xe^{-y} + e^{-y}$ given that $y = 0$ when $x = 0$.

Working

$$2\frac{\mathrm{d}y}{\mathrm{d}x} = 2x\,e^{-y} + e^{-y} = e^{-y}(2x+1)$$

$$\Rightarrow \quad \int \frac{2\mathrm{d}y}{e^{-y}} = \int (2x+1)\mathrm{d}x = \int 2e^{y}\,\mathrm{d}y$$

$$\Rightarrow \quad 2e^{y} = x^2 + x + C \quad \text{where } C \text{ is the constant of integration}$$

When $x = 0, y = 0 \quad \Rightarrow \quad 2 = 0 + C$
$$\Rightarrow \quad C = 2 \quad \Rightarrow \quad 2e^{y} = x^2 + x + 2.$$

(b) The gradient of the tangent to a curve C at any point (x, y) is $3x^2y^2$. Find the equation of C given that the curve passes through the point $(2, 1)$.

Working

The gradient of the curve at any point (x, y) is given by $\dfrac{\mathrm{d}y}{\mathrm{d}x}$, hence

$$\frac{\mathrm{d}y}{\mathrm{d}x} = 3x^2y^2 \quad \Rightarrow \quad \int \frac{\mathrm{d}y}{y^2} = \int 3x^2\,\mathrm{d}x$$

$$\Rightarrow \quad -\frac{1}{y} = x^3 + k \quad \text{where } k \text{ is the constant of integration}$$

When $x = 2, y = 1 \quad \Rightarrow \quad -1 = 2^3 + k \quad \Rightarrow \quad k = -9$, hence the equation of the curve is

$$-\frac{1}{y} = x^3 - 9$$

(c) On 1 January 1990 the population of Townsville was exactly 49 500 and on 1 January 1996 the population was exactly 50 000. It is known that the population at any instant is increasing at a rate which is proportional to the population at that instant. Form a first-order differential equation to model the situation and hence estimate the expected population on 1 January 2000.

Working

Rate of increase of the population is $\dfrac{\mathrm{d}P}{\mathrm{d}t} \propto P \Rightarrow \dfrac{\mathrm{d}P}{\mathrm{d}t} = kP$ where k is a constant. Hence

$$\int \frac{\mathrm{d}P}{P} = \int k\,\mathrm{d}t \quad \Rightarrow \quad \ln P = kt + C$$

where C is the constant of integration.
When $t = 0$, i.e. year 1990 $\qquad P = 49\,500 \quad \Rightarrow \quad \ln 49\,500 = C$
When $t = 6$, i.e. year 1996 $\qquad P = 50\,000$

$$\Rightarrow \quad \ln 50\,000 = 6k + \ln 49\,500 \quad \Rightarrow \quad 6k = \ln \frac{50\,000}{49\,500}$$

$$\Rightarrow \quad k \approx 0.001675$$

So when $t = 10$, i.e. year 2000 $\ln P = (0.001675)(10) + \ln 49\,500$

$\Rightarrow$ $\ln P \approx 10.82648$ $\Rightarrow$ $P = 50\,336$

i.e. in the year 2000 the population of Townsville will be approximately 50 340.

? PRACTICE QUESTIONS

1 Find

  (a) $\displaystyle\int (3x - 2)^{-2}\,dx$ (f) $\displaystyle\int \cos^2 x \sin x\,dx$

  (b) $\displaystyle\int \left(x - \frac{2}{x}\right)^2\,dx$ (g) $\displaystyle\int \frac{e^x}{e^x + 1}\,dx$

  (c) $\displaystyle\int \sin^2 x\,dx$ (h) $\displaystyle\int \frac{x^2}{x + 1}\,dx$

  (d) $\displaystyle\int x^{-\frac{2}{3}}\,dx$ (i) $\displaystyle\int \frac{1}{x} \ln x\,dx$

  (e) $\displaystyle\int \tan^2 x\,dx$ (j) $\displaystyle\int x e^{2x}\,dx$

2 Use the substitution $y = x - 1$ to find $\displaystyle\int \frac{x(x^2 + 1)}{(x - 1)^2}\,dx$.

3 (a) Express $\dfrac{1}{(x + 1)(x + 2)}$ in partial fractions.

  (b) Hence find the area contained between the curve $y = \dfrac{1}{(x + 1)(x + 2)}$, the x and y axes and the straight line $x = 4$.

4 Use integration by parts to find $\displaystyle\int \ln x\,dx$. If $\dfrac{d^2 y}{dx^2} + \dfrac{1}{x} = 0$ find y in terms of x given that $y = e$ when $x = 1$ and $y = 0$ when $x = e$.

5 Prove that the area bounded by the curve $y = x \sin x$ and the segment of the x-axis between $x = 0$ and $x = \pi$ is π.

6 Show that $\sec^6 \theta \equiv (1 + 2 \tan^2 \theta + \tan^4 \theta) \sec^2 \theta$ and hence or otherwise find $\displaystyle\int \sec^6 \theta\,d\theta$.

7 Find the equation of the curve whose gradient at the point (x, y) is $\dfrac{1 - 2x^2}{y}$ and which passes through the point $(0, 2)$.

8 The function f where $y = f(x)$ is such that $\dfrac{dy}{dx} = kx^2 - 2x^{\frac{1}{2}}$ where k is a constant. Find $f(x)$ given that when $x = 1$, $\dfrac{d^2 y}{dx^2} = 5$ and $y = 0$.

9 The area of the finite region contained between the curve $y^2 = 4x$ and the line $x = 4$ is revolved through 2π radians about the y-axis to form a volume of revolution of volume V. Show that $V = \dfrac{512\pi}{5}$.

10 The tangent at any point $P(x, y)$ on the curve shown meets the x-axis at the point T. The distance of T from the origin O is cx where c is a constant and $0 < c < 1$. Determine (a) the gradient of the tangent PT in terms of c and the coordinates of P.
(b) Hence find the equation of the curve given that it passes through the point $(1, 1)$.

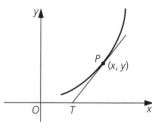

8 *Numerical work*

Absolute and relative errors

In writing final answers to numerical questions, you are often asked to write the answer to a specified degree of accuracy, say 2 significant figures, written as 2 s.f., or 3 decimal places, written 3 d.p.

For example, 31.79 is 32 to 2 s.f. and 31.8 to 1 d.p. You should know how to do this precisely and **do check** at the end of writing out a solution that your answer is given to the degree of accuracy asked for by the examiner.

Suppose you only knew the final answer as 32 to 2 s.f. and that the more detailed information on its accuracy was not available, then you may need to estimate the error involved by taking this approximate answer. Here are the general rules which should be memorized. For numbers x and y whose true values lie in the intervals defined by $x \pm e_1$ and $y \pm e_2$,

1 the sum $x + y$ has a maximum absolute error of $|e_1 + e_2|$ and a relative error of $\dfrac{e_1 + e_2}{x + y}$,

2 the difference $x - y$ has a maximum absolute error of $|e_1 + e_2|$ and a relative error of $\dfrac{e_1 + e_2}{x - y}$,

3 the product xy has a maximum absolute error of approximately $xe_2 + ye_1$ and a relative error of approximately $\dfrac{e_1}{x} + \dfrac{e_2}{y}$,

4 the quotient $\dfrac{x}{y}$ has a maximum absolute error of approximately $\dfrac{x}{y}\left(\dfrac{e_1}{x} + \dfrac{e_2}{y}\right)$ and a relative error of approximately $\dfrac{e_1}{x} + \dfrac{e_2}{y}$.

Worked Example 1

A rectangle measures 7.8 cm by 6.3 cm, where each measurement is correct to 2 s.f. Find the maximum absolute error and the relative error which could arise by using these measurements to calculate (a) the perimeter, (b) the area of the rectangle.

Working
Suppose that x cm and y cm are the correct length and correct breadth of the rectangle, then we have

$$7.75 \leqslant x < 7.85 \quad \text{and} \quad 6.25 \leqslant y < 6.35$$

Using the notation above then

$$x = 7.8, \quad e_1 = 0.05, \quad y = 6.3, \quad e_2 = 0.05$$

(a) We estimate the perimeter of the rectangle as

$$2(x + y)\,\text{cm} = 2(7.8 + 6.3)\,\text{cm} = 28.2\,\text{cm}$$

Maximum absolute error $= 2|e_1 + e_2|\,\text{cm} = 0.2\,\text{cm}$

$$\text{Relative error} = \frac{2(e_1 + e_2)}{2(x + y)} = \frac{0.2}{28.2} \approx 0.0071 \ (2\,\text{s.f.})$$

(b) We estimate the area of the rectangle as

$xy\,\text{cm}^2 = (7.8)(6.3)\,\text{cm}^2 = 49.14\,\text{cm}^2$

Maximum absolute error $\approx (xe_2 + ye_1)\,\text{cm}^2$

$$= \{7.8(0.05) + 6.3(0.05)\}\,\text{cm}^2$$

$$= 0.705\,\text{cm}^2 = 0.71\,\text{cm}^2\ (2\,\text{s.f.})$$

Relative error $\approx \left| \dfrac{0.05}{7.8} + \dfrac{0.05}{6.3} \right|$

$$= 0.0143\ldots = 0.014\ (2\,\text{s.f.})$$

Approximations to roots of equations

Many equations cannot be solved using algebraic methods. Any equation $f(x) = 0$ can be investigated to find the location of its roots by making a sketch of the curve with equation $y = f(x)$. You can do this by plotting points or by using a graphical calculator.

For a continuous function f, where $y = f(x)$, if you find values of x such that $f(\alpha) < 0$ and $f(\beta) > 0$, then in the interval $[\alpha, \beta]$ at least one root of the equation $f(x) = 0$ exists. This is obvious geometrically, as can be seen from the diagram, because the curve must cross the x-axis at least once between the points A and B.

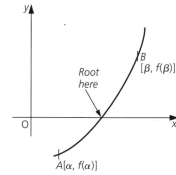

Worked Example 2
$f(x) \equiv e^x + x - 2$

Show that the equation $f(x) = 0$ has a root α in the interval $[0.44, 0.45]$.

Working
$f(0.44) = e^{0.44} + 0.44 - 2 = -0.00729 < 0$

$f(0.45) = e^{0.45} + 0.45 - 2 = 0.0183 > 0$

Since f is continuous in the given interval and there is a sign change, a root α lies in the interval. Once an approximation to a root has been found, there are various methods available to obtain greater accuracy of the root by finding further approximations.

Worked Example 3
Use the iterative relation $x_{n+1} = \ln(2 - x_n)$ with $x_0 = 0.44$ to find the root α of the equation $e^x + x - 2 = 0$, correct to 3 d.p.

Working
$x_1 = \ln(2 - 0.44) = 0.444\ 685\ 8$

$x_2 = \ln(2 - x_1) = 0.441\ 677\ 5$

$x_3 = \ln(2 - x_2) = 0.443\ 609\ 8$

$x_4 = \ln(2 - x_3) = 0.442\ 369\ 1$

$x_5 = \ln(2 - x_4) = 0.443\ 166$

$x_6 = \ln(2 - x_5) = 0.442\ 654\ 2$

Successive iterations are converging on α from above and below and the root α lies in the interval $[0.4426, 0.4431]$ from the values found for x_5 and x_6.

$\therefore\quad \alpha = 0.443$ **correct** to 3 d.p.

Newton–Raphson method

The iterative procedure defined by $x_{n+1} = x_n - \dfrac{f(x_n)}{f'(x_n)}$ and known as the Newton–Raphson method will usually improve an approximation to a root of the equation $f(x) = 0$ very rapidly, provided that a satisfactory first approximation x_0 is used.

Worked Example 4

Consider again the equation $f(x) = 0$, where $f(x) = e^x + x - 2$ with $x_0 = 0.44$ (see worked example 2).

$f'(x) = e^x + 1$ by differentiation with respect to x

Hence $f(x_0) = f(0.44) = -0.00729$

$\qquad\quad f'(x_0) = f'(0.44) = 2.5527$

Using the Newton–Raphson process, we have

$$x_1 \approx 0.44 - \frac{(-0.00729)}{2.5527}$$

$$= 0.44 + 0.002856 = 0.443 \text{ (3 d.p.)}$$

The Newton–Raphson method is very important because of the rapid convergence it usually provides towards the root. We can check in the above case that 0.4429 is, in fact, the root **correct** to 4 d.p.
  Consider the interval [0.44285, 0.44295]

$f(0.44285) = -0.000011 < 0$

$f(0.44295) = 0.00024 > 0$

Therefore the root lies in this interval because of the sign change and is 0.4429 **correct** to 4 d.p.

PRACTICE QUESTIONS

1 The measurements x and y, in seconds, are 1.2 and 3.7 respectively, correct to 1 d.p. Giving your answers to 1 d.p., find the least possible value of
(a) $y - x$,   (b) $\dfrac{x}{y}$.

2 A cylindrical hollow gun barrel has internal radius 8 cm and length 140 cm, where each measurement has been taken to the nearest centimetre. Find, to the nearest cubic centimetre (cm^3), the greatest possible volume of the gun barrel.

3 A wall is measured as 37 m long and 2 m high where each measurement is to the nearest metre.
(a) State the maximum possible absolute error in each of these measurements.
(b) Find the corresponding relative error in each case, giving your answer to 2 s.f.

4 $f(x) \equiv 2(\sin x \cos x + \sin x + x) - 3$.
(a) Show that the equation $f(x) = 0$ has a root α in the interval [0.5, 0.6].
(b) State the values of $f(0.5)$ and $f(0.6)$ and use these with linear interpolation to find α to 2 d.p.
(c) Show that this volume of α is in fact correct to 2 d.p.

5 $f(x) \equiv \arctan x - \frac{11}{12}x$.
(a) Show that the equation $f(x) = 0$ has a root β in the interval [0.5, 0.6].
(b) Using the method of interval bisection twice on [0.5, 0.6] as the initial interval, show that β lies in [m, 0.55] and state the value of m.

(c) Using 0.55 as a first approximation to β, use the Newton–Raphson procedure once to find β, giving your answer to 3 d.p.

6 $f(x) \equiv x^3 - 6x + 3$.

    (a) Show that the equation $f(x) = 0$ has a negative root γ in the interval $[-3, -2]$.

    (b) Use the iterative relation $x_{n+1} = (6x_n + 3)^{\frac{1}{3}}$, $x_0 = -3$ to find γ *correct* to 3 d.p.

Mathematics of uncertainty

Types of data

This concerns the collection, study and interpretation of information or data on which important decisions have to be made. The information to be observed and studied is known as the **variate** or **variable**. Some of it is **qualitative**, e.g. the colour of a car, some of it is **quantitative**, e.g. the heights of children in a class or the number of children in the different classes of a school. You should note that of the two quantitative examples one is discrete i.e. it is always a whole number of children, and one is continuous, i.e. it can take any value in the range between the height of the shortest child and the height of the tallest child in the class.

You need to be familiar with ways of collecting information or data, that is, terms like **sample**, **random sample**, **census**, and the ways in which the information or data can be presented – by means of **pie charts**, **histograms**, **bar charts**, **frequency polygons**, **cumulative frequency curves**, and **scatter diagrams** – should all be completely familiar to you.

Histogram

Remember that in a histogram the height of each rectangle is obtained by dividing the area of the rectangle which is the frequency (or some constant factor times the frequency) by the length of the class interval. The frequency polygon can then be obtained by joining the midpoints of the tops of each rectangle in the histogram by straight lines. The cumulative frequency curve, on the other hand, represents a running total of the frequencies plotted against the upper class boundaries, and these are joined by a smooth curve, except for a very small sample when straight line segments may be used.

Worked Example 1

The table below shows the number of pairs of shoes and their values rounded to the nearest pound, sold by a shoe shop on a particular day. Represent these data by a histogram showing clearly the relative heights of the rectangles representing each class interval.

Cost per pair of shoes, £x	$10 \leqslant x < 20$	$20 \leqslant x < 25$	$25 \leqslant x < 35$	$35 \leqslant x < 40$	$40 \leqslant x < 45$	$45 \leqslant x < 60$
Number sold	6	12	28	26	16	6

Working

£x	$10 \leqslant x < 20$	$20 \leqslant x < 25$	$25 \leqslant x < 35$	$35 \leqslant x < 40$	$40 \leqslant x < 45$	$45 \leqslant x < 60$
Frequency	6	12	28	26	16	6
Class width	10	5	10	5	5	15
Height	0.6	2.4	2.8	5.2	3.2	0.4

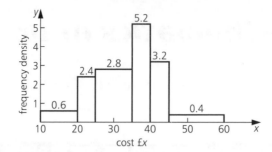

Cumulative frequency curve

Worked Example 2

The percentage marks obtained by 80 students in an English examination are given in the table below. Draw a cumulative frequency curve for these data.

Marks, x	$x \leqslant 20$	$20 < x \leqslant 30$	$30 < x \leqslant 40$	$40 < x \leqslant 60$	$60 < x \leqslant 80$	$80 < x \leqslant 100$
Number	3	7	18	36	10	6
Students' marks	$\leqslant 20$	$\leqslant 30$	$\leqslant 40$	$\leqslant 60$	$\leqslant 80$	$\leqslant 100$
Cumulative frequency	3	10	28	64	74	80

Working

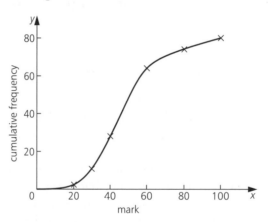

When joined by straight lines the curve is usually referred to as a cumulative frequency polygon. Do make sure you plot the cumulative frequency against the *upper* class boundary of an interval.

Remember that the summary measures of the location and dispersion of data are given by the mean, median, mode, range, interquartile range and standard deviation. You must be able to state or calculate these.

Measures of central location

The **mean** is the arithmetic mean. The **median** is obtained by arranging the data in ascending order and taking the middle value. The **mode** is the value which occurs most frequently.

Worked Example 3

John's score for each of the 18 holes of a golf course were

3, 4, 4, 5, 3, 6, 4, 4, 3, 5, 4, 4, 2, 7, 5, 3, 4, 5

Find (a) his modal score, (b) his median score, (c) his mean score.

Working

First rearrange the scores in ascending order of magnitude, thus

2, 3, 3, 3, 3, 4, 4, 4, 4, 4, 4, 4, 5, 5, 5, 5, 6, 7

(a) The most frequently occurring score is 4 $\Rightarrow$ modal score = 4.

(b) The middle scores are the 9th and 10th $\Rightarrow$ median score = $\dfrac{4+4}{2}$ = 4.

(c) The mean score is $\dfrac{\text{sum of all scores}}{18} = \dfrac{75}{18} \approx 4.17$ $\Rightarrow$ mean score ≈ 4.17.

(Learn how to use your calculator to obtain this last measure.)

Measures of dispersion

To measure the dispersion you must be able to calculate the variance and standard deviation. The variance of a set of data $x_1, x_2, x_3, \ldots, x_n$, occurring with frequencies $f_1, f_2, f_3, \ldots, f_n$, respectively and mean $\mu = \sum_{r=1}^{n} x_r f_r / \sum_{r=1}^{n} f_r$ is given by

$$\textbf{Variance } \sigma^2 = \frac{\sum_{r=1}^{n} f_r (x_r - \mu)^2}{\sum_{r=1}^{n} f_r} = \frac{\sum_{r=1}^{n} f_r (x_r)^2}{\sum_{r=1}^{n} f_r} - \mu^2$$

The **standard deviation** is the square root of the variance.

Worked Example 4

Thirty anglers participated in a fishing competition with the results as shown in the table below. Calculate the mean and the standard deviation for the number of fish caught

Number of fish caught	1	2	3	4	5	6	7	8	9	10
Number of people catching them	2	5	2	2	1	2	3	6	2	5

Working

x	f	fx	fx^2
1	2	2	2
2	5	10	20
3	2	6	18
4	2	8	32
5	1	5	25
6	2	12	72
7	3	21	147
8	6	48	384
9	2	18	162
10	5	50	500
	30	180	1362

$$\text{Mean} = \frac{180}{30} = 6 \text{ fish}$$

$$\text{Variance} = \frac{1\,362}{30} - 6^2 = 45.4 - 36 = 9.4$$

Standard deviation = $\sqrt{9.4} \approx 3.1$

Learn to obtain this answer directly from your calculator.

Probability

You must ensure that you are familiar with the elementary rules of probability, including the combined probabilities of both independent and dependent events together with simple ideas of conditional probability.

If a sample space consists of n events, all of which are equally likely and r of the events are considered a success then the probability of choosing a successful event is defined as

$$\frac{\text{number of ways of choosing a successful event}}{\text{total number of events in the sample space}}$$

or, in short $\quad\dfrac{\text{number of successful outcomes}}{\text{total number of possible outcomes}}$

Worked Example 5
Find the probability P of throwing a 2 or a 4 with a single throw of an unbiased die.

Working
For the throwing of an unbiased die, the sample space is the numbers 1, 2, 3, 4, 5 and 6. Thus the total number of possible outcomes is 6. A successful outcome would be if a 2 or a 4 were thrown. Thus the total number of successful outcomes is 2.

Hence P (Event A) where A represents the throwing of a 2 or a 4 is given by

$P(A) = \frac{2}{6} = \frac{1}{3}$

The complementary event to A, called 'not A', notation A', will occur if a score of 1, 3, 5 or 6 is obtained

$P(A') = \frac{4}{6} = \frac{2}{3}$

You should note that $P(A) + P(A') = \frac{1}{3} + \frac{2}{3} = 1 = $ certainty. It is true for all events that $P(A) + P(A') = 1$.

You may find it helpful to use a Venn diagram to illustrate the situation. The rectangle contains the whole of the sample space. The circle contains the successful events.

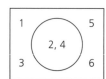

Summary of rules
Other notations and rules which you must know and be able to use are

1   $A \cup B$ Either A or B or both,

2   $A \cap B$ Both A and B

3   $A|B$ A given that B has already occurred

4   $P(A \cup B) = P(A) + P(B) - P(A \cap B)$

5   $P(A|B) = \dfrac{P(A \cap B)}{P(B)}$ and $P(B|A) = \dfrac{P(A \cap B)}{P(A)}$

6   For mutually exclusive events, $P(A \cup B) = P(A) + P(B)$ since $P(A \cap B) = 0$

7   For independent events, $P(A \cap B) = P(A) \times P(B)$

8   For independent events, $P(A|B) = P(A)$ whilst $P(B|A) = P(B)$

The rule $P(A \cap B) = P(A) \times P(B)$ is often referred to as the *product rule*, but it is valid *only* when A and B are independent events.

Worked Example 6

A card is selected at random from a pack of 52 playing cards. When a card is selected from the pack the event A is 'an ace is selected' and the event H is 'a heart is selected'. The diagram shows the events A and H, $A \cup H$ and $A \cap H$. (Note the overlap of the two events H and A to contain the ace of hearts.)

(a) Find the probability of drawing an ace or a heart from the pack.
(b) Given that the first card drawn was the ace of hearts, find the probability of drawing a second card which is an ace when the first card is not returned to the pack.

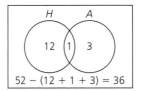

Working

(a) $P(A \cup H) = \dfrac{3 + 1 + 12}{52} = \dfrac{16}{52} = \dfrac{4}{13}.$

(b) When the ace of hearts is drawn there will be 3 aces left in the pack which now contains only 51 cards. Hence

$P(A \mid \text{ace of hearts drawn}) = \frac{3}{51}.$

Independent events

Two events A and B are said to be **independent** if the occurrence of one event A does not depend upon the occurrence of B or vice versa.

Worked Example 7

A box contains 10 fuses, 3 of which are broken and the others good. Two fuses are drawn from the box in succession without replacement. Find the probability that both fuses are good.

Working

Probability of drawing a good fuse $= \frac{7}{10}$. If this is not replaced, there will be 9 fuses left in the box, 6 of which will be good, therefore the probability of drawing a second good fuse $= \frac{6}{9}$. As the two events are completely independent

$P(2 \text{ good fuses}) = \frac{7}{10} \times \frac{6}{9} = \frac{7}{15}$

Mutually exclusive events

When two events A and B cannot both happen together they are said to be **mutually exclusive**. In such cases, $P(A \cap B) = 0$. The Venn diagram for such a situation shows two non-intersecting circles.

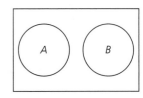

When events A and B are mutually exclusive then $P(A \cup B) = P(A) + P(B)$.

Worked Example 8

Find the probability of obtaining a total of 7 or 11 when two unbiased dice are thrown.

Working

Let A be the event of a total of 7. The total of 7 can come from $3 + 4$, $4 + 3$, $2 + 5$, $5 + 2$, $1 + 6$ and $6 + 1$. Therefore

$P(A) = \frac{6}{36} = \frac{1}{6}$

Let B be the event of a total of 11. The total of 11 can come from $5 + 6$ or $6 + 5$. Therefore

$$P(B) = \tfrac{2}{36} = \tfrac{1}{18}$$

Now events A and B are mutually exclusive since a total of 7 and a total of 11 cannot both occur at the same time. Hence

$$P(7 \text{ or } 11) = P(A) + P(B) = \tfrac{1}{6} + \tfrac{1}{18} = \tfrac{4}{18} = \tfrac{2}{9}$$

Tree diagrams

A very useful notation for solving some probability questions is the tree diagram.

Worked Example 9

A bag contains 5 red balls and 4 white balls. Two balls are drawn from the bag, one after the other, without replacement. Find the probability of drawing two balls of the same colour.

Working
Represent different ways of drawing the balls by the branches of a tree and on the branches write the probability for that section. From the diagram we can see that

$$P(2R \text{ or } 2W) = \tfrac{5}{18} + \tfrac{1}{6} = \tfrac{8}{18} = \tfrac{4}{9}$$

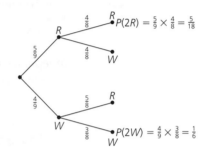

 PRACTICE QUESTIONS

1   The height of 10 girls were each measured to the nearest millimetre as:

    $1\,686,\ 1\,721,\ 1\,711,\ 1\,726,\ 1\,701,\ 1\,676,\ 1\,761,\ 1\,741,\ 1\,746,\ 1\,741$

    Find (a) the mean,   (b) the standard deviation of these heights.

2   In a county election, 75% of those eligible to vote did in fact vote. If three of those eligible are selected at random, find the probability that
    (a) at least two voted,
    (b) only one, at most voted.

3   One hundred children from school A and sixty children from school B were each set the same investigation to write up. The times (in minutes) which they took are given in the table.

Time	0–	50–	100–	150–	200–	300–400
School A	4	18	60	10	5	3
School B	2	13	26	17	0	2

    (a) By drawing a cumulative frequency curve for each school on the same axes, estimate the interquartile ranges.
    (b) What deductions can you make from your calculations?

4   Nine balls numbered $1, 2, 3, \ldots, 9$, are placed in a box. Three balls are drawn from the box at random and without replacement. The number on the first ball drawn is called n and S is the sum of the numbers on the balls drawn. Find the probability that (a) $S = 10$ (b) $S = 10$ *and* $n = 2$,   (c) $S = 10$ given that $n = 2$.

5   Two sets of data are such that

	Frequency	Mean	Standard deviation
X	24	15.5	0.5
Y	30	15.5	0.67

Find the standard deviation of the group $X + Y$ giving your answer to 2 s.f.

6   (a) The events A and B are mutually exclusive. $P(A) = \frac{1}{3}$ and $P(A \cup B) = \frac{1}{2}$.
     Find (i) $P(B)$ and (ii) $P(A' \cap B')$.
    (b) The events C and D are independent. $P(C) = \frac{2}{5}$ and $P(D \cap C') = \frac{3}{40}$.
     Find (i) $P(D)$, (ii) $P(C \cap D)$ (iii) $P(C|D)$ and (iv) $P(D|C)$.
    (c) For two events E and F it is known that $P(E) = \frac{3}{5}$, $P(F) = \frac{1}{5}$ and
     $P(E|F) = \frac{1}{10}$.
     Find (i) $P(E \cap F)$ and (ii) $P(E \cap F') + P(E' \cap F)$.

7   The table shows the amount of money collected by 250 children involved in a sponsored swim.

Amount collected, £	$0 \leqslant x < 2$	$2 \leqslant x < 5$	$5 \leqslant x < 9$	$9 \leqslant x < 14$	$14 \leqslant x < 20$
Number of children	10	83	80	48	29

Draw a histogram to represent these data.

10 Vectors

Properties of vectors

- The vector $\overrightarrow{OA}$ is a **directed line segment** having both magnitude (length) and direction. $\overrightarrow{AO} = -\overrightarrow{OA}$.
- The unit vectors $\mathbf{i}, \mathbf{j}$ and $\mathbf{k}$ are taken to be parallel to the x, y and z axes respectively.
- If $\overrightarrow{OP} = x\mathbf{i} + y\mathbf{j} + z\mathbf{k}$, then the position vector of P referred to O as origin is $x\mathbf{i} + y\mathbf{j} + z\mathbf{k}$ and the length (or magnitude) of $\overrightarrow{OP}$ is $\sqrt{(x^2 + y^2 + z^2)}$.
- The vector of length 1 unit, that is the **unit vector**, in the direction $\overrightarrow{OP}$ is
  $$\frac{x\mathbf{i} + y\mathbf{j} + z\mathbf{k}}{\sqrt{(x^2 + y^2 + z^2)}}.$$
- Two vectors are equal if, and only if, they are equal in magnitude and have the same direction.

Triangle law

Vectors are added by adding respective x, y and z components of each or by using the *triangle law* which is equivalent.

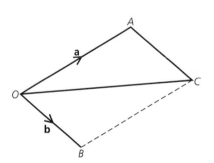

For vectors $\overrightarrow{OA}$ and $\overrightarrow{OB}$ in the diagram, complete $\triangle OAC$ where $\overrightarrow{OB} = \overrightarrow{AC}$. Then,

$$\overrightarrow{OA} + \overrightarrow{OB} = \overrightarrow{OA} + \overrightarrow{AC}$$
$$= \overrightarrow{OC}$$

Journey from O to A + journey from A to $C \equiv$ journey from O to C, i.e.

$$\overrightarrow{OA} + \overrightarrow{OB} = \overrightarrow{OC}$$

(Notice that $OACB$ is a *parallelogram*.)

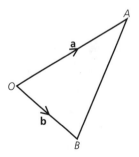

Also $\overrightarrow{OB} - \overrightarrow{OA} = \overrightarrow{OB} + \overrightarrow{AO} = \overrightarrow{AO} + \overrightarrow{OB} = \overrightarrow{AB}$

So $\overrightarrow{AB} = \mathbf{b} - \mathbf{a}$, where $\overrightarrow{OB} = \mathbf{b}$ and $\overrightarrow{OA} = \mathbf{a}$

If $\mathbf{a} = a_1\mathbf{i} + a_2\mathbf{j} + a_3\mathbf{k}$ and
$\mathbf{b} = b_1\mathbf{i} + b_2\mathbf{j} + b_3\mathbf{k}$, then
$\mathbf{a} + \mathbf{b} = (a_1 + b_1)\mathbf{i} + (a_2 + b_2)\mathbf{j} + (a_3 + b_3)\mathbf{k}$, and
$\mathbf{a} - \mathbf{b} = (a_1 - b_1)\mathbf{i} + (a_2 - b_2)\mathbf{j} + (a_3 - b_3)\mathbf{k}$.

Referred to O as origin, the line AB has equation

$$\mathbf{r} = \mathbf{a} + t(\mathbf{b} - \mathbf{a}),$$

where t is a scalar parameter, that is, as t takes different values, the point with position vector $\mathbf{r}$ lies at different points on the line. In component form, the equation of the line is often written as

$$\mathbf{r} = \begin{pmatrix} a_1 \\ a_2 \\ a_3 \end{pmatrix} + t \begin{pmatrix} b_1 - a_1 \\ b_2 - a_2 \\ b_3 - a_3 \end{pmatrix}, \quad \text{where} \begin{pmatrix} a_1 \\ a_2 \\ a_3 \end{pmatrix} \equiv a_1\mathbf{i} + a_2\mathbf{j} + a_3\mathbf{k}$$

Scalar product

The scalar product $\mathbf{a} \times \mathbf{b}$ of the vectors $\mathbf{a}$ and $\mathbf{b}$ is defined as $a_1b_1 + a_2b_2 + a_3b_3$ and the scalar product is also the same as $|\mathbf{a}|\,|\mathbf{b}|\cos\theta$, where θ is the angle between the vectors $\mathbf{a}$ and $\mathbf{b}$. (The scalar product is also called the **dot product**.) So we have

$$\cos\theta = \frac{a_1b_1 + a_2b_2 + a_3b_3}{\sqrt{(a_1^2 + a_2^2 + a_3^3)}\,\sqrt{(b_1^2 + b_2^2 + b_3^2)}}$$

If $\theta = 90°$, $\mathbf{a} \times \mathbf{b} = 0$, and if $\mathbf{a} \times \mathbf{b} = 0$, then $\theta = 90°$.

Worked Example 1

Referred to an origin O, the points A and B are given by $\overrightarrow{OA} = (3\mathbf{i} + 4\mathbf{j} - 5\mathbf{k})$ and $\overrightarrow{OB} = (4\mathbf{i} - 2\mathbf{j} - 4\mathbf{k})$. Find (a) an equation, in vector form, of the line AB, and (b) the size of $\angle AOB$ to the nearest degree.

Working

(a) Now $\overrightarrow{AB} = \overrightarrow{OB} - \overrightarrow{OA} = \mathbf{i} - 6\mathbf{j} + \mathbf{k}$

Equation of AB is $\mathbf{r} = (3\mathbf{i} + 4\mathbf{j} - 5\mathbf{k}) + t(\mathbf{i} - 6\mathbf{j} + \mathbf{k})$

(b) $\mathbf{a} \times \mathbf{b} = 12 - 8 + 20 = 24$

$|\mathbf{a}| = \sqrt{(3^2 + 4^2 + 5^2)} = 5\sqrt{2}, \quad |\mathbf{b}| = \sqrt{(4^2 + 2^2 + 4^2)} = 6$

$\cos\angle AOB = \dfrac{24}{6 \times 5\sqrt{2}} = \dfrac{4}{5\sqrt{2}}$

$\Rightarrow \angle AOB = 56°$ (nearest degree)

PRACTICE QUESTIONS

1 (a) By using the scalar product, or otherwise, show that the points with position vectors $\mathbf{i} + 2\mathbf{j}$, $4\mathbf{i} + 6\mathbf{j}$, $5\mathbf{i} - \mathbf{j}$ are the vertices of an isosceles right-angled triangle.
   (b) Given that the three given points in (a) are three vertices of a square, find the position vector of the fourth vertex.
   (c) Find, to the nearest degree, the acute angle between the line joining the points with position vectors $4\mathbf{i} + 6\mathbf{j}$ and $5\mathbf{i} - \mathbf{j}$ and the line $y = 2x$.

2 Given that the points X, Y and Z have position vectors
$$\begin{pmatrix} 2 \\ 1 \\ -1 \end{pmatrix}, \begin{pmatrix} 1 \\ 3 \\ 3 \end{pmatrix} \text{ and } \begin{pmatrix} -1 \\ 1 \\ 5 \end{pmatrix}$$ respectively referred to an origin O, calculate
   (a) the angle YXZ to $0.1°$, and (b) the area of $\triangle XYZ$, to 2 d.p.

3 (a) Given that $\overrightarrow{OA} = \begin{pmatrix} 3 \\ 4 \\ -5 \end{pmatrix}$ and $\overrightarrow{OB} = \begin{pmatrix} 4 \\ 2 \\ -3 \end{pmatrix}$, where O is the origin, find an equation for the line AB in vector form.

(b) The point C is such that $\overrightarrow{OC} = \frac{1}{3} \begin{pmatrix} 14 \\ 2 \\ -5 \end{pmatrix}$. Show that OC is perpendicular to

the line AB and that C lies on the line AB.

4 Referred to an origin O, the points P and Q have position vectors

$\begin{pmatrix} 2 \\ 3 \\ 6 \end{pmatrix}$ and $\begin{pmatrix} 2 \\ 4 \\ 4 \end{pmatrix}$ respectively.

(a) Calculate $\angle OPQ$ to $0.1°$.

(b) The point R is such that $\overrightarrow{OR} = \begin{pmatrix} 5 \\ 12 \\ 6 \end{pmatrix}$. Show that OR and PQ are

perpendicular.

(c) Show also that the lines OR and PQ intersect and find $\overrightarrow{OS}$, where S is the intersection point.

Mechanics

✓ TOPIC OUTLINE AND REVISION TIPS

Modelling

In modelling practical situations we assume that:

1 a body which has mass but whose dimensions are small in comparison to the surroundings is modelled as a particle,
2 ropes and strings which only stretch marginally are taken to be **light** (no mass) and **inextensible** (no stretching),
3 elastic strings and springs are assumed to obey **Hooke's law** and have negligible mass,
4 any surface described as **smooth** is **frictionless**,
5 smooth **pegs** and **pulleys** allow a string to retain a tension of constant magnitude when it passes around them,
6 uniform bodies have constant mass per unit volume and retain their shape under external forces,
7 any surface described as rough requires frictional forces to be considered in its associated model.

Assumptions

As part of the solution to a problem, examiners may ask you to state any assumptions that you make, such as those outlined in 1–7 above. Some worked examples in this chapter show you how to do this.

Worked Example 1

For the path of a golf ball passing over horizontal ground, the time of flight and the horizontal range are measured. State what modelling assumptions should be made in order to estimate the speed and the direction of the velocity of projection.

Working

The following assumptions are relevant
(a) the force of gravity is constant,
(b) the ball is modelled as a particle,
(c) air resistance is neglected,
(d) there is no wind blowing.

Having made these assumptions, the equations

$$T = \frac{2v \sin \alpha}{g} \quad \text{and} \quad R = \frac{2v^2 \sin \alpha \cos \alpha}{g},$$

where T is the time of flight and R is the horizontal range, can be solved simultaneously to find v, the speed, and α, the angle of elevation, at projection.

Motion in a straight line under constant acceleration

$$A \xrightarrow{\quad\quad\quad\quad \gg a \quad\quad\quad\quad} B$$
$$\xrightarrow{} u \qquad\qquad \text{distance } S \text{ in time } t \qquad\qquad \xrightarrow{} v$$

A particle moves in a straight line AB under constant acceleration a ms^{-2}, where $AB = S$ m. The velocity at A is u ms^{-1} and after t seconds the velocity at B is v ms^{-1}. For this motion, the following formulae are applicable:

1 $V = u + at,$

2 $S = ut + \frac{1}{2}at^2,$

3 $S = vt - \frac{1}{2}at^2,$

4 $V^2 = u^2 + 2aS,$

5 $S = \left(\dfrac{u+v}{2}\right)t$

Note: In practical problems we take $g \approx 10$ ms^{-2}.

Worked Example 2
A pebble P is falling vertically with acceleration 10 ms^{-2}. Initially, P was released from rest from a stationary balloon at a height of 200 m above horizontal ground. Find the speed of P after 5 seconds and its height above the ground at this instant.

Working
Here we have $u = 0$, $a = 10$ and $t = 5$ and using $V = u + at = 0 + 50$
  So speed of P is 50 ms^{-1} after $5\,s$.
  Using $S = ut + \frac{1}{2}at^2 = 0 + \frac{1}{2} \times 10 \times 25 = 125.$
  Height of P above the ground is $(200 - 125)$m $= 75$ m after $5\,s$.
(Notice that in the solution we have neglected air resistance and the pebble is modelled as a particle.)

Projectiles

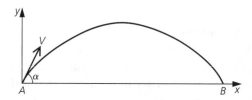

Consider a particle moving from A to B in the path shown, starting with velocity of magnitude V at an angle of elevation α. The particle moves freely under gravity (no air resistance).

Time of flight T from A to $B = \dfrac{2V \sin \alpha}{g}$

Horizontal range $AB = \dfrac{2V^2 \sin \alpha \cos \alpha}{g} = \dfrac{V^2 \sin 2\alpha}{g}$

Greatest height above AB is $\dfrac{V^2 \sin^2 \alpha}{2g}$.

All of these formulae can be obtained by resolving V into $V \sin \alpha$ vertically and $V \cos \alpha$ horizontally. Remember that g, the acceleration due to gravity, only affects the vertical component of the motion.
  For a given value of V and variable α, the greatest horizontal range is obtained when $\alpha = 45°$ and this greatest range is V^2/g since $\sin 2\alpha = 1$ when $\alpha = 45°$.

At time t in the motion of the particle from A to B suppose it has reached the point (x, y) where x is measured along AB and y is measured vertically upwards. Then

$$x = (V \cos \alpha)t \quad \text{and} \quad y = (V \sin \alpha)t - \tfrac{1}{2}gt^2$$

By eliminating t, we obtain the cartesian equation of the path

$$y = x \tan \alpha - \frac{gx^2}{2V^2 \cos^2 \alpha}$$

which is a **parabola**.

When answering questions on projectiles, **always draw a neat freehand diagram** and write on it the given information.

Worked Example 3

A ball is thrown with velocity $20 \, \text{ms}^{-1}$ at $30°$ above the horizontal from an edge E of a roof, which is $15 \, \text{m}$ above horizontal street level. The ball hits the street at the point S. Find

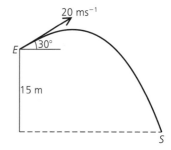

(a) the time taken by the ball to reach S from E,
(b) the horizontal distance between S and E.

Working

(a) Considering the vertical component of motion from E to S, we have

$$u = 20 \sin 30° = 10, \quad a = -g = -10, \quad s = -15$$
$$s = ut + \tfrac{1}{2}at^2 \quad \Rightarrow \quad -15 = 10t - 5t^2 \quad \Rightarrow \quad t^2 - 2t - 3 = 0$$

Factorising $(t - 3)(t + 1) = 0 \quad \Rightarrow \quad t = 3$

The ball takes $3 \, \text{s}$ to move from E to S.

(b) The horizontal component of the velocity $= 20 \cos 30°$ and this value is constant.

Horizontal distance between E and S is

$$ut = (20 \cos 30°) \, 3 \text{ metres}$$
$$= 52 \, \text{m to the nearest metre}$$

Notice that in the solution, the ball is taken to be a particle and air resistance is neglected.

Uniform circular motion

A particle P describes a circle, centre O and radius a, with constant angular speed w. The linear speed of P is aw. You should appreciate that the velocity of P is **continuously changing** but the magnitude is constant.

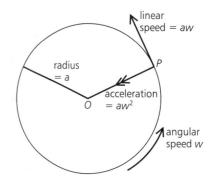

1 If the linear speed is v, then $\boxed{v = aw}$

2 The acceleration of P is of magnitude $aw^2 \equiv \dfrac{v^2}{a}$.

3 The direction of the velocity of P is along the tangent and the direction of the acceleration is towards the centre O of the circle.

Worked Example 4

A particle moves in a circular path of radius 6 m with constant angular speed $7 \, \text{rad s}^{-1}$. Find the linear speed of P, the acceleration of P and the time taken by P to complete one orbit.

Working

Speed $= (wa) \, \text{ms}^{-1} = (6 \times 7) \, \text{ms}^{-1} = 42 \, \text{ms}^{-1}$

Acceleration $= (aw^2) \, \text{ms}^{-2} = (6 \times 7^2) \, \text{ms}^{-2} = 294 \, \text{ms}^{-2}$

Time for one orbit $= \left(\dfrac{2\pi}{w} \right)$ seconds $= \left(\dfrac{2\pi}{7} \right)$ seconds $= 0.9$ seconds (1 d.p.)

Note: In non-uniform circular motion, the velocity **v** changes continuously in both magnitude and direction. At any instant, at the point P, where O is the centre of the circle of radius a, we have

1 **v** is directed along the tangent at P,

2 the acceleration of P has a component of $\left| \dfrac{d\mathbf{v}}{dt} \right|$ along the tangent and a component of $\dfrac{\mathbf{v}^2}{a}$ along $\overrightarrow{PO}$.

Questions on this topic are usually solved by using conservation of energy and Newton's 2nd law (see question 15 in the exercises at the end of this chapter).

Non-uniform motion in a straight line

Suppose a particle P is moving along the x-axis from the origin O and that, at time t, its velocity is v when at a distance x from O. Then we have

$$\frac{dx}{dt} = v = \text{velocity of } P \text{ at time } t$$

$$\frac{d^2x}{dt^2} = \frac{dv}{dt} = \frac{dv}{dx} \times \frac{dx}{dt} = v\frac{dv}{dx} = \text{acceleration of } P \text{ at time } t$$

Simple harmonic motion (SHM)

SHM is an important example of non-uniform motion in a straight line.

$$A \text{———————} \underset{O}{\mid} \;\; x \;\; \underset{P}{\mid} \text{———} B$$

A particle P moves along the x-axis in such a way that its acceleration is always directed towards O and is of magnitude $w^2|x|$, where $OP = x$ and w is a constant. When this occurs, P is said to move with SHM. $OA = OB = a$ is called the **amplitude** of the motion.

The time taken for P to move from B to A and back to B, or equivalent, is called the **period** and is $\dfrac{2\pi}{w}$.

Learn these important results (for $x = a$, $v = 0$ at $t = 0$)

1 $\dfrac{d^2x}{dt^2} = v\dfrac{dv}{dx} = -w^2x,$

2 $v^2 = w^2(a^2 - x^2),$

3 $x = a \cos wt,$

4 Period $= \dfrac{2\pi}{w},$

5 Amplitude of SHM $= a.$

Worked Example 5

A particle moves with SHM such that when it is at the points C and D on the x-axis, the speed at C is $1\,\text{ms}^{-1}$, where $OC = 2\,\text{m}$, and the speed at D is $2\,\text{ms}^{-1}$, where $OD = 1\,\text{m}$. C and D are on opposite sides of the centre of motion O. Find the amplitude, period, greatest speed and greatest acceleration of the particle. Find also the time taken to move from C to D.

Working

Using the formula $v^2 = w^2(a^2 - x^2)$, we have for C and D

$$v = 2, x = 1 \quad \Rightarrow \quad 4 = w^2(a^2 - 1) \tag{1}$$

$$v = 1, x = -2 \quad \Rightarrow \quad 1 = w^2(a^2 - 4) \tag{2}$$

Taking equation [2] from equation [1] gives $\quad 3 = 3w^2 \quad \Rightarrow \quad w = 1$.
Substituting in [1] gives $\quad 4 = 1^2(a^2 - 1) \quad \Rightarrow \quad a^2 = 5 \quad \Rightarrow \quad a = \sqrt{5}$

$\text{Period} = \dfrac{2\pi}{w} = 2\pi$ seconds and amplitude $= \sqrt{5}$ metres

Greatest speed is at O (when $x = 0$) and is $wa = \sqrt{5}\,\text{ms}^{-1}$
Greatest acceleration is at A (or B) and is $w^2a = \sqrt{5}\,\text{ms}^{-2}$

$$\text{Time from } C \text{ to } D = \frac{1}{w} \arccos \frac{OC}{a} + \frac{1}{w} \arccos \frac{OD}{a}$$

$$= \left(\arccos \frac{2}{\sqrt{5}} + \arccos \frac{1}{\sqrt{5}} \right) \text{ seconds} \approx 1.57 \text{ seconds}$$

Differentiation and integration of vectors

Referred to an origin O, the point P has position vector $\mathbf{r}$ and $\mathbf{r} = x\mathbf{i} + y\mathbf{j} + z\mathbf{k}$ where x, y and z are variables which are functions of the time variable t only.
The velocity of P is $\mathbf{v}$, where

$$\mathbf{v} = \frac{d\mathbf{r}}{dt} = \frac{dx}{dt}\mathbf{i} + \frac{dy}{dt}\mathbf{j} + \frac{dz}{dt}\mathbf{k}$$

and the acceleration of P is $\mathbf{a}$, where

$$\mathbf{a} = \frac{d\mathbf{v}}{dt} = \frac{d^2\mathbf{r}}{dt^2} = \frac{d^2x}{dt^2}\mathbf{i} + \frac{d^2y}{dt^2}\mathbf{j} + \frac{d^2z}{dt^2}\mathbf{k}$$

Worked Example 6

A particle P starts from the origin O and at time t seconds the velocity of P is $\left\{ (\cos t)\mathbf{i} + \left(e^{\frac{t}{2}}\right)\mathbf{j} \right\} \text{ms}^{-1}$. Find (a) the speed of P when $t = \pi$, (b) the position vector of P at time $t = \dfrac{\pi}{2}$.

Working

(a) At $t = \pi$, $\mathbf{v} = \left(-\mathbf{i} + e^{\frac{\pi}{2}}\mathbf{j} \right) \text{ms}^{-1}$

Speed of $P = \sqrt{(1 + e^{\pi})}\,\text{ms}^{-1} = 4.91\,\text{ms}^{-1}$

(b) Integrating $\mathbf{v}$ with respect to t gives

$\mathbf{r} = (\sin t)\mathbf{i} + 2e^{\frac{t}{2}}\mathbf{j} + \mathbf{c}$ where $\mathbf{c}$ is a constant vector. $e^{\frac{t}{2}}$

At the origin $(0, 0)$, $t = 0 \quad \Rightarrow \quad 0 = 0\mathbf{i} + 2\mathbf{j} + \mathbf{c} \quad \Rightarrow \quad \mathbf{c} = -2\mathbf{j}$

$\mathbf{r} = (\sin t)\mathbf{i} + 2\left(e^{\frac{t}{2}} - 1\right)\mathbf{j}$

At $t = \dfrac{\pi}{2}$, $\mathbf{r} = \mathbf{i} + 2\left(e^{\frac{\pi}{4}} - 1\right)\mathbf{j}$.

At $t = \dfrac{\pi}{2}$, the position vector of P is $(\mathbf{i} + 1.19\mathbf{j})$ metres.

Relative motion

At time t, referred to an origin O, the points P and Q have position vectors $\mathbf{p}$ and $\mathbf{q}$ respectively.

The position of Q relative to P is $\mathbf{q} - \mathbf{p}$.

The velocity of Q relative to P is $\dfrac{d\mathbf{q}}{dt} - \dfrac{d\mathbf{p}}{dt} = \mathbf{v}_Q - \mathbf{v}_P$.

The acceleration of Q relative to P is $\dfrac{d^2\mathbf{q}}{dt^2} - \dfrac{d^2\mathbf{p}}{dt^2} = \mathbf{a}_Q - \mathbf{a}_P$.

Worked Example 7

The velocity of P is $(5\mathbf{i} - 7\mathbf{j})\,\text{ms}^{-1}$ and the velocity of Q is $(-3\mathbf{i} + 8\mathbf{j})\,\text{ms}^{-1}$. Find (a) the velocity of Q relative to P, and (b) the speed of Q relative to P.

Working
(a) Velocity of Q relative to $P = -3\mathbf{i} + 8\mathbf{j} - (5\mathbf{i} - 7\mathbf{j})\,\text{ms}^{-1}$

$$= (-8\mathbf{i} + 15\mathbf{j})\,\text{ms}^{-1}.$$

(b) Speed of Q relative to $P = \sqrt{(8^2 + 15^2)}\,\text{ms}^{-1} = 17\,\text{ms}^{-1}$ in the direction of the vector $(-8\mathbf{i} + 15\mathbf{j})$.

Newton's laws of motion

1 Every body stays at rest or in uniform motion in a straight line unless it is made to change that state by external forces.
2 The rate of change of linear momentum of a body is proportional to the force being applied to the body and acts in the same direction as the force. In symbols, $\mathbf{F} = m\mathbf{a}$ where $\mathbf{F}$ is the force, m the mass of the body and $\mathbf{a}$ the acceleration.
3 The force exerted by body A on body B is equal in magnitude and opposite in direction to the force exerted by B on A.

Worked Example 8

A force of $1.2\,\text{N}$ (newtons) acts on a particle P of mass $0.4\,\text{kg}$ for $4\,\text{s}$. Starting from rest, P moves through $x\,\text{m}$ in a straight line. Find the acceleration of P and the value of x.

Working
From $\mathbf{F} = m\mathbf{a} \quad \Rightarrow \quad 1.2 = 0.4a \quad \Rightarrow \quad a = 3$

Using $s = ut + \frac{1}{2}at^2$, where $u = 0$, $a = 3$, $t = 4$

$\Rightarrow \quad s = 0 + \frac{1}{2}(3)(16) = 24$

The acceleration of P is $3\,\text{ms}^{-2}$ and the distance covered is $24\,\text{m}$.

Worked Example 9

Two particles, A of mass $0.1\,\text{kg}$ and B of mass $0.2\,\text{kg}$, are connected by a light, inextensible string passing over a smooth, fixed pulley. The particles are released from rest, as shown. Find the acceleration of A and the tension in the string.

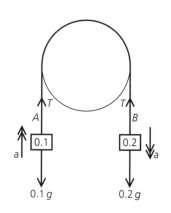

Working

Using Newton's second law for A and B, in turn, where A moves upwards and B moves downwards

$$T - 0.1g = 0.1a \qquad [1]$$

$$0.2g - T = 0.2a \qquad [2]$$

Solving [1] and [2] we have $a = \frac{1}{3}g$ and $T = \frac{2}{15}g$.

So if we take $g \approx 10\,\mathrm{ms}^{-2}$, the acceleration is $3\frac{1}{3}\,\mathrm{ms}^{-2}$ and the tension in the string is $1\frac{1}{3}\,\mathrm{N}$.

Energy

For a particle of mass m kg moving with speed $v\,\mathrm{ms}^{-1}$ the kinetic energy (KE) is $\frac{1}{2}mv^2$, measured in **joules** (J).

If a point B is h metres *vertically* higher than a point A, the potential energy (PE) of a particle of mass m at B with respect to the level of A is mgh. That is, the PE is equivalent to the **work done** on the particle in moving it from A to B.

For an elastic string or spring with **modulus of elasticity** λ and natural length l, **Hooke's law** gives the **tension** T as

$$T = \frac{\lambda x}{l}$$

for an extension of x. The **energy** in this string is $\frac{1}{2}\lambda x^2/l$.

The **work–energy** principle states that:

$$\text{Increase in mechanical energy} = \begin{array}{c}\text{work done by} \\ \text{external forces}\end{array} - \begin{array}{c}\text{work done} \\ \text{against friction}\end{array}$$

Worked Example 10

The vertical distance between the top and bottom of a helter-skelter is 15 m but the actual track is of length 64 m. A child with a mat has mass 36 kg and starts with speed $2\,\mathrm{ms}^{-1}$ at the top and finishes with speed $11\,\mathrm{ms}^{-1}$ at the bottom. Taking $g = 10\,\mathrm{ms}^{-2}$, find the constant frictional force.

Working

Increase in KE $= \frac{1}{2} \times 36 \times (11^2 - 2^2)\,\mathrm{J} = 2\,106\,\mathrm{J}$.

Decrease in PE $= 36 \times 10 \times 15\,\mathrm{J} \qquad = 5\,400\,\mathrm{J}$.

Work done against friction $= 64F$ (where F newtons is the friction)

Using the work–energy principle then

$$64F = 5\,400 - 2\,106 \quad \Rightarrow \quad F = 51.5 \quad (3\,\text{s.f.})$$

The frictional force is 51.5 N.

■ Worked Example 11

A light, elastic string has modulus 16 N, natural length 0.8 m and it has one end fixed at a point A. A particle P of mass 0.4 kg is tied to the other end. The particle is held at A and released to fall vertically. Find the greatest length of the string in the ensuing motion.

Working

The loss in potential energy from the start to maximum extension will be the same as the work done in stretching the string to its extension.

Suppose greatest length is x metres then, taking $g = 10\,\mathrm{ms}^{-2}$,

$$0.4 \times 10 \times x = \frac{1}{2} \times 16 \times \frac{(x - 0.8)^2}{0.8}$$

$$(x - 0.8)^2 = 0.4x \quad \Rightarrow \quad x^2 - 2x + 0.64 = 0$$

$$x = \frac{2 \pm \sqrt{(4 - 2.56)}}{2} = \frac{2 \pm 1.2}{2} = 1.6 \quad (\text{or } 0.4)$$

The greatest length of AP is 1.6 m.

Power

Power is defined as the rate of doing work. The units are **watts** or **kilowatts**.

Worked Example 12
The engine of a pump is required to lift 120 kg of water per minute through a verticle height of 15 m and to discharge it with a speed of 8 ms⁻¹. Find the rate of working of the engine of the pump. (Take $g = 10\,\text{ms}^{-2}$)

Working
In 1 second the pump raises 2 kg of water through a height of 15 m, so

PE increase $= 2 \times 10 \times 15\,\text{J} = 300\,\text{J}$

Also in 1 second 2 kg of water is given a speed of 8 ms⁻¹, so

KE increase $= \frac{1}{2} \times 2 \times 8^2 = 64\,\text{J}$

Total work done in 1 second $= (300 + 64)\,\text{J} = 364\,\text{J}$.

Rate of working $= 364\,\text{W}$ or $0.364\,\text{kW}$.

Worked Example 13
A lorry of mass 5 000 kg is climbing a hill inclined at $\arcsin\frac{1}{20}$ to the horizontal with constant speed 15 ms⁻¹. The non-gravitational resistance is of magnitude 640 N. Find the rate of working of the engine of the lorry. (Take $g = 10\,\text{ms}^{-2}$)

Working
Work done in overcoming resistance each second $= 640 \times 15\,\text{J}$
Work done in overcoming gravitational force in each
second $= 5\,000 \times 10 \times \frac{1}{20} \times 15\,\text{J}$
Rate of working of engine of lorry in
1 second $= \left(640 \times 15 + 5\,000 \times 10 \times \frac{1}{20} \times 15\right)\text{J}$
$= 47\,100\,\text{W} = 47.1\,\text{kW}$

Impulse

The **impulse** of a force is measured by the change in momentum it produces over a time interval t when acting on a particle of mass m.
For example, if the force **F** is constant then

$\mathbf{F}t = m(\mathbf{v}_2 - \mathbf{v}_1)$

where $\mathbf{v}_1$ and $\mathbf{v}_2$ are the initial and final velocities of the particle on which the impulse has been enacted.

Worked Example 14
A particle P of mass 0.3 kg is moving with velocity $(3\mathbf{i} - 4\mathbf{j})\,\text{ms}^{-1}$. As a result of an impulse, P now moves with velocity $6\mathbf{i}\,\text{ms}^{-1}$. Find the magnitude of the impulse.

Working
Impulse $=$ change in momentum
$= 0.3(6\mathbf{i} - 3\mathbf{i} + 4\mathbf{j})$ Newton-seconds
$= 0.3(3\mathbf{i} + 4\mathbf{j})\,\text{Ns}$
Magnitude of impulse $= 0.3\sqrt{(3^2 + 4^2)}\,\text{Ns} = 1.5\,\text{Ns}$

Principle of conservation of linear momentum

The total momentum in a given direction of all the bodies in a system is not changed by any interaction between them.

Worked Example 15

A capsule, of mass 1 100 kg, is moving in space in a straight line with speed $400 \, \text{ms}^{-1}$ at an instant when a retrorocket, of mass 200 kg, is fired directly backwards with speed $950 \, \text{ms}^{-1}$. Find the new speed of the capsule, whose mass is now 900 kg.

Working

Using the conservation of linear momentum principle

$$1\,100 \times 400 = 900\,v - 200 \times 950$$
$$900\,v = 440\,000 + 190\,000 = 630\,000$$
$$\Rightarrow \quad v = 700$$

Now speed of capsule is $700 \, \text{ms}^{-1}$.

Collisions and Newton's experimental law

Consider two particles of mass m_1 and m_2 moving in the same line and the same direction with speeds u_1 and u_2. They collide and afterwards the speeds are v_1 and v_2, as shown.

Clearly, momentum is conserved:

$$m_1 u_1 + m_2 u_2 = m_1 v_1 + m_2 v_2 \qquad\qquad\qquad [1]$$

Newton's experimental law for collisions of particles states that

Relative speed of separation $= e$ (Relative speed of approach)

where e is a constant, $0 \leqslant e \leqslant 1$, called the coefficient of restitution.

Using this law

$$v_2 - v_1 = e(u_1 - u_2)$$

These topics are very popular with examiners. Always draw a diagram and mark on it the relevant masses and speeds. Then your strategy should be to form the two equations from conservation of momentum and Newton's experimental law and solve them.

The loss in KE is also often required and is

$$\tfrac{1}{2} m_1 u_1^2 + \tfrac{1}{2} m_2 u_2^2 - \tfrac{1}{2} m_1 v_1^2 - \tfrac{1}{2} m_2 v_2^2$$

The impulse exerted by one particle on the other in a collision is found by obtaining the change in momentum of one particle $= m_1(u_1 - v_1)$ (or $m_2(v_2 - u_2)$).

Equilibrium

A particle is in equilibrium if and only if the vector sum of the forces acting on it is zero.

Worked Example 16

The three forces $(5\mathbf{i} + 7\mathbf{j})$ newtons, $(4\mathbf{i} - p\mathbf{j})$ newtons and $(-3q\,\mathbf{i} + 2p\,\mathbf{j})$ newtons are in equilibrium. Find the values of p and q.

Working

For equilibrium $\qquad 5\mathbf{i} + 7\mathbf{j} + 4\mathbf{i} - p\mathbf{j} - 3q\mathbf{i} + 2p\mathbf{j} = 0$

For the **i** components $\quad 5 + 4 - 3q = 0 \quad \Rightarrow \quad q = 3$

For the **j** components $\quad 7 - p + 2p = 0 \quad \Rightarrow \quad p = -7$

Resolutions of a force

A force P acting at an angle α to the horizontal is equivalent to the forces $P\cos\alpha$ and $P\sin\alpha$, as shown.

Resultant of two (or more) coplanar forces

Each force is resolved into components in two fixed directions, horizontal and vertical say, and the corresponding components added to give F_x and F_y. The resultant force R is then found by taking

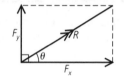

$R^2 = F_x^2 + F_y^2$ (Pythagoras).

The angle θ is given by the equation

$$\tan\theta = \frac{F_y}{F_x}$$

Triangle of forces

If three forces can be represented by the sides of a triangle taken in order in both *magnitude* and *direction*, the forces are in equilibrium. The converse result is also true. This result can be extended to a closed polygon.

In the diagram, the forces $\mathbf{F}_1$, $\mathbf{F}_2$ and $\mathbf{F}_3$ are represented completely by $\overrightarrow{AB}$, $\overrightarrow{BC}$ and $\overrightarrow{CA}$. The forces are in **equilibrium**.

Note also that $-\mathbf{F}_3$ is the resultant of $\mathbf{F}_1 + \mathbf{F}_2$.

Friction

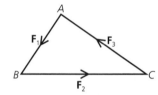

Suppose that at the contact point between a particle and a plane, the frictional force is F and the normal contact force is N. The coefficient of friction between the particle and the plane is μ.

1 For non-limiting equilibrium, $F < \mu N$,
2 For limiting equilibrium $F = \mu N$.

Worked Example 17

A small box, of mass 4 kg, is standing on a rough horizontal floor. A force of magnitude 22 N acts on the box at $33°$ to the horizontal. Equilibrium is limiting with the box about to slide across the floor. Find the coefficient of friction between the box and the floor.

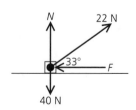

Working

Resolving vertically $N + 22 \sin 33° = 40$ $\Rightarrow$ $N = 28.02$ N

Resolving horizontally $F = 22 \cos 33°$ $\Rightarrow$ $F = 18.45$ N

Since equilibrium is limiting $\dfrac{F}{N} = \mu$ $\Rightarrow$ $\mu = 0.66$ (2 d.p.)

Moment of a force

The moment of a force **F** about a point A is the product of the magnitude of **F** and the perpendicular distance from A to the line of action of **F**.

A **rigid body** is in equilibrium provided that (1) the vector sum of the coplanar forces acting on it is zero, **and** (2) the sum of the moments of all the forces about any point is also zero.

In solving problems on the equilibrium of a body you need to form three equations relating the various forces acting on the body. Usually these are formed from two resolution equations and a moments equation.

Worked Example 18

A uniform rod AB rests in limiting equilibrium with A on rough horizontal ground and B against a smooth vertical wall, as shown. The coefficient of friction between the rod and the ground is 0.2. Find the angle between BA and the horizontal.

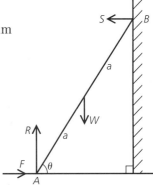

Working

The forces acting on the rod are shown in the diagram.

The rod is inclined at an angle θ to the horizontal and $AB = 2a$.

Resolving vertically   Forces upwards = Forces downwards $\Rightarrow$ $R = W$

Resolving horizontally   Forces to left = Forces to right $\Rightarrow$ $S = F$

Moments about A $S(2a \sin \theta) = W(a \cos \theta)$

$2S \sin \theta = W \cos \theta$

Since equilibrium is limiting, $F = 0.2R$

Processing the equations gives

$0.4 \sin \theta = \cos \theta$

$\Rightarrow$ $\tan \theta = \dfrac{1}{0.4}$ $\Rightarrow$ $\theta = 68.2°$

Centres of mass

The centres of mass of many symmetrical uniform bodies such as rods, circular laminas, cuboids, etc. can be located by inspection. Others, like hemispheres, cones and sectors, need integration. The centre of mass for many composite bodies can be found by taking moments for the parts and equating their sum to the moment of the whole body.

Worked Example 19

A light triangular frame ABC has a right angle at B, $AB = 6\,\text{cm}$ and $BC = 8\,\text{cm}$. Particles of mass $4\,M$, $5\,M$ and $6\,M$ are attached to A, B and C respectively. Find the distance of the centre of mass of the loaded frame from (a) AB, (b) BC.

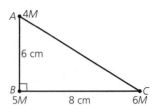

Working

Draw a diagram, as shown, and mark on it all the given information. Let the centre of mass be at a distance of $\bar{x}$ from AB and $\bar{y}$ from BC.

Taking moments from the line AB

$$15\,M\bar{x} = 6\,M \times 8 \quad \Rightarrow \quad \bar{x} = \frac{48}{15} = 3.2$$

Taking moments from the line BC

$$15\,M\bar{y} = 4\,M \times 6 \quad \Rightarrow \quad \bar{y} = 1.6$$

The centre of mass of the triangular frame is $3.2\,\text{cm}$ from AB and $1.6\,\text{cm}$ from BC.

Worked Example 20

The loaded frame in worked example 19 above is hung by a string attached to the point B and rests in equilibrium.

Find the angle BC makes with the vertical, giving your answer to the nearest degree.

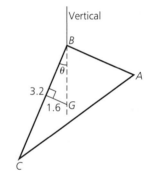

Working

In equilibrium, G is vertically below B, and G is $3.2\,\text{cm}$ from AB, $1.6\,\text{cm}$ from BC, as shown in the diagram. Hence, the required angle θ is given by

$$\tan\theta = \frac{1.6}{3.2} = \frac{1}{2} \quad \Rightarrow \quad \theta = 27° \text{ (nearest degree)}$$

? PRACTICE QUESTIONS

Take $g = 10\,\text{ms}^{-2}$ in numerical questions.

1 A girl of mass $45\,\text{kg}$ stands in a lift which descends vertically directly from the penthouse to the basement. The lift first moves with acceleration $3.5\,\text{ms}^{-2}$, then with constant speed and finally with retardation $5\,\text{ms}^{-2}$. Find the magnitude of the force exerted on the girl by the floor of the lift during each of the three stages in the descent.

2 A particle P is dropped from rest at a height of $100\,\text{m}$ above the ground. Find
   (a) the time taken for P to reach the ground,
   (b) the speed at which P hits the ground.
   State any assumption you made in your solutions to (a) and (b).

3 A ball B is thrown from a point O with velocity V ms^{-1} at an angle of elevation $\alpha°$. After 0.4 s, B is at a point which is 12 m horizontally from O and 12 m vertically higher than O. Find
 (a) the value of V,
 (b) the value of α,
 (c) the greatest height achieved by B above the level of O.

4 A particle P is moving between two fixed points C and D in a straight line with simple harmonic motion. The greatest speed of P is 0.6 ms^{-1} and its greatest acceleration is 2.4 ms^{-2}. Find
 (a) the amplitude and
 (b) the period of the motion.

5 At all speeds and on all roads a car of mass 640 kg has a resistance to motion of magnitude 870 N.
 (a) Find, in kW, the power being generated when the car moves at constant speed 25 ms^{-1} on a level road.
 (b) When the power being generated is 24 kW the car ascends a straight road inclined at arcsin $\frac{1}{25}$ to the horizontal. Find the acceleration of the car when its speed is 6 ms^{-1}, giving your answer in ms^{-2} to 2 s.f.

6 Forces of magnitude 7 N and 12 N act along OA and OB as shown, where $\angle AOB = 50°$. The resultant of these forces is R newtons acting at an angle $\alpha°$ to OB. Find the values of (a) R and (b) α.

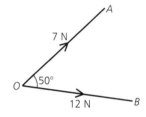

7 Two particles P and Q of mass 0.3 kg and 0.2 kg respectively are tied at the ends of a light, inextensible string passing over a small, smooth, fixed pulley. The particles are released from rest with the string taut. Find
 (a) the acceleration of P,
 (b) the tension in the string,
 (c) the force exerted by the string on the pulley.

8 Three particles X, Y and Z, each of the same mass m, lie on a smooth horizontal floor in a straight line. X is given a velocity u towards Y.
 (a) Show that after colliding with Y, the velocity of Y is $\frac{u}{2}(1+e)$ towards Z, where e is the coefficient of restitution between any two of the particles.
 (b) After the collision between Y and Z, Z moves with velocity $\frac{9u}{16}$. Find (i) the value of e and (ii) the total kinetic energy lost in the two collisions.

9 A particle is hung from a fixed point A by a light, elastic string of natural length l which obeys Hooke's law. The length of the string is $\frac{5l}{4}$ when the particle hangs in equilibrium. If the particle is released from rest at A, find the distance it falls before it comes to rest instantaneously.

10 A uniform ladder, of length $2a$ and mass M, rests in equilibrium with its lower end A on rough horizontal ground and its upper end B resting against a smooth vertical wall. The ladder is inclined at an angle α to the horizontal. Show that $2\mu \geqslant \cot\alpha$, where μ is the coefficient of friction between the ladder and the ground.

11 A particle P, of mass 0.3 kg, moves on a smooth horizontal floor with velocity $(13\mathbf{i} + 6\mathbf{j})$ ms^{-1}, where $\mathbf{i}$ and $\mathbf{j}$ are unit vectors in the plane of the floor. An impulse is applied to P so that its velocity is now $(\mathbf{i} - 3\mathbf{j})$ ms^{-1}. Find
 (a) the magnitude of the impulse, and
 (b) the change in kinetic energy due to the impulse.

12 A uniform rod AB, of mass $14\,\text{kg}$, is smoothly hinged to a vertical wall at A. The rod makes an angle of $60°$ to the wall and is kept in equilibrium by a horizontal force of magnitude T newtons.

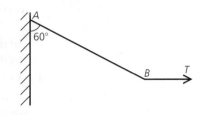

(a) Find the value of T to 3 s.f.

(b) Determine the magnitude and direction of the force exerted by the hinge on the rod at A.

13 At time t seconds, the velocity $v\,\text{ms}^{-1}$ of a particle P, moving along the positive x-axis O_x, is given by

$$v = \mathrm{e}^{-\frac{x}{2}},$$

where $OP = x$ metres. Given that $x = 0$ at $t = 0$, find

(a) an expression for x in terms of t,

(b) the acceleration of P when $x = 3$.

14 A marble falls vertically and strikes a horizontal floor with speed u and rebounds with speed $\dfrac{4u}{5}$. The coefficient of restitution between the marble and the floor is e and the marble rises to a height h metres after the first bounce. Calculate

(a) the value of e,

(b) the height in terms of h from which the marble was dropped.

(c) State two modelling assumptions which you have made in solving this problem.

15 A particle is placed inside and at the lowest point of a fixed sphere whose inside surface is smooth. The particle is projected horizontally with speed $\sqrt{(7ga/2)}$, where a is the radius of the sphere. Show that the particle leaves the sphere at a vertical height of $\dfrac{3a}{2}$ above its point of projection.

12 Random variables and probability distributions

TOPIC OUTLINE AND REVISION TIPS

Types of random variable

In considering random variables it is necessary to distinguish between those which form a **discrete sample space** and those which form a **continuous sample space**. Discrete random variables represent count data such as the number of defectives in a sample of N items or the number of heads obtained when an unbiased coin is tossed twice in succession. Continuous random variables tend to represent measured data such as the heights of children in a class which may take any value within a particular range of values. We cannot find the probability of John being exactly 5 feet tall, but only the probability of him being less than or greater than 5 feet or say between 5 ft and 5 ft 2 in.

Discrete probability distribution

A table or formula listing all possible values that a discrete variable can take together with the associated probabilities is called a **discrete probability distribution**.

Example
An unbiased coin is tossed twice in succession. The number of heads obtained together with their associated probabilities is therefore

$X = x$	0	1	2
$P(X = x)$	$\frac{1}{4}$	$\frac{1}{2}$	$\frac{1}{4}$

Note: We use X to denote the discrete random variable, x to denote its value and $P(X = x) = p(x)$ as the probability that X has a value x.

Note also that $\sum P(X = x) = \frac{1}{4} + \frac{1}{2} + \frac{1}{4} = 1$.

You must also know that for a discrete probability function or distribution

1 the **mean** μ or **expectation** of X i.e. $E(X)$ is defined as

$$\mu = E(X) = \sum_{r=1}^{n} x_r\, p(x_r)$$

2 the **variance** σ^2 is

$$\text{Var}(X) = \sum_{r=1}^{n} (x_r - \mu)^2 p(x_r)$$

which can be shown to be

$$\sum_{r=1}^{n} x_r^2\, p(x_r) - \mu^2$$

which is the formula that you will nearly always need to use.

The **standard deviation** of X is the square root of the variance.

Worked Example 1

The discrete random variables X and Y are independent and have the following probability distributions

X	x	1	2
	$P(X = x)$	$\frac{1}{3}$	$\frac{2}{3}$

Y	y	1	2	3
	$P(Z = y)$	$\frac{1}{8}$	$\frac{3}{8}$	$\frac{1}{2}$

The random variable Z is the product of one observation from X and one observation from Y

(a) Show that $P(Z = 2) = \dfrac{5}{24}$.

(b) Find the probability distribution for Z and hence or otherwise find $E(Z)$.

(c) Find the standard deviation of Z.

Working

A score of 2 for Z is obtained in two ways. Either $x = 1$ and $y = 2$ or $x = 2$ and $y = 1$ and the corresponding probabilities are

$$\frac{1}{3} \times \frac{3}{8} \quad \text{and} \quad \frac{2}{3} \times \frac{1}{8}$$

As they are mutually exclusive events, $P(Z = 2) = \dfrac{1}{8} + \dfrac{1}{12} = \dfrac{5}{24}$.

The other possible scores for Z are 1, 3, 4 and 6 and their probabilities are found similarly

z	1	2	3	4	6
$P(Z = z)$	$\frac{1}{24}$	$\frac{5}{24}$	$\frac{4}{24}$	$\frac{6}{24}$	$\frac{8}{24}$

$$E(Z) = \frac{1}{24}[(1 \times 1) + (2 \times 5) + (3 \times 4) + (4 \times 6) + (6 \times 8)] = \frac{95}{24} = 3.96$$

$$\text{Var}(Z) = \frac{1}{24}\left[(1 \times 1^2) + (5 \times 2^2) + (4 \times 3^2) + (6 \times 4^2) + (8 \times 6^2)\right] - \left(\frac{95}{24}\right)^2$$

$$= \frac{1}{24}\left(441 - \frac{95^2}{24}\right) = \frac{1559}{24^2}$$

Hence $\sigma = \dfrac{\sqrt{1559}}{24} \approx 1.645$

You should note the following properties of expected values and variance of simple functions of the variables

1   $E(aX \pm b) = aE(X) \pm b$,

2   $\text{Var}(aX \pm b) = a^2 \text{Var}(X)$,

3   $E(aX \pm bY) = aE(X) \pm bE(Y)$,

4   $\text{Var}(aX \pm bY) = a^2 \text{Var}(X) + b^2 \text{Var}(Y)$, provided that X and Y are independent.

Worked Example 2

The random variable X has mean 2 and variance 5 and the independent random variable Y has mean 4 and variance 3. Find (a) $E(3Y - 2X)$, (b) $\text{Var}(3Y - 2X)$.

Working

$E(3Y - 2X) = 3E(Y) - 2E(X) = 3 \times 4 - 2 \times 2 = 8$

$\text{Var}(3Y - 2X) = 3^2 \text{Var}(Y) + 2^2 \text{Var}(X) = 3^2 \times 3 + 2^2 \times 5 = 47$

Worked Example 3

The probability distribution of the discrete random variable X is given below.

X	1	2	3
p(X)	a	b	c

Given that $E(X) = 1.8$ and $\text{Var}(X) = 0.76$ find a, b and c.

Working

Sum of probabilities $= 1 \quad \Rightarrow \quad a + b + c = 1$ [1]

$$E(X) = a + 2b + 3c = 1.8 \qquad\qquad [2]$$

$$\text{Var } X = a + 2^2 b + 3^2 c - 1.8^2 = 0.76$$

$$\Rightarrow \quad a + 4b + 9c = 0.76 + 3.24 = 4 \qquad\qquad [3]$$

$[2] - [1]$ gives $b + 2c = 0.8$ [4]

$[3] - [1]$ gives $3b + 8c = 3$ [5]

$[5] - 3[4]$ gives $2c = 0.6 \quad \Rightarrow \quad c = 0.3$

Substitute in [4] to give $b + 0.6 = 0.8 \quad \Rightarrow \quad b = 0.2$

Substitute in [1] to give $a = 1 - b - c = 1 - 0.2 - 0.3 = 0.5$

Binomial distribution

The binomial distribution concerns experiments each of which requires repetition of the same test a specific number of times, say n. Each test must be independent of all the other tests and can only have two possible outcomes, one of which we call a success and the other a failure. The probability of a success (p) is constant for each test. The probability of a failure $q = 1 - p$.

Under these conditions the probability distribution of the binomial random variable X, the number of successes in n independent tests is

$$B(r; n, p) = \binom{n}{r} p^r (1 - q)^{n-r} \qquad (r = 0, 1, 2, \ldots, n)$$

We write $X \sim B(n, p)$ i.e. X is distributed binomially with n independent tests, each test having a constant probability p of success and $q = 1 - p$ of failure.

The mean μ or expected value of X, $E(X)$ is np.

The variance, $\sigma^2 = \text{Var}(X)$ is $npq = np(1 - p)$.

Worked Example 4

It is known that 10% of a large batch of components are defective. Eight of the components are selected at random. Estimate the probability that of the eight components (a) two will be defective, (b) at most two will be defective.

Working

$X \sim B(8, 0.1)$

$$\Rightarrow \quad P(x = 2) = \binom{8}{2}(0.1)^2 (0.9)^6 = \frac{8.7}{1.2}(0.1)^2 (0.9)^6$$

$$\approx 0.1488$$

If at most two are defective then we may have none defective, 1 defective or 2 defective

$$P(\text{at most two defective}) = P(x \leqslant 2) = P(0) + P(1) + P(2)$$

$$= (0.9)^8 + \binom{8}{1}(0.1)^1 (0.9)^7 + \binom{8}{2}(0.1)^2 (0.9)^6$$

$$= 0.4305 + 0.3826 + 0.1488 = 0.9619 \approx 0.962 \text{ (3 s.f.)}$$

Poisson distribution

The arithmetic involved in a binomial distribution can be quite considerable, especially if n is large. Fortunately, if n is large $(n \geqslant 20)$ and p is small $(p \leqslant 0.05)$ the Poisson distribution gives a good approximation to the binomial distribution. The larger the value of n or the smaller the value of p, the closer the approximation.

The Poisson distribution states that for a discrete random variable X the probability function is

$$P(X = r) = P(r) = \frac{\lambda^r e^{-\lambda}}{r!}$$

where $r = 0, 1, 2, \ldots$, and λ is a positive constant. We write $X \sim \text{Poi}(\lambda)$.

The mean μ of the distribution is $\mu = E(x) = \lambda = np$.

The variance σ^2 of the distribution is $\sigma^2 = \text{Var}(X) = \lambda$.

Worked Example 5

A pair of unbiased dice are thrown 20 times. Find, using a Poisson distribution, an estimate of the probability that double six will be obtained three times out of the 20. Explain why these data are appropriate for using a Poisson distribution as an approximation of the binomial distribution.

Working

Probability of throwing a six with a single die is $\frac{1}{6}$, therefore the probability of throwing a double six is $\frac{1}{6} \times \frac{1}{6} = \frac{1}{36}$.

$$n = 20, p = \frac{1}{36} \quad \Rightarrow \quad np = 20 \times \frac{1}{36} = \frac{5}{9} = \lambda$$

$$\Rightarrow \quad P(X = 3) = \frac{\lambda^3 e^{-\lambda}}{3!} = \left(\frac{5}{9}\right)^3 e^{-\frac{5}{9}} \times \frac{1}{3!}$$

$$= 0.0164$$

The Poisson distribution is appropriate since $n = 20$ and $p = \frac{1}{36} \approx 0.028$ which is less than 0.05.

Worked Example 6

It is estimated that 1 person in every 1 000 will at some stage of their life require an extended stay in hospital. Find the probability that in a random sample of 8 000 people less than 7 will require an extended stay in hospital.

Working

This is essentially a binomial distribution problem, but as $n = 8\,000$ and the probability p is 0.001 the Poisson distribution is most appropriate.

$$\lambda = np = 8\,000 \times 0.001 = 8$$

Hence if X represents the number requiring extended stay

$$P(X < 7) = P(0) + P(1) + P(2) + P(3) + P(4) + P(5) + P(6)$$

$$= e^{-8} + \frac{8e^{-8}}{1!} + \frac{8^2 e^{-8}}{2!} + \frac{8^3 e^{-8}}{3!} + \ldots + \frac{8^6 e^{-8}}{6!}$$

Fortunately there are cumulative probability tables for both the binomial distribution and the Poisson distribution so rather than work out each of the above probabilities we can look up the answer in the tables for $n = 6$ and $\mu = \lambda = 8$.

This gives that the probability of less than 7 out of the 8 000 requiring extended stay is 0.313.

The probability of 7 or more requiring extended stay is $1 - 0.313 = 0.687$.

Probability functions of a continuous random variable

The **probability density function** (p.d.f.) of a continuous variable X, usually written $f(x)$, satisfies the conditions

1 $f(x) \geqslant 0$ for all x,

2 $\displaystyle\int_{-\infty}^{\infty} f(x)\,dx = 1$,

3 $\displaystyle P(a \leqslant X \leqslant b) = \int_{a}^{b} f(x)\,dx$.

In other words, probabilities are given by the area under the curve of the probability density function between appropriate limits. When given a problem in which X takes values only in a finite interval we assume that the p.d.f. is zero everywhere else. Then

$$\int_{-\infty}^{\infty} f(x)\,dx = 1 \qquad \text{(certainty)}$$

The mean μ, the expected value $E(X)$, is given by $\displaystyle\int_{-\infty}^{\infty} xf(x)\,dx$.

The variance σ^2 of $X = \text{Var}\,(X) = \displaystyle\int_{-\infty}^{\infty} x^2 f(x)\,dx - \mu^2$.

Worked Example 7

A random variable X has probability density function given by

$$f(x) = \begin{cases} k(2-x) & 0 \leqslant x \leqslant 2,\ k \text{ a positive constant} \\ 0 & \text{otherwise} \end{cases}$$

Show that $k = \frac{1}{2}$.
    Find (a) $E(X)$,   (b) $\text{Var}\,(X)$,   (c) $P(X > \mu)$.

Working

$$\int_{0}^{2} f(x)\,dx = \int_{0}^{2} k(2-x)\,dx = k\left[2x - \frac{x^2}{2}\right]_{0}^{2} = k[4-2] = 2k$$

$$\Rightarrow \quad k = \frac{1}{2} \quad \text{since } \int_{0}^{2} f(x)\,dx = 1$$

(a) $E(X) = \dfrac{1}{2}\displaystyle\int_{0}^{2} x(2-x)\,dx = \dfrac{1}{2}\left[x^2 - \dfrac{x^3}{3}\right]_{0}^{2} = \dfrac{1}{2}\left[4 - \dfrac{8}{3}\right] = \dfrac{2}{3}.$

(b) $\text{Var}\,(X) = \dfrac{1}{2}\displaystyle\int_{0}^{2} x^2(2-x)\,dx - \left(\dfrac{2}{3}\right)^2 = \dfrac{1}{2}\left[\dfrac{2}{3}x^3 - \dfrac{x^4}{4}\right]_{0}^{2} - \dfrac{4}{9} = \dfrac{8}{3} - 2 - \dfrac{4}{9} = \dfrac{2}{9}.$

(c) $P(X \leqslant \mu) = P\left(X \leqslant \dfrac{2}{3}\right) = \dfrac{1}{2}\displaystyle\int_{0}^{\frac{2}{3}} (2-x)\,dx = \dfrac{1}{2}\left[2x - \dfrac{x^2}{2}\right]_{0}^{\frac{2}{3}}$

$$= \dfrac{1}{2}\left[\dfrac{4}{3} - \dfrac{1}{2}\times\dfrac{4}{9}\right] = \dfrac{5}{9}.$$

$$\Rightarrow \quad P\left(X > \dfrac{2}{3}\right) = 1 - \dfrac{5}{9} = \dfrac{4}{9}.$$

It is often worth sketching the p.d.f. as this can sometimes help to shorten the work. For instance, in worked example 7

Area of triangle $= 1 = \frac{1}{2} \times 2 \times 2k$

$$\Rightarrow k = \tfrac{1}{2}$$

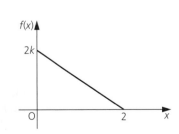

Cumulative distribution function (c.d.f.)

The **cumulative distribution function** $F(x_0)$ of the random variable X is $F(x_0) = P(X \leqslant x_0)$.

For the continuous distribution, $F(x_0)$ is given by

$$F(x_0) = P(X \leqslant x_0) = \int_{-\infty}^{x_0} f(x)\, dx$$

Note that capital F is used to denote the c.d.f. and small f for the p.d.f., and that the c.d.f. $F(x)$ and p.d.f. $f(x)$ are related by $f(x) = F'(x)$.

When answering questions involving the p.d.f. and the c.d.f., do read the question carefully as many students mix up the two functions. Remember:

1 when f is defined and F is asked for, use integration, taking particular care over the limits,
2 when F is defined and f is asked for, use differentiation. The p.d.f. and the c.d.f. can be useful in finding the mode and the median of a continuous random variable as will be seen in the following examples. The modal value of X is where the p.d.f. has its maximum value. The median value is m where $F(m) = \frac{1}{2}$.

Worked Example 8

The cumulative distribution function of a random variable X is given by

$$F(x) = \begin{cases} 0 & x < 1 \\ \dfrac{x^2 - 1}{3} & 1 \leqslant x \leqslant 2 \\ 1 & x > 2 \end{cases}$$

Find

(a) the p.d.f. of the random variable X and sketch the graph of f,
(b) the mode of X,
(c) the median of X.

Working

(a) The p.d.f. of X is given by $F'(X)$:

$$f(x) = \begin{cases} 0 & x < 1 \\ \dfrac{2x}{3} & 1 \leqslant x \leqslant 2 \\ 0 & x > 2 \end{cases}$$

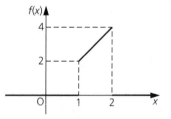

(b) From the graph, the maximum value of f occurs at $x = 2$, therefore

$$\text{mode of } X = \frac{2 \times 2}{3} = \frac{4}{3} \text{ at } x = 2$$

(c) The median of X is m where $m^2 - 1 = \dfrac{3}{2} \quad \Rightarrow \quad m = \sqrt{\dfrac{5}{2}}.$

Worked Example 9

The time to service a car in hours is modelled by the random variable T with probability density function

$$f(t) = \begin{cases} \dfrac{3}{4}(2t^2 - t^3) & 0 \leqslant t \leqslant 2 \\ 0 & \text{otherwise} \end{cases}$$

Find

(a) the cumulative distribution function of T,
(b) $P(T \leqslant 1.5)$,
(c) the modal time.

Working

$$F(t) = \int_0^t \frac{3}{4}\left(2t^2 - t^3\right) dt \qquad \text{for} \quad 0 \leqslant t \leqslant 2$$

$$= \frac{3}{4}\left(\frac{2}{3}t^3 - \frac{t^4}{4}\right) = \frac{1}{2}t^3 - \frac{3}{16}t^4 = \frac{t^3}{16}(8 - 3t)$$

$$\therefore \quad \text{c.d.f. is } F(t) = \begin{cases} 0 & t < 0 \\ \dfrac{1}{2}t^3 - \dfrac{3}{16}t^4 & 0 \leqslant t \leqslant 2 \\ 1 & t > 2 \end{cases}$$

$$\Rightarrow \quad P(T \leqslant 1.5) = \frac{1}{2}(1.5)^3 - \frac{3}{16}(1.5)^4 \approx 0.738$$

Modal time is when $\dfrac{3}{4}\left(2t^2 - t^3\right)$ is maximum:

$$\frac{d}{dt}\left\{\frac{3}{4}\left(2t^2 - t^3\right)\right\} = \frac{3}{4}\left(4t - 3t^2\right) \quad \Rightarrow \quad t = \frac{4}{3}$$

Normal distribution

The most important of the continuous distributions is the normal distribution. Its equation is of the form

$$y = a \exp\left\{-b(x - c)^2\right\}$$

where a, b and c are constants, or alternatively

$$y = \frac{1}{\sigma\sqrt{(2\pi)}} \exp\left\{-(x - \mu)^2/(2\sigma^2)\right\}$$

where μ is the mean and σ is the standard deviation of the distribution. Its graph is bell shaped.

The mode, median and mean are all equal owing to the symmetry about the mean. The range of X is from $-\infty$ to $+\infty$ and the total area under the curve is constant, equal to 1.

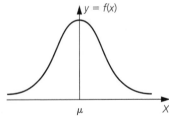

In order to find probabilities related to X we make the transformation $Z = \dfrac{x - \mu}{\sigma}$ so that the graph becomes the graph of the probability density function of a continuous random variable Z which is normally distributed, i.e.

$$\phi(z) = \frac{1}{\sqrt{(2\pi)}} \exp\left(-z^2/2\right) \qquad (z \in \mathbb{R})$$

and this is known as the **standardised normal probability function**. Its mean is 0 and its variance is 1.
Hence we write $Z \sim N(0, 1^2)$.

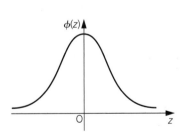

The curve is symmetrical about $z = 0$.
The area enclosed by the curve and the z-axis is 1.

We cannot integrate the probability density function $\phi(z)$, but fortunately there are tables of values provided for the cumulative probability function $\Phi(z)$ where

$$\Phi(z) = P(Z \leqslant z) = \int_{-\infty}^z \phi(z) \, dz$$

There are several different forms of the tables so you must ensure that you are very familiar with the one used by your examining board.

Geometrically $\Phi(z)$ represents the shaded area as shown, the unit along the z-axis being the standard deviation which is 1.

To help in the use of the tables *it is always* advisable to draw a clear diagram showing the area under consideration.

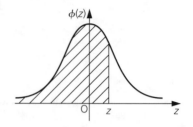

Worked Example 10

The random variable $Z \sim N(0, 1^2)$. Find (a) $P(z \leqslant 0.7)$, (b) $P(z \geqslant 0.7)$, (c) $P(-0.5 \leqslant z \leqslant 0.7)$.

Working

(a) $P(z \leqslant 0.7) = \int_{-\infty}^{0.7} \phi(z) \, dz = \Phi(0.7) = 0.7580.$

(b) $P(z \geqslant 0.7) = \int_{0.7}^{\infty} \phi(z) \, dz = 1 - 0.7580$
$$= 0.242$$

(c) $P(-0.5 \leqslant z \leqslant 0.7) = \int_{-0.5}^{0.7} \phi(z) \, dz$

$$= \Phi(0.7) - \Phi(-0.5)$$
$$= \Phi(0.7) - \{1 - \Phi(0.5)\}$$
$$= 0.7580 - 1 + 0.6915$$
$$= 0.4495$$

Worked Example 11

The random variable X is normally distributed with mean 50 and variance 100, i.e. $X \sim N(50, 100)$. Find $P(40 < X < 65)$. As we are not concerned directly with a standardised normal probability function we must use the transformation

$$Z = \frac{X - \mu}{\sigma} = \frac{X - 50}{10}$$

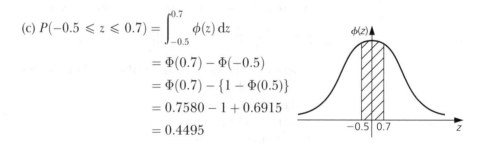

$$\Rightarrow \quad P(40 < X < 65) = P\left(\frac{40 - 50}{10} < Z < \frac{65 - 50}{10}\right)$$

$$= P(-1 < Z < 1.5) = \Phi(1.5) - \Phi(-1)$$
$$= \Phi(1.5) - \{1 - \Phi(1)\} = 0.9332 - 1 + 0.8413$$
$$= 0.7745$$

You need to be able to use the tables in the reverse order and to know when to apply continuity connections.

Worked Example 12

In an examination, 5% of the candidates scored more than 80 marks and 7% of the candidates scored less than 35 marks. Given that the marks of the candidates taking the examination are approximately normally distributed, find estimates for the mean and standard deviation of the mark distribution.

Working
Examination marks are usually awarded as integers, i.e. discrete quantities so, as we are using a continuous distribution, it is necessary to apply continuity corrections at both limits. Thus at the 80% mark we consider all those scoring less than 80.5 marks and at the 35% mark we consider all those scoring more than 34.5 marks. Let the mean be μ and the standard deviation σ.

At the 80 mark, $P(\text{mark} < 80.5) = 0.95$.

Now, $Z = \dfrac{X - \mu}{\sigma}$ so $P\left(z = \dfrac{80.5 - \mu}{\sigma} \leqslant 1.645\right) = 0.95$

the 1.645 coming from reading the tables in reverse. Hence

$$\frac{80.5 - \mu}{\sigma} = 1.645$$

$$\Rightarrow \quad 80.5 - \mu = 1.645\,\sigma \qquad\qquad [1]$$

At the 35 mark, $P(\text{mark} > 34.5) \quad \Rightarrow \quad 0.93$. Hence

$$P\left(z = \frac{34.5 - \mu}{\sigma} \geqslant -1.475\right) = 0.93 \qquad \text{(again using the tables in reverse)}$$

$$\Rightarrow \quad \frac{34.5 - \mu}{\sigma} = -1.475 \quad \Rightarrow \quad 34.5 - \mu = -1.475\sigma \qquad\qquad [2]$$

Solving [1] and [2] gives $\quad \sigma \approx 14.7 \quad$ and $\quad \mu \approx 56.2$.

Binomial distribution and Poisson distribution

The normal distribution can be used as an approximation to both the binomial and Poisson distributions under certain conditions, but in both cases continuity corrections are needed. The conditions are:

▶ Binomial $B(n, p) \quad \Rightarrow \quad X \sim N(\mu, \sigma^2)$ where $\mu = np$ and $\sigma^2 = npq$ provided n is fairly large and p not too near 0 or 1 – a good working rule being when np and nq are both greater than 5.
▶ Poisson $\text{Poi}(\mu) \quad \Rightarrow \quad X \sim N(\mu, \mu)$ provided the mean $\mu > 20$, though the approximation is quite good when $\mu > 10$.

Worked Example 13
An unbiased die is to be thrown 240 times. Using the normal distribution approximation to the binomial distribution, estimate to 2 decimal places the probability that between 36 and 43 sixes inclusive will be obtained.

Working
$B\left(240, \frac{1}{6}\right)$

Take normal distribution $N(np, npq) = N\left(40, \frac{100}{3}\right)$.

$$Z = \frac{x - 40}{\sqrt{\frac{100}{3}}} \quad \Rightarrow \quad P(35.5 \leqslant x \leqslant 43.5) = P(-0.7794 \leqslant z \leqslant 0.6062)$$

$$= -(1 - 0.7820) + 0.7277$$

$$= 0.5097 \approx 0.51$$

Linear combinations of independent normal variables

Provided that $X_1 \sim N(\mu_1, \sigma_1^2)$, $X_2 \sim N(\mu_2, \sigma_2^2)$ and X_1 and X_2 are independent then

$$X_1 \pm X_2 \sim N(\mu_1 \pm \mu_2, \sigma_1^2 + \sigma_2^2)$$

More generally

$$aX_1 \pm bX_2 \sim N(a\mu_1 \pm b\mu_2, a^2\sigma_1^2 + b^2\sigma_2^2) \qquad (a, b \text{ constants})$$

Worked Example 14

Cartons of sugar are delivered to supermarkets in boxes containing 20 cartons each. The cartons of sugar are normally distributed with mean weight $1\frac{1}{2}$ kg and standard deviation 0.05 kg. The weights of the empty boxes are also normally distributed with mean 1 kg and standard deviation 0.2 kg.

(a) Find the probability that a full box weighs more than $31\frac{1}{2}$ kg.
(b) Two cartons of sugar are taken at random from a box. Find the probability that they differ in weight by more than 0.05 kg.

Working
The mean weight of a full box of sugar $= 20 \times 1\frac{1}{2} + 1 \times 1 = 31$.
The variance of a full box of sugar $= 20 \times 0.05^2 + 0.2^2 = 0.09$.

$$P(\text{Weight} > 32) = P\left(Z > \frac{31\frac{1}{2} - 31}{\sqrt{0.09}}\right) = P\left(Z > \frac{\frac{1}{2}}{0.3}\right) = 1 - \Phi(1.667) \Rightarrow 1 - 0.9522$$

$$\Rightarrow P\left(\text{Weight} > 31\frac{1}{2}\right) \approx 0.048$$

Mean $C_1 - C_2 = 0$, $\quad \text{Var}(C_1 - C_2) = 0.05^2 + 0.05^2 = 0.005$

$$P(|C_1 - C_2| > 0.05) = 2P(C_1 - C_2 > 0.05) = 2P(z > 0.7071)$$

$$= 2\{1 - \Phi(0.7797)\} = 0.4406 \approx 0.44$$

Distribution of sample means

The **central limit theorem** gives information concerning the distribution of sample means.

1 If the original population is distributed $X \sim N(\mu, \sigma^2)$ then the distribution of sample means of samples of size n is distributed

$$\overline{X} \sim N\left(\mu, \frac{\sigma^2}{n}\right)$$

2 If the original population has mean μ and variance σ^2, but is not normally distributed then the distribution of sample means is approximately

distributed $N\left(\mu, \dfrac{\sigma^2}{n}\right)$ provided $n \geqslant 30$.

Worked Example 15

A firm produces batteries which are known to have a mean lifetime of 96 hours. Forty samples of 36 batteries each are tested. Estimate the number of samples in which the average lifetime of the 36 batteries is greater than 98 hours if the standard deviation of the batteries is 6 hours.

Working

$$X \sim N\left(96, \frac{6^2}{36}\right)$$

$$\Rightarrow \quad P(\overline{X} < 98) = \Phi\left(\frac{98 - 96}{\sqrt{\dfrac{6^2}{36}}}\right) = \Phi\left(\frac{2 \times 6}{6}\right) = \Phi(2) = 0.977$$

$$\Rightarrow \quad 40 \times 0.977 = 39.08 \text{ samples would be expected to have a mean lifetime of less than 98 hours.}$$

Confidence intervals

The mean and variance of a population can be estimated from the data of a random sample size n taken from the population.

The unbiased estimates are

▶ $\hat{\mu} = \bar{x}$ the sample mean,

▶ $\hat{\sigma} = \dfrac{n}{n-1} \times s^2$ where s^2 is the sample variance.

Using the central limit theorem we try to find a symmetrical interval within which we can say with a given degree of confidence (e.g. 90%, 95%, 98%) that the population mean will be. This is called the confidence interval for the population mean.

Worked Example 16

In a survey of the male population a random sample of 81 males had a mean height of 174.3 cm and a variance of 2.25.

(a) Find unbiased estimates of (i) the mean and (ii) variance of the population from which the sample was taken.

(b) Find (i) a 92% and (ii) a 95% confidence interval for the mean height.

Working

(a) (i) Estimated mean height of population = 174.3.

 (ii) Estimated variance of population = $\frac{81}{80} \times 2.25$

$$\Rightarrow \quad \text{standard deviation} = 1.5\sqrt{\tfrac{81}{80}}.$$

(b) (i) 92% confidence interval requires $0.50 + 0.46 = 0.96$

$$\Rightarrow \quad \Phi\left(\frac{x - 174.3}{\dfrac{1.5\sqrt{\frac{81}{80}}}{\sqrt{81}}}\right) = 0.96 = \Phi(1.751) \text{ using the tables in reverse}$$

$$\Rightarrow \quad (x - 174.3) = 1.751 \times \frac{1.5}{\sqrt{80}} = 0.294$$

$$\Rightarrow \quad 92\% \text{ confidence interval} = 174.3 \pm 0.294 \approx 174.3 \pm 0.3$$

 (ii) 95% confidence interval requires 0.975

$$\Rightarrow \quad \Phi\left(\frac{x - 174.3}{\left(\dfrac{1.5\sqrt{\frac{81}{80}}}{\sqrt{81}}\right)}\right) = 0.975 = \Phi(1.960)$$

$$\Rightarrow \quad x - 174.3 = 1.960 \times \frac{1.5}{\sqrt{80}} = 0.329$$

$$\Rightarrow \quad 95\% \text{ confidence interval} = 174.3 \pm 0.329$$

Sample sums and differences

If the populations from which the samples are taken are normally distributed then so will the distribution of the sums or differences of sample means from the populations.

$$X_1 \sim N(\mu_1, \sigma_1^2), X_2 \sim N(\mu_2, \sigma_2^2) \quad \Rightarrow \quad X_1 \pm X_2 \sim N\left(\mu_1 \pm \mu_2, \frac{\sigma_1^2}{n_1} + \frac{\sigma_2^2}{n_2}\right)$$

Worked Example 17

Firms X and Y produce radio batteries. Samples of 50 batteries are taken from each firm and tested for longevity with the following results

> Firm X mean life 320 hours,   standard deviation 8 weeks
>
> Firm Y mean life 325 hours,   standard deviation 10 hours

Determine the 90% confidence interval for the mean life difference D between the batteries from the two firms.

Working
Mean life difference = 5 hours

Standard deviation of the difference in the means $= \sqrt{\left(\dfrac{8^2 + 10^2}{50}\right)} = 1.81$

Hence at 90% confidence

$$\Phi\left(\frac{D-5}{1.81}\right) = 0.95 = \Phi(1.645) \quad \Rightarrow \quad D = 5 \pm 2.977$$

$\Rightarrow$ 90% confidence interval $5 \pm 2.98 = (2.02, 7.98)$

Hence it appears that the difference of 5 hours has some statistical significance since the 90% level does not include zero, i.e. batteries from firm Y do really have a longer mean life.

Hypothesis testing

We often wish to test whether or not a set of sample data provides sufficient evidence to say that the sample has come from a particular population with known or assumed parameter values (mean, variance). For instance, the manager of a factory producing electric light bulbs may wish to investigate whether there have been slight alterations to their processing plant which have resulted in a change in the mean lifetime of the bulbs. To do this he would carry out a **significance test**. This would involve setting up two hypotheses about the population H_0, the null hypothesis and H_1 the alternative hypothesis. The latter, as you will see, can be one of two kinds: one-tailed or two-tailed, depending on the problem being investigated. It would then be necessary to decide on the level of significance required. In the examination question this will be given. The sample value is tested and any probability value smaller than the acceptable significance level will lead to the rejection of H_0 and the acceptance of H_1. Any probability greater than the acceptable significance level will lead to the acceptance of H_0.

Worked Example 18
Factory records over a long period of time show that the breaking strength of a particular synthetic fishing line has a mean value of 18 kg with a variance of 1.3 kg^2. A random sample of 50 lines was tested after the machines had been modified and they were found to have a mean breaking strength of 18.2 kg. Investigate at the 5% level of significance whether or not the mean breaking strength has increased.

Working
Null hypothesis H_0 $\mu = 18.0$.
Alternative hypothesis H_1 $\mu > 18.00$.
The factory is only concerned with an *increase* in strength, so this is said to be a one-tailed test.

$$P(x) \geqslant 18.2 = \Phi\left(\frac{18.0 - 18.2}{\frac{1.3}{\sqrt{50}}}\right) = \Phi(-1.088) = 1 - 0.8515 = 0.1385$$

Since $0.1385 > 0.05$ we cannot reject H_0 at the 5% level.

Hence the mean breaking strength does not appear to have increased.

Note: You must always end with a conclusion otherwise you will lose marks.

Worked Example 19

A random sample of 100 electric motors produced by a company making washing machines is taken from a population which is normally distributed. They are computed to have a mean lifetime of 6 500 hours and a standard deviation of 210 hours. Test the hypothesis that the mean lifetime of all the electric motors produced by the company is 6 650 hours against the alternative hypothesis that $\mu \neq 6\,650$ hours using a 5% level of significance.

Working

This problem requires a two-tailed test since $\mu \neq 6\,650$ includes $\mu < 6\,650$ and $\mu > 6\,650$.

$$H_0 : \mu = 6\,650$$

$$H_1 : \mu \neq 6\,650$$

A 5% level of significance with a two-tailed test gives critical limits of ± 1.960. Hence if the $\bar{z}$ score of the sample does not lie within $-1.960 < \bar{z} < 1.960$ we reject H_0. If it does we accept H_0.

$$\bar{z} = \frac{6\,500 - 6\,650}{\frac{210}{\sqrt{100}}} = -7.14$$

This lies outside the range $-1.960 < \bar{z} < 1.960$ so we reject H_0 at the 5% level and accept H_1, i.e. that the mean lifetime of all the electric motors is not 6 650.

Significance testing can also be applied to the binomial and Poisson distributions.

Worked Example 20

The number of motor accidents happening in the city of Townsville has been found to average 1.5 per week. After an extensive road safety campaign 4 motor accidents happened in the next four weeks. Investigate whether the mean number of motor accidents in Townsville has changed, using a 5% level of significance.

Working

$$H_0 : \lambda = 1.5 \qquad \text{(i.e. there is no change)}$$

$$H_1 : \lambda \neq 1.5$$

This is a two-tailed test since we are looking for a change in λ.
    Under H_0 we would expect $4 \times 1.5 = 6.0$ accidents in 4 weeks.

$$P(x \leqslant 4) = e^{-6.0}\left(1 + \frac{6}{1} + \frac{6^2}{2!} + \frac{6^3}{3!} + \frac{6^4}{4!}\right) = 0.285$$

At the 5% significance level for a two-tailed test we require the probability to be < 0.025 for H_0 to be rejected. Since $0.285 > 0.025$ we accept H_0, i.e. the mean number of motor accidents in Townsville is unchanged.

There are two types of errors one can make when concerned with significance testing. They are referred to as

Type 1 error	Rejecting a null hypothesis which should be accepted,
Type 2 error	Accepting an alternative hypothesis which should have been rejected.

The χ^2 (chi-squared) test

This is a test used to determine how well a theoretical distribution (e.g. binomial or Poisson for discrete distribution, normal for continuous distribution) models a given practical situation.

We assume (H_0) that the chosen theoretical distribution fits the same data. We calculate $E_1, E_2, E_3, \ldots, E_n$ the expected frequencies under this assumption and then calculate the statistic

$$\chi^2 = \sum_{i=1}^{n} \frac{(O_i - E_i)^2}{E_i}$$

We then see how many 'degrees of freedom v' there are where $v = n - 1 -$ (number of population parameters estimated) and n is the number of frequencies (or cells).

If any of the expected frequencies are less than 5 then cells must be combined. If $v = 1$, as is the case for a 2×2 contingency table, Yates' correction should be used and the test statistic is

$$\sum_{i=1}^{n} \frac{(|O_i - E_i| - 0.5)^2}{E_i}$$

Worked Example 21

A random number table of 200 digits showed the following distribution of the digits 1 to 10

1	2	3	4	5	6	7	8	9	10
17	24	30	16	20	21	15	16	19	22

Determine whether the observed distribution differs significantly from the expected distribution. Use a 5% level of significance.

	1	2	3	4	5	6	7	8	9	10
O	17	24	30	16	20	21	15	16	19	22
E	20	20	20	20	20	20	20	20	20	20
$(O-E)^2$	9	16	100	16	0	1	25	16	1	4

$$\Rightarrow \sum_{1}^{10} \frac{(O - E)^2}{E} = \frac{188}{20} = 9.4 \quad \Rightarrow \quad \chi^2 = 9.4$$

Number of degrees of freedom $= v = n - 1 = 10 - 1 = 9$
Hence for a significance level $P = 0.05$ (5%) the cricital χ^2 value $= 16.92$ and since $9.4 < 16.92$ we accept H_0 and reject H_1 that the difference is significant.

Worked Example 22

The number of errors made by 100 infant school children in taking a simple basic mental arithmetic test are shown in the table below.

No. of errors	0	1	2	3	$\geqslant 4$
No of children	56	30	10	6	0

(a) Show that the population mean is 0.68.
(b) Use a Poisson distribution to calculate the expected frequencies.
(c) Use the χ^2 test to assess whether or not the difference between the observed and calculated numbers of children is significant at the 10% level.

Working
Estimate of the population mean $= \frac{1}{100}(1 \times 30 + 2 \times 10 + 3 \times 6) = 0.68$.
Under H_0 the expected frequencies are

$$E_0 = e^{-0.68} \times 100 = 50.66, \quad E_1 = 0.68 E_0 = 34.45, \quad E_2 = \frac{0.68}{2} E_1 = 11.71, \quad E_3 = 3.18$$

Since $E_3 < 5$ we must combine cells to avoid distortion of the χ^2 value.

No. of errors	0	1	$\geqslant 2$
O_r	56	30	16
E_r	50.66	34.45	14.89

$$\chi^2 = \frac{(56 - 50.66)^2}{50.66} + \frac{(30 - 34.45)^2}{34.45} + \frac{(16 - 14.89)^2}{14.89} \approx 1.221$$

Now $v = 3 - 1 - 1$ (the mean was estimated), but at the 10% level the critical χ^2 value is 2.706 and since $1.221 < 2.706$ we accept H_0 that the results do not differ significantly from a Poisson distribution.

In this problem the number of degrees of freedom is 1 so Yates' correction should be used. However, decreasing each of the terms in the numerator e.g. $(|56 - 50.66| - 0.5)^2$ would simply decrease the value of χ^2 slightly so that the conclusion reached above is still valid.

Contingency tables

Here the sample and population are recorded for more than one attribute. Consider the following problem. In a recent council election the way that 300 people voted was recorded along with their age range. We wish to find if there is any significant difference in voting pattern between ages.

Age	Vote Conservative	Vote Labour	Vote Lib Democrate	Total
18–30	23 $\left(35\frac{1}{3}\right)$	49 (36)	28 $\left(28\frac{2}{3}\right)$	100
30–45	37 $\left(35\frac{1}{3}\right)$	28 (36)	35 $\left(28\frac{2}{3}\right)$	100
>45	46 $\left(35\frac{1}{3}\right)$	31 (36)	23 $\left(28\frac{2}{3}\right)$	100
Total	106	108	86	300

H_0: There is no significant difference in voting pattern between ages.
Under H_0, 106 out of 300 vote Conservative. Thus out of 100 people in the 18–30 age group we would expect $\frac{100}{300} \times 106$ to vote Conservative, i.e. $35\frac{1}{3}$. This we write in brackets beside the 23. Now fill in the remaining 8 expected totals

$$\chi^2 = \frac{12\frac{1}{3}^2}{35\frac{1}{3}} + \frac{1\frac{2}{3}^2}{35\frac{1}{3}} + \frac{10\frac{2}{3}^2}{35\frac{1}{3}} + \frac{13^2}{36} + \frac{8^2}{36} + \frac{5^2}{36} + \frac{\left(\frac{2}{3}\right)^2}{28\frac{2}{3}} + \frac{\left(6\frac{1}{3}\right)^2}{28\frac{2}{3}} + \frac{\left(5\frac{2}{3}\right)^2}{28\frac{2}{3}} \approx 17.30$$

The number of degrees of freedom is 4, i.e. $(3 - 1) \times (3 - 1)$. This is because each of the first two rows has one constraint whilst the last row has three constraints. Hence the total number of constraints is 5. As there are 9 cells, the number of degrees of freedom $= 9 - 5 = 4$. (Generally, for an $n \times m$ contingency table the number of degrees of freedom is $(n - 1)(m - 1)$.)

Now, the critical value of χ^2 for 4 degrees of freedom at the 1% level of significance is 13.28. Hence as $17.30 > 13.28$ we must reject H_0 and accept H_1 that there is a difference in the voting pattern between the ages at the 1% level of significance.

Worked Example 23

Of the 140 trains arriving at one London station on a particular day, 95 were on time and 45 were late. At another London station on the same day, out of 156 trains arriving 87 were on time and 69 were late. Test at the 2.5% significance level whether there is any difference in the proportions arriving late at the two terminals.

Working

	Terminal A	Terminal B	Total
Late	45 (53.92)	69 (60.08)	114
On time	95 (86.08)	87 (95.92)	182
Total	140	156	296

As the number of degrees of freedom $v = (2-1)(2-1) = 1$ we will apply Yates' correction.

$$\chi^2 = \frac{(8.92 - 0.5)^2}{53.92} + \frac{(8.92 - 0.5)^2}{86.08} + \frac{(8.92 - 0.5)^2}{60.08} + \frac{(8.92 - 0.5)^2}{95.92} \approx 4.058$$

The critical value of χ^2 at the 2.5% level for one degree of freedom is 5.024 and as $4.058 < 5.024$ we conclude that H_0, there is no difference in the proportions arriving late, must be accepted. H_1, there is a difference in the proportions arriving late, is rejected.

Linear regression

Apart from dealing with distributions of a single variate, we often need to concern ourselves as to whether there is any relationship between two variates, i.e. bivariate data, $(x_1, y_1)(x_2, y_2)(x_3, y_3), \ldots, (x_n, y_n)$. The bivariate data can be represented on a 'scatter diagram' which will give some indication as to whether any relationship does exist.

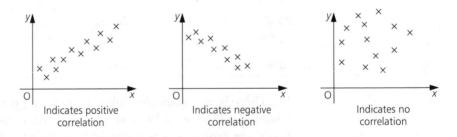

Indicates positive correlation	Indicates negative correlation	Indicates no correlation

If there is a relationship between x and y then one can draw by eye the best straight line through the points so that there is an even spread of points above and below the line. However, we need to do this more scientifically and we do so by means of the method of **least squares**. This gives the least squares regression line of y on x as

$$y - \bar{y} = \frac{S_{xy}}{S_x^2}(x - \bar{x})$$

or x on y as

$$x - \bar{x} = \frac{S_{xy}}{S_y^2}(y - \bar{y})$$

where S_{xy} is known as the **regression coefficient**, S_y^2 is the variance of y and S_x^2 is the variance of x.

You are not required to be able to establish these equations, but simply to be able to use them and understand their significance.

Both lines go through $(\bar{x}, \bar{y})$,

$$S_{xy} = \frac{\Sigma xy - n\bar{x}\bar{y}}{n},$$

$$S_x^2 = \frac{\Sigma x^2 - n\bar{x}^2}{n},$$

$$S_y^2 = \frac{\Sigma y^2 - n\bar{y}^2}{n}$$

Note that

1 You can use the regression equation y on x to estimate y for given x but not to estimate x for given y.

2 You can use the regression equation x on y to estimate x for given y but not to estimate y for given x.

3 You must only estimate x or y for values within or close to the range of the sample. Conditions outside the sample may be very different.

Worked Example 24

Find the equation of the regression line of y on x for the four pairs of values of the variables given in the table

x	1	2	3	4
y	2	4	5	7

Working

$$\bar{x} = \frac{1+2+3+4}{4} = 2.5, \quad \bar{y} = \frac{2+4+5+7}{4} = 4.5$$

					Totals
x	1	2	3	4	10
y	2	4	5	7	18
xy	2	8	15	28	53
x^2	1	4	9	16	30

$$S_{xy} = \frac{\Sigma xy - n\bar{x}\bar{y}}{n} = \frac{53 - 4 \times 2.5 \times 4.5}{4} = 2$$

$$S_x^2 = \frac{\Sigma x^2 - n\bar{x}^2}{n} = \frac{30 - 4 \times 2.5^2}{4} = 1.25$$

$\Rightarrow$ regression line of y on x is $y - 4.5 = \dfrac{2}{1.25}(x - 2.5)$

or $y = 1.6x + 0.5$.

Show that the regression line of x on y has equation $x = 0.615y - 0.269$.

Worked Example 25

The following table shows the number of road vehicles ($x \times 10^{-6}$) and the related number of road casualties ($y \times 10^{-5}$) each year for six consecutive years.

(a) Find the equation of the regression line of y on x in the form $y = mx + c$.

(b) Give an interpretation of your value of m and estimate the number of casualties when the number of road vehicles is 8 million.

(c) State, giving reasons, whether you would use the regression equation to predict the number of road casualties when the number of vehicles on the road reaches 12 million.

x	4.8	5.2	5.7	6.5	7.0	7.6
y	2.0	2.2	2.3	2.7	2.8	2.9

Working

x	y	xy	x^2
4.8	2.0	9.60	23.04
5.2	2.2	11.44	27.04
5.7	2.3	13.11	32.49
6.5	2.7	17.55	42.25
7.0	2.8	19.60	49.00
7.6	2.9	22.04	57.76
36.8	14.9	93.34	231.58

$$\Rightarrow \quad \bar{x} = 6.133 \quad \bar{y} = 2.483, \quad S_{xy} = \frac{1.9533}{6}, \quad S_x^2 = \frac{5.8733}{6}$$

$$\Rightarrow y - 2.483 = \frac{1.9533}{5.8733}(x - 6.133) \quad \Rightarrow \quad y \approx 0.3326x + 0.4433$$

$m \Rightarrow$ for every extra million cars on the road there will most likely result in an extra 330 000 road casualties.

When $x = 8$, $y = 3.1041$, i.e. the number of road casualties is approximately 310 000.

It would not be safe to use the regression equation as $x = 12$ is well outside the range and road conditions may have changed considerably by then.

Product–moment correlation coefficient

The gradients of the two regression lines can be used to measure the degree of the relationship between the two variables. We establish what is known as the product–moment correlation coefficient

$$r = \frac{S_{xy}}{S_x S_y} = \frac{\sum xy - n\bar{x}\bar{y}}{\sqrt{\{(\sum x^2 - n\bar{x}^2)(\sum y^2 - n\bar{y}^2)\}}}$$

If $r = 1$ there is perfect positive correlation, i.e. the two regression lines have a positive gradient and are coincident.

If $r = -1$ there is perfect negative correlation, i.e. the two regression lines have a negative gradient and are coincident.

If $r = 0$ there is no correlation.

Worked Example 26

Determine the correlation coefficient for worked example 25.

Working

We found $S_{xy} = \dfrac{1.9533}{6}$ and $S_x^2 = \dfrac{5.8733}{6}$. All that is necessary is to

calculate $S_y^2 = \dfrac{\sum y^2 - n\bar{y}^2}{n}$.

$$\sum y^2 = 4.00 + 4.84 + 5.29 + 7.29 + 7.84 + 8.41 = 37.67$$

$$\Rightarrow \quad S_y^2 = \frac{37.67 - 6 \times \left(\frac{14.9}{6}\right)^2}{6} = \frac{0.6683}{6}$$

$$\Rightarrow \quad r = \frac{S_{xy}}{S_x S_y} = \frac{1.9533}{\sqrt{5.8733} \times \sqrt{0.6683}} \approx 0.986 \text{ (almost perfect positive correlation)}$$

Rank correlation

When the data are not given in the form of exact measurements but in the form of an order or a rank then it is possible, by using Spearman's rank correlation coefficient, to obtain some measure of correlation. The formula, which you are not required to be able to derive, is

$$r_S = 1 - \frac{6 \sum\limits_{r=1}^{n} d_r^2}{n(n^2 - 1)}$$

where d_r is the difference in rank between the rth pair. In the case of tied ranks, the convention of giving the mean rank of each equal item is used, though some examination boards do not include tied ranks within their syllabus.

Worked Example 27

The marks obtained by 10 students in the biology and chemistry examination were as shown in the table.

	A	B	C	D	E	F	G	H	J	K
Biology	61	39	81	86	20	50	56	47	35	17
Chemistry	43	40	82	93	34	40	46	22	42	20

Determine Spearman's rank correlation and comment upon your result.

Working
First place the marks in order of rank. We shall use 1 for the highest mark, and where two gain the same mark they will each be given the mean of the ranks which they occupy, i.e. B and F both obtained 40 marks in chemistry, 40 represents the 6th and 7th positions in rank so each are given a ranking of $6\frac{1}{2}$.

	A	B	C	D	E	F	G	H	J	K
Rank in biology	3	7	2	1	9	5	4	6	8	10
Rank in chemistry	4	$6\frac{1}{2}$	2	1	8	$6\frac{1}{2}$	3	10	5	9
d	-1	$\frac{1}{2}$	0	0	1	$-1\frac{1}{2}$	1	-4	3	1
d^2	1	$\frac{1}{4}$	0	0	1	$2\frac{1}{4}$	1	16	9	1

$$\Rightarrow \quad r_S = 1 - \frac{6 \times 31\frac{1}{2}}{10(10^2 - 1)} = 1 - 0.1909 \approx 0.81$$

0.81 is a high value which therefore indicates strong positive correlation between these students' ability in biology and chemistry.

Significance testing of a rank correlation coefficient

If in doubt about the result, we can always look up the significance of the value of r_S in the appropriate tables.

The null hypothesis will always be H_0 (no correlation exists). We then look up in the appropriate tables the probability that the result could have occurred by chance.

For $n = 10$, $\Sigma d^2 = 31.5$, the tables give

$P(\Sigma d^2 \leqslant 30)$ is 0.0029, $P(\Sigma d^2 \leqslant 36)$ is 0.0053

Interpolating $\Rightarrow$ $P(\Sigma d^2 = 31.5) = 0.0035$. This is indeed very small so we conclude therefore that there is strong positive correlation between the rankings of the students in biology and chemistry.

? PRACTICE QUESTIONS

1 The random variable X has the probability distribution shown.

X	1	2	3	4	5
$P(X)$	0.15	0.20	p	0.35	0.10

where p is a positive constant.
(a) Find the value of p.
(b) Find the expected value of X.
(c) Find $P(X > \mu)$, where μ is the mean.

2 Two events A and B are such that $P(A) = \frac{1}{5}$, $P(B) = \frac{3}{5}$ and $P(B|A) = \frac{1}{10}$.
Find
(a) P (Both A and B occur)
(b) P (Just one event A or B occurs)

3 (a) Two events X and Y are mutually exclusive. Given that $P(X) = 0.2$ and $P(X \cup Y) = 0.7$, find $P(Y)$.
(b) Two events A and B are independent. Given $P(A) = 0.25$ and $P(A \cup B) = 0.6$, find $P(B)$.

4 The following table refers to the number of births to women in a particular county in 1975 related to the age of the mother. All births to women under 16 have been discounted.

Age of mother	16–22	23–26	27–31	32 and over
No. of births	4 856	2 281	1 425	683

(a) Draw a cumulative frequency curve for these data and estimate the median and interquartile range.
(b) The corresponding data for 1995 revealed a median of 20.5 and an interquartile range of 6 years and 7 months. Compare these values with those you obtained for 1975 and state any conclusions that can be made concerning the two sets of figures.
(c) Why is it better to use the median and interquartile range rather than the mean and standard deviation for making this comparison?

5 A well known tyre was used on the front wheels of cars of the same make and design. The number of kilometres covered by the tyres before replacement was required is shown in the table below.

Mileage x	No. of tyres
$14\,000 \leqslant x < 17\,000$	3
$17\,000 \leqslant x < 20\,000$	7
$20\,000 \leqslant x < 23\,000$	21
$23\,000 \leqslant x < 26\,000$	98
$26\,000 \leqslant x < 29\,000$	123
$29\,000 \leqslant x < 32\,000$	62
$32\,000 \leqslant x < 35\,000$	36

(a) Estimate the mean and standard deviation of the number of miles covered for this distribution.
(b) It was later revealed that all of the mileages should have been increased by 1 000. What effect does this have on the estimated mean and the standard deviation?

6 A machine produces rivets whose lengths are normally distributed with mean 2 cm and standard deviation 0.01 cm. The rivets can only be used provided their lengths are not greater than 2.015 cm and not less than 1.996 cm.
(a) Find the probability that a rivet chosen at random is acceptable.

(b) Given that the machine is capable of sorting out the rivets greater than 2 cm in length, find the probability that the randomly chosen rivet from this section is satisfactory.

7 The equation of two regression lines of a bivariate distribution are given by

$$y = 1.5x + 0.3, \quad x = 0.6y - 0.1$$

(a) Show that the arithmetic means of each distribution are $\bar{x} = 0.8$, and $\bar{y} = 1.5$.

(b) Find the product–moment correlation coefficient between the two distributions.

8 The number of accidents at a busy road junction has been found to follow a Poisson distribution with a mean of 0.8 accidents per week. Estimate to 3 significant figures the probability that there will be

(a) at least 2 accidents in a particular week,

(b) exactly 3 accidents in a particular 4 week period.

9 The table shows the ranking of 10 football players by two football managers asked to consider the player of the year award.

	A	B	C	D	E	F	G	H	J	K
Manager I	1	2	3	4	5	6	7	8	9	10
Manager II	2	4	3	1	7	5	6	10	8	9

(a) Calculate Spearman's coefficient of rank correlation between the two managers.

(b) Using a table of critical values comment on the significance of your result stating clearly your null hypothesis.

10 The random variable X has probability density function $f(x)$ given by

$$f(x) = \begin{cases} 3x^{\alpha} & 0 \leqslant x \leqslant 1, \ \alpha \text{ a positive integer} \\ 0 & \text{otherwise} \end{cases}$$

Find

(a) the value of α,

(b) the expected value of X,

(c) the variance of X,

(d) the value of x such that $P(X \leqslant x) = 0.8$.

11 A bag contains a large number of different coins, 40% of which are British. A random sample of 20 coins is taken from the bag. Use the binomial distribution to calculate the probability that the sample contains

(a) fewer than 8 British coins,

(b) exactly 8 British coins.

12 The stem and leaf diagram below shows the marks obtained by 41 students in a mathematics examination

```
3 | 0 3 7                      (3)
4 | 1 2 6 8                    (4)
5 | 0 3 5 6 7 9                (6)
6 | 1 1 4 5 7 8 8 9            (8)
7 | 0 0 1 1 3 3 4 6 6 8       (10)
8 | 1 2 2 3 6 8                (6)
9 | 0 1 3 6                    (4)
```

(a) Calculate the median and the lower and upper quartiles.

(b) Show the data on a box and whiskers plot and comment on the skewness of the distribution.

13 A variate X is $N(80, 25)$. Find the probabilities (a) $P(X) < 75$,

(b) $P(X) \geqslant 90$,   (c) $P(76 < x < 86)$.

14 Certain newspapers are printed with an average of 30 errors per paper.
   (a) Using the normal approximation of the Poisson distribution find the probability that one of the newspapers chosen at random will have more than 35 errors.
   (b) Why is it possible to use the normal approximation of the Poisson distribution in this case?

15 When analysing the results of a 3×2 contingency table the value of
$$\sum_{1}^{6} \frac{(O_i - E_i)^2}{E_i}$$ was found to be 3.52. State
   (a) the number of degrees of freedom,
   (b) the critical values appropriate to these data in order to carry out a χ^2 test of significance at (i) the 5% level, (ii) the 2.50% level.

16 One hundred boys and one hundred girls were questioned as to whether they walked or travelled to school by public transport. Sixty per cent of the boys answered that they walked whilst only 45% of the girls answered that they walked. Find the probability that if one of them were chosen at random that person
   (a) walked to school,
   (b) was a girl who travelled to school by public transport,
   (c) was a boy, given that it was known that the person walked to school.

Here you will find hints and outline solutions to the practice questions found in Part II. Try not to look at these answers until you have completed your own answers, but if you get into difficulty, look at the hints for suggestions on approaching the question.

1 Solutions
Algebra

HINTS AND OUTLINE SOLUTIONS

1   You are likely to make fewer errors substituting $x = 1 + 2y$ in $3xy - y^2 = 8$ than substituting $y = \frac{1}{2}(x - 1)$. Do not forget that you have to pair the values of x and y.

2   Show that $f\left(\frac{2}{3}\right) = 0$. To factorise, use $(3x - 2)(2x^2 + ax - 1)$. To fix the x term in the x^2 bracket consider the x^2 terms, i.e. $-4x^2 + 3ax^2 = -7x^2 \quad \Rightarrow$ $a = -1$ (or the x terms $-2ax - 3x = -x \quad \Rightarrow \quad a = -1$). This is an easier method than dividing. Do not mix up factors with roots.

3   Be careful to distinguish between the $\leqslant$ and $<$ signs.

4   For (a) the partial fractions are $\dfrac{A}{x} + \dfrac{Bx + C}{x^2 + 2}$.

   For (b) the partial fractions are $\dfrac{A}{x} + \dfrac{B}{x + 2} + \dfrac{C}{(x + 2)^2}$.

5   Note that y has a minimum value of zero at A. The curve is tangential to the x-axis, therefore $ax^2 + bx + c = 0$ has equal roots.

6   (a) (i) Take logarithms of both sides.
      (ii) Quadratic in 2^y. Let $x = 2^y$, then solve $x^2 - x = -\frac{3}{16}$.
   (b) Use change of base formula or note

   $$\log_8 2 = \log_8\left(8^{\frac{1}{3}}\right) = \frac{1}{3} \quad \Rightarrow \quad \log_8\left(\frac{t}{2}\right) = 3\log_8 t = \log_8 t^3.$$

7   (a) Use formula $\dfrac{-b \pm \sqrt{(b^2 - 4ac)}}{2a}$.

   (b) Use the factor theorem to show that $(x + 2)$ is a factor.
      (i) Then show $f(x) = (x + 2)(x^2 - 2x - 24) = (x + 2)(x + 4)(x - 6)$.
      (ii) Partial fractions are $\dfrac{A}{x + 2} + \dfrac{B}{x + 4} + \dfrac{C}{x - 6}$.

8   Use $y = kx^n \quad \Rightarrow \quad \ln y = \ln k + n \ln x$.

9 Sketch the graphs and consider their points of intersection.

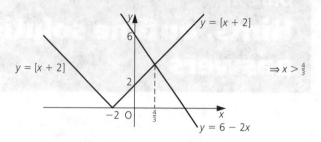

10 (a) Rationalise the denominators

$$\frac{1}{3-\sqrt{2}}+\frac{1}{3+\sqrt{2}}=\frac{1}{3-\sqrt{2}}\left(\frac{3+\sqrt{2}}{3+\sqrt{2}}\right)+\frac{1}{3+\sqrt{2}}\left(\frac{3-\sqrt{2}}{3-\sqrt{2}}\right)$$

(b) Substitute $x=5-\sqrt{3}$ in $x^2-10x+p=0$ in order to find p and then

use $\dfrac{-b\pm\sqrt{(b^2-4ac)}}{2a}$.

ANSWERS

1 $(3,1)$ $(-2.2,-1.6)$

2 (a) $\frac{2}{3}$, $-\frac{1}{2}$, 1

   (b) $-\frac{4}{3}$, $-\frac{5}{2}$, -1

3 (a) 2 only, (b) $-2<x<6$

4 (a) $\dfrac{1}{x}-\dfrac{x}{x^2+2}$

   (b) $\dfrac{1}{2x}-\dfrac{1}{2(x+2)}-\dfrac{1}{(x+2)^2}$

5 (b) $\left(\dfrac{-b}{2a},0\right)$

6 (a) (i) 5.58, (ii) -2 or 1.58

   (b) ±0.707

7 (a) 1.71, -3.21

   (b) (i) $(x+4)(x+2)(x-6)$

     (ii) $\dfrac{1}{20(x+4)}-\dfrac{1}{16(x+2)}+\dfrac{1}{80(x-6)}$

8 $n=-3.12$, $k=217$

9 (a) $x>\frac{4}{3}$, (b) $-\frac{8}{3}\leqslant x\leqslant0$

10 (a) $\frac{6}{7}$, (b) $p=22$, $5+\sqrt{3}$

2 Sequences and series

HINTS AND OUTLINE SOLUTIONS

1 (a) $(1-x)^6=1-\binom{6}{1}x+\binom{6}{2}x^2-\binom{6}{3}x^3+\binom{6}{4}x^4-\binom{6}{5}x^5+x^6.$

Make sure you know how to use your calculator efficiently to evaluate $\binom{6}{3}$ etc. Most have a key specifically for this.

$$(1-x)^6=1-6x+15x^2-20x^3+15x^4-6x^5+x^6$$

(b) Since $0.997=1-0.003$, we take $x=0.003$ in the series

$$(0.997)^6\approx1-0.018+0.000\,135-0.000\,000\,54\quad\text{(next terms too small)}$$
$$=0.982\,134\,46\quad\text{(8 d.p.)}$$

2 (a) For the GP $\frac{1}{2} + \frac{1}{2^2} + \frac{1}{2^3} + \ldots, a = \frac{1}{2}$ and $r = \frac{1}{2}$

$$S_n = \frac{a(1 - r^n)}{1 - r} = \frac{\frac{1}{2}\left(1 - \frac{1}{2^n}\right)}{\frac{1}{2}} = 1 - \frac{1}{2^n}$$

(b) $S_\infty = \dfrac{a}{1 - r} = \dfrac{\frac{1}{2}}{1 - \frac{1}{2}} = 1.$

(c) We require $1 - \dfrac{1}{2^n} > 0.9999 \quad \Rightarrow \quad \dfrac{1}{2^n} < 0.0001.$ That is

$$2^n > 10\,000 \quad \Rightarrow \quad n > \frac{\log 10\,000}{\log 2} \quad \Rightarrow \quad n \geqslant 14$$

3 (a) $\displaystyle\sum_{n=1}^{80}(2n - 1) = 1 + 3 + \ldots + 159$

This is an AP of 80 terms: $a = 1, \quad d = 2, \quad n = 80.$ Use

$$S = \frac{n}{2}\{2a + (n - 1)d\} = 40(2 + 2 \times 79) = 6\,400$$

(b) $\displaystyle\sum_{n=1}^{9} 144(2^{-n}) = 72 + 36 + \ldots$

This is a GP of 9 terms: $a = 72, \quad r = \frac{1}{2}, \quad n = 9.$ Use

$$S = \frac{a(1 - r^n)}{1 - r} = \frac{72\left(1 - \frac{1}{2^9}\right)}{1 - \frac{1}{2}} = \frac{144 \times 511}{512} = 143.7$$

4 (a) Terms get bigger positively without limit. Sequence diverges to $+\infty$.
(b) Successive terms are 2 and -2. Sequence oscillates between 2 and -2.
(c) Terms are $\frac{1}{2}, 0, \frac{1}{2}, 1$ and then repeated. Sequence is periodic over 4
terms.
(d) $3^{3-n} \to 0$ as $n \to \infty$. Sequence converges to 2 as $n \to \infty$.

5 (a) $3\,000 \,(0.88)^9 = 949 \quad \Rightarrow \quad$ Value after 9 years is £949 (nearest £1).

(b) $3\,000\,(0.88)^r = 375 \quad \Rightarrow \quad r = \dfrac{\log\left(\frac{375}{3000}\right)}{\log(0.88)} \approx 16.2\ldots$

After 17 years, value is £375.

6 (a) Use $(1 + x)^n$ with $n = \frac{1}{3}$ to obtain $1 + \frac{1}{3}x - \frac{1}{9}x^2 + \frac{5}{81}x^3.$
(b) Put $x = 0.02$ in your series.

7 (a) Write $\dfrac{2 - 3x}{(1 - x)(1 - 2x)} = \dfrac{A}{1 - x} + \dfrac{B}{1 - 2x}$ and obtain $A = 1, B = 1.$

(b) Expand $(1 - x)^{-1} + (1 - 2x)^{-1} = 1 + x + x^2 + x^3 + \ldots + 1 + 2x + 4x^2 + 8x^3 + \ldots$

to obtain $1 + 3x + 5x^2 + 9x^3$ as first 4 terms of the series for $\dfrac{2 - 3x}{1 - 3x + 2x^2}.$

$(1 - x)^{-1}$ series is valid for $|x| < 1.$
$(1 - 2x)^{-1}$ series is valid for $|2x| < 1$, i.e. $|x| < \frac{1}{2}.$
So overall combined series $(1 - x)^{-1} + (1 - 2x)^{-1}$ valid for $|x| < \frac{1}{2}.$

8 Write down a few terms to help you decide the behaviour of each sequence.
(a) $\left(\frac{1}{3}\right)^n \to 0$ as $n \to \infty \quad \therefore$ sequence converges to 4.
(b) Successive terms are $3, 5, 3, 5, \ldots, \quad \therefore$ sequence oscillates between 3
and 5.
(c) $2^n \to \infty$ as $n \to \infty, \quad \therefore$ sequence diverges to $-\infty$.

(d) $\displaystyle\sum_{n=1}^{N}\left[4-\left(\frac{1}{3}\right)^{n}\right]=\sum_{n=1}^{N}4-\sum_{n=1}^{N}\left(\frac{1}{3}\right)^{n}$

$$\sum_{n=1}^{N}4=4+4+4+\ldots=4N$$

$$\sum_{n=1}^{N}\left(\frac{1}{3}\right)^{n}=\frac{1}{3}+\left(\frac{1}{3}\right)^{2}+\left(\frac{1}{3}\right)^{3}+\ldots \quad \left(\text{a GP with } a=\frac{1}{2}, r=\frac{1}{2}, n=N\right)$$

$$=\frac{\frac{1}{3}\left(1-\frac{1}{3^{n}}\right)}{1-\frac{1}{3}}=\frac{1}{2}\left(1-\frac{1}{3^{n}}\right)$$

$$\therefore \quad \sum_{n=1}^{N}U_{n}=4N+\frac{1}{2}-\frac{1}{2}\left(\frac{1}{3^{N}}\right)$$

ANSWERS

1 (a) $1-6x+15x^{2}-20x^{3}$
   $+15x^{4}-6x^{5}+x^{6}$
   (b) $0.98\,213\,446$

2 (a) $1-\dfrac{1}{2^{n}}$, (b) 1, (c) 14 terms.

3 (a) $6\,400$, (b) 143.7

4 (a) Divergent to $+\infty$
   (b) Oscillating finitely between -2
   and 2.
   (c) Periodic over the 4 terms
   $\frac{1}{2}$, 0, $\frac{1}{2}$, 1.
   (d) Convergent to 2.

5 (a) £949, (b) 17 years

6 (a) $1+\frac{1}{3}x-\frac{1}{9}x^{2}+\frac{5}{81}x^{3}$
   (b) $1.006\,623$

7 (a) $\dfrac{1}{1-x}+\dfrac{1}{1-2x}$
   (b) $1+3x+5x^{2}+9x^{3}$, $|x|<\frac{1}{2}$

8 (a) Converges to 4.
   (b) Oscillates finitely between 3 and
   5.
   (c) Diverges to $-\infty$.
   (d) $4N+\frac{1}{2}-\frac{1}{2}(3)^{-N}$.

3 Coordinate geometry

HINTS AND OUTLINE SOLUTIONS

1 (a) Do not forget to add the coordinates, not subtract.
   (b) Show $m_{1}m_{2}=-1$ if the lines are perpendicular.
   (c) Use $\frac{1}{2}$ (length of base $PQ \times$ height RM).

2 Substitute $y=1-2x$ in $4x^{2}+y^{2}=13$ and solve the quadratic.

3 Solve the simultaneous equations, find the gradient of the tangent at A and
   use the equation $y-y_{1}=m(x-x_{1})$.

4 Note that the circles pass through the origin so the general equation of the
   circle reduces to $x^{2}+y^{2}+2gx+2fy=0$. Hence for (a) substitute the
   coordinates of A and B and solve for g and f. For (b) note the midpoint of OA
   is the centre of the circle, i.e. $\left(\frac{3}{2}, 1\right)$, radius of circle $=\frac{1}{2}(AO)^{2}$. Alternatively,
   use $(x-x_{1})(x-x_{2})+(y-y_{1})(y-y_{2})=0$.

5 (a) The gradients of the lines are 3, 2. They pass through (4, 3) so use
   $y-y_{1}=m(x-x_{1})$, i.e. draw a diagram of the parallelogram and determine
   the coordinates of all the vertices by solving the necessary simultaneous
   equations.

(b)

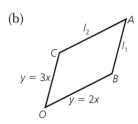

6

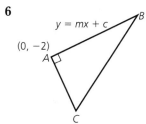

Sketch triangle ABC making sure that B is in the first quadrant. Let equation of AB be $y = mx - 2$; then equation of AC is $y = -\dfrac{1}{m}x - 2$. Use

$$AB^2 = AC^2 \quad \Rightarrow \quad m = \dfrac{3}{5}.$$

ANSWERS

1 (a) $(5, 4)$
(c) 20 units^2
2 $(-1, 3)$, $(\frac{3}{2}, -2)$
3 $A(2, 1)$, $B(-1, 4)$, $y = 2x - 3$
4 (a) $x^2 + y^2 + x - 7y = 0$
(b) $x^2 + y^2 - 3x - 2y = 0$

5 (a) $y = 3x - 9$, $y = 2x - 5$
(b) (i) 45
(ii) 5, $\sqrt{1\,285}$
6 (a) $3x - 5y = 10$, $5x + 3y = -6$
(b) $(5, 1)$
(c) 17

4 Functions

HINTS AND OUTLINE SOLUTIONS

1 (a) Since $x^2 \geqslant 0$, range of f is y where $0 < y \leqslant 5$.

(b) $y = \dfrac{5}{1 + x^2} \quad \Rightarrow \quad x^2 = \dfrac{5}{y} - 1 \quad \Rightarrow \quad x = \left(\dfrac{5}{y} - 1\right)^{\frac{1}{2}}$

$$f^{-1} : x \mapsto \left(\dfrac{5}{x} - 1\right)^{\frac{1}{2}} \qquad x \in \mathbb{R}, \quad 0 < x \leqslant 5$$

(c) See diagram.

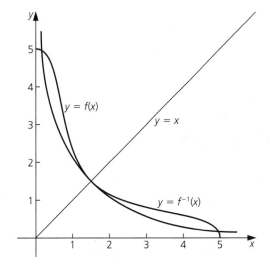

2 (a) (i) $fg(x) = f[g(x)] = f(x-3) = (x-3)^2 + 2 = x^2 - 6x + 11.$

    (ii) $gf(x) = g[f(x)] = g(x^2 + 2) = x^2 + 2 - 3 = x^2 - 1.$

    (iii) $ff(x) = f[f(x)] = f(x^2 + 2) = (x^2 + 2)^2 + 2 = x^4 + 4x^2 + 6.$

  (b) Now $g^{-1}(x) = x + 3,$ hence

$$fg^{-1}(x) = f(x+3) = (x+3)^2 + 2$$

$$fg^{-1}(x) \leqslant 6 \quad \Rightarrow \quad (x+3)^2 + 2 \leqslant 6$$

$$\Rightarrow \quad x^2 + 6x + 5 \leqslant 0 \quad \Rightarrow \quad (x+5)(x+1) \leqslant 0$$

$$\Rightarrow \quad -5 \leqslant x \leqslant -1$$

3   Start with curve $y = \cos x \rightarrow y = \cos 2x \rightarrow y = -\cos 2x.$ Then you can sketch the curve $y = 3 - \cos 2x.$

4 (a)

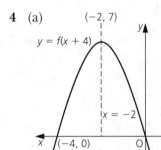

   (b)

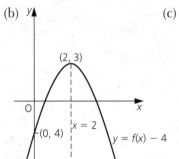

   (c)

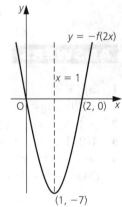

   (d)

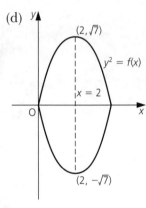

5 (a)

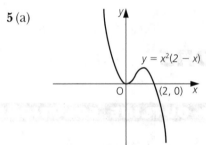

  (b) (i)

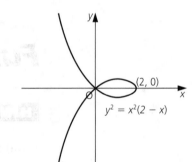

  (b) (ii)

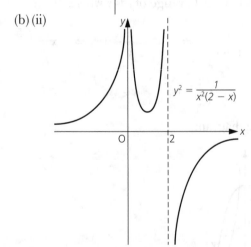

ANSWERS

1 (a) $0 < y \leqslant 5$

   (b) $f^{-1} : x \mapsto \left(\dfrac{5}{x} - 1\right)^{\frac{1}{2}}$

     $x \in \mathbb{R}, \quad 0 < x \leqslant 5$

   (c) See diagram above.

2 (a) $x^2 - 6x + 11$ (b) $x^2 - 1$

   (c) $x^4 + 4x^2 + 6$

3 See diagram above.

4 See diagram above.

5 See diagram above.

5 Trigonometry

HINTS AND OUTLINE SOLUTIONS

1 (a) Solved by using the factors, $\cos x = \frac{1}{2}$, $\sin x = -\frac{1}{2}$.

  (b) Convert to a quadratic in $\sin x$ using $\cos^2 x = 1 - \sin^2 x$.

  (c) Convert to a quadratic in $\sec^2 x$ using $\tan^2 x = \sec^2 x - 1$.

  (d) Use $\cosec x = \dfrac{1}{\sin x}$ then $2\sin x \cos x = \sin 2x$

2 Sketch $\triangle ABC$.

  (a) Use the cosine rule remembering that $\cos 120° = -\cos 60°$.

  (b) Use the sine rule remembering $\sin 120° = \sin 60°$.

3 (a) Sketch the situation after two hours, use the cosine rule remembering
     $\cos 164° = -\cos 16°$.

  (b) Use the sine rule to calculate $\angle\text{PBA}$. The bearing of A from B is
     $\{180° - (\angle\text{PBA} + 36°)\}$.

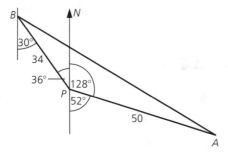

4 (a) (i) Use $\sin 3x = \sin(2x + x)$. Expand and use $\cos 2x = 1 - 2\sin^2 x$,
       $\sin 2x = 2\sin x \cos x$ and $\cos^2 x = 1 - \sin^2 x$.

   (ii) Use $\cos 2y = 2\cos^2 y - 1$, $\cos 4y = 2\cos^2 2y - 1$.

  (b) Expand $\sin(x + 60°)$ then use $\sin x = \dfrac{2t}{1 + t^2}$, $\cos x = \dfrac{1 - t^2}{1 + t^2}$

   where $t = \tan\dfrac{x}{2}$.

5 Solve by using the tan half angle formulae.

6 (a) Use $\triangle CGA$ and $AG^2 = AC^2 + CG^2$,

  (b) Use $\triangle HEC$ and $CE^2 = EH^2 + CH^2$ where $CH^2 = HD^2 + DC^2$.

  (c) Use the isosceles $\triangle EMH$ where $EM = MH$ and $EM^2 = 2.5^2 + 3^2 + 2^2$.

  (d) Use the rectangle $BEHC$ and let BH and CE intersect at X. Then

$$EX = HX = \frac{1}{2}BH \quad \text{and} \quad CH = 2^2 + 3^3 \quad \Rightarrow \quad \tan\left(\frac{1}{2}E\widehat{X}H\right) = \frac{5}{\sqrt{13}}$$

$$\Rightarrow \frac{1}{2}E\widehat{X}H = 54.2° \quad \Rightarrow \quad \text{Required angle} = 108.4°.$$

7 (a) Use arc length $= r\theta$, do not forget θ is in radians.

$$r = 12, \quad \theta = \frac{5\pi}{3} \quad \Rightarrow \quad S = 20\pi.$$

  (b) Use required area $= \pi r^2 - \dfrac{1}{2}r^2\theta = 144\pi - \dfrac{1}{2} \times 144\left(\dfrac{\pi}{3}\right) = 377\,\text{cm}^2$.

  (c) Use area of segment $= \dfrac{1}{2}r^2(\theta - \sin\theta) = \dfrac{1}{2} \times 12^2\left(\dfrac{\pi}{3} - \sin\dfrac{\pi}{3}\right) = 13.0\,\text{cm}^2$.

8 Draw diagrams.

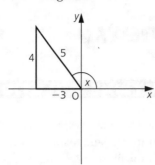 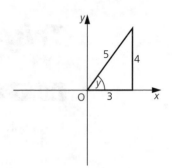

Use the trigonometric formulae.

(a) $\sin 2x = 2 \sin x \cos x = 2 \times \left(\dfrac{4}{5}\right)\left(-\dfrac{3}{5}\right) = -\dfrac{24}{25}$.

(c) $\cos 2y = 2 \cos^2 y - 1 = 2 \times \left(\dfrac{3}{5}\right)^2 - 1 = \dfrac{18}{25} - 1 = -\dfrac{7}{25}$.

(e) $\cos(2y - x) = \cos 2y \cos x + \sin 2y \sin x = \left(-\dfrac{7}{25}\right)\left(-\dfrac{3}{5}\right) + 2 \sin y \cos y \sin x$

$$= \dfrac{21}{125} + 2 \times \left(\dfrac{4}{5}\right)\left(\dfrac{3}{5}\right)\left(\dfrac{4}{5}\right) = \dfrac{21 + 96}{125} = \dfrac{117}{125}.$$

ANSWERS

1 (a) $60°$, $300°$, $210°$, $330°$
   (b) $30°$, $150°$
   (c) $60°$, $109.5°$
   (d) $15°$, $75°$, $195°$, $255°$

2 (a) 4.61, (b) $26°$

3 (a) $83.2\,\text{km}$, (b) $134°$

4 (b) $-113.8°$, $66.2°$

5 0.60, 2.86, 3.75, 6.00

6 (a) $60.9°$, (b) $35.6°$,
   (c) $69.5°$, (d) $108.4°$

7 (a) $20\,\pi\,\text{cm}$, (b) $377\,\text{cm}^2$,
   (c) $13.0\,\text{cm}^2$

8 (a) $\dfrac{-24}{25}$, (b) 0, (c) $\dfrac{-7}{25}$,
   (d) 0, (e) $\dfrac{117}{125}$

6 *Differentiation*

HINTS AND OUTLINE SOLUTIONS

1 (a) Use function of function rule $\Rightarrow$ $3(2x + 1)^2 \times 2$, or alternatively multiply out although this will give you more work.

(b) Use quotient rule. $\left(\text{Remember } \dfrac{\mathrm{d}}{\mathrm{d}x} \sin x = \cos x.\right)$

(c) Use product rule.

(d) Use function of function rule $\Rightarrow$ $3 \sin^2 2x\,(2 \cos 2x.)$

(e) Use quotient rule. $\left(\text{Remember } \dfrac{\mathrm{d}}{\mathrm{d}x} \cos x = -\sin x.\right)$

2 Use quotient rule on $\dfrac{3 \sin x}{2 + \cos x}$.

3 (a) Equate $\dfrac{dy}{dx} = 0$. Do not forget to test for max or min. The easiest test here

is to consider the sign of $\dfrac{d^2y}{dx^2}$.

4 Remember $\dfrac{d}{dx}\,e^{ax} = ae^{ax}$, and that if $e^{ax} = c$, $ax = \ln c$.

5 Remember to start with $\dfrac{d}{dx}\left(3x^2\right) + \dfrac{d}{dx}\left(5xy\right) - \dfrac{d}{dx}\left(2y^2\right) = \dfrac{d}{dx}\left(8\right)$ and that

when differentiating the terms involving y you will need $\dfrac{dy}{dx}\dfrac{d}{dy}\left(2y^2\right)$.

6 (a) Find the value of $\dfrac{dy}{dx}$ at $(-1, 0)$ $\Rightarrow$ $\dfrac{dy}{dx} = 3x^2 + 2x = 1$ at $(-1, 0)$.

(b) Equate $\dfrac{dy}{dx}$ in terms of x to this value, i.e. $3x^2 + 2x - 1 = 0$. Solve

$(3x - 1)(x + 1)$ $\Rightarrow$ $x = \frac{1}{3}$ $\Rightarrow$ $y = \frac{4}{27}$. Hence the equation of

parallel tangent is $y - \frac{4}{27} = 1\left(x - \frac{1}{3}\right)$ $\Rightarrow$ $y = x + \frac{5}{27}$.

7 Write down information given and information required.

Given $\dfrac{dV}{dt} = 4$. Require $\dfrac{dS}{dt}$ where $S = 4\pi r^2$ and $V = \frac{4}{3}\pi r^3$.

Now connect: $\dfrac{dS}{dt} = \dfrac{dS}{dr} \times \dfrac{dr}{dV} \times \dfrac{dV}{dt}$

8 Solve inequalities $\dfrac{df}{dx} > 0$ and $\dfrac{df}{dx} < 0$

9 (a) Use $\dfrac{dy}{dx} = 0$ at $x = 2$, $y = 20$ when $x = 2$, and $y = 8$ when $x = 0$ to find

the values of a, b and c.

(b) Solve $\dfrac{dy}{dx} < 0$.

10 Sketch the box to enable you to find the surface area $= 108$ in terms of x and y.

ANSWERS

1 (a) $6(2x + 1)^2$

(b) $\dfrac{1}{x^2}\left(x\cos x - \sin x\right)$

(c) $e^{2x}\left(2\ln x + \dfrac{1}{x}\right)$

(d) $6\sin^2 2x \cos 2x$

(e) $\dfrac{1}{x\cos^2 x}\left(\cos x + x\sin x\ln x\right)$

3 (a) max $(1, 2)$, min $(-1, -2)$

4 Min $\left(\ln\frac{4}{3}, \frac{16}{9}\right)$, Max $\left(\ln\frac{2}{3}, \frac{20}{9}\right)$

5 $\dfrac{6x + 5y}{4y - 5x}$

6 (a) $y = x + 1$

(b) $y = x - \frac{5}{27}$

(c) Max $\frac{4}{27}$, Min 0

7 $\frac{8}{3}\,\text{cm}^2\,\text{s}^{-1}$

8 (a) Increasing for $x > 4$

and $x < \frac{2}{3}$

(b) Decreasing for $\frac{2}{3} < x < 4$

9 (a) $a = -3$, $b = 12$, $c = 8$

(b) $x > 2$

10 $108\,\text{cm}^3$

Integration

HINTS AND OUTLINE SOLUTIONS

1 (a) Use $\displaystyle\int (ax+b)^n \, dx = \frac{1}{n+1}(ax+b)^{n+1} \cdot \frac{1}{a}$.

(b) Multiply out, then integrate.

(c) Use $\sin^2 x = \frac{1}{2}(1 - \cos 2x)$.

(d) Use $\displaystyle\int x^n \, dx = \frac{1}{n+1} \cdot x^{n+1}$

(e) Use $\tan^2 x = \sec^2 x - 1$.

(f) Use $\displaystyle\int \cos^2 \, d(-\cos x)$

(g) Use $\displaystyle\int \frac{f'(x)}{f(x)} \, dx = \ln f(x)$.

(h) Divide and then integrate.

(i) Use the substitution $t = \ln x$.

(j) Use integration by parts.

3 (a) Show $\displaystyle\frac{1}{(x+1)(x+2)} = \frac{1}{x+1} - \frac{1}{x+2}$.

(b) Integrate using the limits 0 and 4.

4 Use integration by parts. Show $\displaystyle\frac{dy}{dx} + \ln x = $ constant c and use $y = 0$ when

$x = e, y = e$ when $x = 1$ to find the constants of integration.

5 Use integration by parts to find $\displaystyle\int_0^\pi x \sin x \, dx$.

6 Use $\sec^6 \theta = \left(\sec^2 \theta\right)^2 \sec^2 \theta$ together with $\sec^2 \theta = 1 + \tan^2 \theta$.

7 Form the equation $\displaystyle\frac{dy}{dx} = \frac{1 - 2x^2}{y}$, separate the variables and integrate.

8 Differentiate to obtain $\displaystyle\frac{d^2 y}{dx^2}$ and use $\displaystyle\frac{d^2 y}{dx^2} = 5$ when $x = 1$ to find the value of

k. Then integrate $\displaystyle\frac{dy}{dx}$ and use $x = 1, y = 0$ to obtain the constant of

integration.

9 Sketch the area of finite region to show that the required volume of revolution is that of a cylinder, radius 4 height 8

less $\displaystyle\pi \int_{-4}^{4} x^2 \, dy = \pi \int_{-4}^{4} \frac{1}{16} y^4 \, dy$.

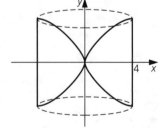

10 Use gradient $\displaystyle= \frac{dy}{dx} = \frac{y}{x - cx}$. Separate the variables and integrate each side, using $x = 1$,

$y = 1$ to find the constant of integration.

(a) The gradient of tangent at P is $\displaystyle\frac{y}{x - c}$.

1 (a) $-\dfrac{1}{3(3x-2)}$ (b) $\dfrac{1}{3}x^3 - 4x - \dfrac{4}{x}$

(c) $\dfrac{1}{2}\left(x - \dfrac{1}{2}\sin 2x\right)$ (d) $3x^{\frac{1}{3}}$

(e) $\tan x - x$ (f) $-\dfrac{1}{3}\cos^3 x$

(g) $\ln(e^x + 1)$

(h) $\dfrac{1}{2}x^2 - x + \ln(x-1)$

(i) $\dfrac{1}{2}(\ln x)^2$ (j) $\dfrac{1}{2}x\,e^{2x} - \dfrac{1}{4}e^{2x}$

2 $\dfrac{1}{2}x^2 + 2x - \dfrac{2}{x-1} + 4\ln(x-1)$

3 (a) $\dfrac{1}{x+1} - \dfrac{1}{x+2}$ (b) $\ln\frac{5}{3}$

4 $y = e - x\ln x$

6 $\dfrac{1}{5}\tan^5\theta + \dfrac{2}{3}\tan^3\theta + \tan\theta$

7 $y^2 = 2x - \dfrac{4x^3}{3} + 4$

8 $3y = 3x^3 - 4x^{\frac{3}{2}} + 1$

10 (a) Gradient of tangent at P is $\dfrac{y}{x-c}$

(b) Equation of curve is $y^{1-c} = x$

8 Numerical work

1 (a) Least possible y – Greatest possible $x = (3.65 - 1.25)\,\text{s} = 2.4\,\text{s}$

(b) $\dfrac{\text{Least }x}{\text{Greatest }y} = \dfrac{1.15}{3.75} \approx 0.3$ (1 d.p.)

2 Use $\pi r^2 h$ with $r = 8.5$ and $h = 140.5$ to obtain $31\,890\,\text{cm}^3$.
(Remember, strictly $r < 8.5$ and $h < 140.5$ so correct your final answer *downwards* to give nearest $31\,890\,\text{cm}^3$; $31\,891$ is not attainable.)

3 (a) Absolute error in each case is $0.5\,\text{m}$.

(b) Relative errors are $\dfrac{0.5}{37}$ and $\dfrac{0.5}{2}$ $\Rightarrow$ 0.014 and 0.25 to 2 s.f.

4 (a) $f(0.5) = -0.1997$, $f(0.6) = 0.2613$ $\Rightarrow$ sign change $\therefore$ root.

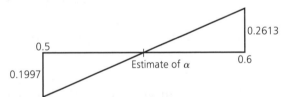

(b) Estimate of $\alpha \approx 0.5 + \dfrac{0.1997}{0.4610} \times 0.1 \approx 0.54$ (2 d.p.)

(c) $f(0.535) < 0$, $f(0.545) > 0$ $\therefore$ 0.54 correct for α to 2 d.p.

5 (b) $m = 0.525$

(c) $f(0.55) \approx -0.001323$, $f'(x) = \dfrac{1}{1+x^2} - \dfrac{11}{12}$, $f'(0.55) = -0.1489$

apply Newton–Raphson procedure to obtain $\beta = 0.541$ (3 d.p.)

6 (a) $\gamma = -3$

(b) -2.669 (correct to 3 d.p.). Use sufficient iterations to obtain this degree of accuracy.

1 (a) $2.4\,\text{s}$, (b) 0.3

2 $31\,890\,\text{cm}^3$

3 (a) $0.5\,\text{m}$ for each

(b) 0.014, 0.25

4 (b) $f(0.5) \approx -0.1997$,

$f(0.6) \approx 0.2613$, $\alpha = 0.54$

5 (b) $m = 0.525$, (c) 0.541

6 (b) -2.669

9 *Mathematics of uncertainty*

1 You will ease your working if you code about $1\,720$.

2 (a) For at least 2 voting we have 3 arrangements of V, V, NV together with V, V, V, i.e. $3\left(\frac{3}{4} \times \frac{3}{4} \times \frac{1}{4}\right) + \left(\frac{3}{4} \times \frac{3}{4} \times \frac{3}{4}\right) \Rightarrow \frac{54}{64}$.

(b) For only one at most voting we have 3 arrangements of V, NV, NV together with NV, NV, NV.

3 (a) Do not forget to use the same graph paper for each school and to join the points by smooth curves. Remember also that the cumulative frequencies are plotted against corresponding upper class boundaries.

$$\text{IQR} = Q_3 - Q_1 \text{ where } 75\% \text{ of the observations} \leqslant Q_3$$
$$\text{and } 25\% \text{ of the observations} \leqslant Q_1.$$

4 (a) $S = 10$ obtained by arrangements of $1, 2, 7 \quad 2, 3, 5 \quad 1, 3, 6$ and $1, 4, 5$.

Each can be arranged in 6 ways $\Rightarrow \dfrac{24}{9 \times 8 \times 7}$.

(b) For $S = 10$ and $n = 2$ we need $2, 1, 7 \quad 2, 7, 1 \quad 2, 3, 5$ or

$2, 5, 3 \Rightarrow \dfrac{4}{9 \times 8 \times 7}$.

(c) $P(S = 10 | n = 2) = \dfrac{P(S = 10 \cap n = 2)}{P(2)} = \dfrac{\frac{1}{126}}{\frac{1}{9}} = \dfrac{9}{126}$

5 Note that the two sets of data have the same mean.

6 (a) A and B mutually exclusive $\Rightarrow P(A) + P(B) = P(A \cup B)$,
i.e. $P(A \cap B) = 0$.
Draw a Venn diagram and see $P(A' \cap B') = 1 - P(A \cup B)$.

(b) C and D are independent $\Rightarrow P(C) \times P(D) = P(C \cap D)$. Again draw a Venn diagram to assist you in your reasoning. Use $P(C') = 1 - P(C)$,

$P(C|D) = \dfrac{P(C \cap D)}{P(D)}$, etc.

(c) Use a Venn diagram and mark on it the relevant probabilities starting with $P(E \cap F)$ derived from $P(E|F) = \frac{1}{10}$. From this you can fit in all of the other probabilities.

7 Calculate the class widths $\Rightarrow 2, 3, 4, 5, 6$. Divide these into the corresponding frequencies in order to get the corresponding height of each rectangle:

$5, \quad 27\frac{2}{3}, \quad 20, \quad 9\frac{3}{5}, \quad 4\frac{5}{6}$.

ANSWERS

1 (a) 1721 mm, (b) 26.1 mm

2 (a) $\frac{27}{32}$, (b) $\frac{5}{32}$

3 (a) School A, IQR $= 35$
School B, IQR $= 63$

4 (a) $\frac{1}{21}$, (b) $\frac{1}{126}$, (c) $\frac{1}{14}$

5 0.60

6 (a) (i) $\frac{1}{6}$, (ii) $\frac{1}{2}$

(b) (i) $\frac{1}{8}$, (ii) $\frac{1}{20}$, (iii) $\frac{2}{5}$, (iv) $\frac{1}{8}$

(c) (i) $\frac{1}{50}$, (ii) $\frac{19}{25}$

10 Vectors

HINTS AND OUTLINE SOLUTIONS

1 (a) Draw a diagram

$$\overrightarrow{AB} = \begin{pmatrix} 4 \\ 6 \end{pmatrix} - \begin{pmatrix} 1 \\ 2 \end{pmatrix} = \begin{pmatrix} 3 \\ 4 \end{pmatrix}$$

$$\overrightarrow{AC} = \begin{pmatrix} 5 \\ -1 \end{pmatrix} - \begin{pmatrix} 1 \\ 2 \end{pmatrix} = \begin{pmatrix} 4 \\ -3 \end{pmatrix}$$

$$\overrightarrow{AB} \times \overrightarrow{AC} = \begin{pmatrix} 3 \\ 4 \end{pmatrix} \times \begin{pmatrix} 4 \\ -3 \end{pmatrix} = 12 - 12 = 0$$

$\therefore \quad \angle BAC = 90°$

Also $|\overrightarrow{AB}| = \sqrt{(3^2 + 4^2)} = 5$ and $|\overrightarrow{AC}| = \sqrt{(4^2 + (-3)^2)} = 5$

$\therefore \quad \triangle ABC$ is isosceles and has a right angle at A.

2 $\overrightarrow{XY} = \begin{pmatrix} 1 \\ 3 \\ 3 \end{pmatrix} - \begin{pmatrix} 2 \\ 1 \\ -1 \end{pmatrix} = \begin{pmatrix} -1 \\ 2 \\ 4 \end{pmatrix}, \quad \overrightarrow{XZ} = \begin{pmatrix} -1 \\ 1 \\ 5 \end{pmatrix} - \begin{pmatrix} 2 \\ 1 \\ -1 \end{pmatrix} = \begin{pmatrix} -3 \\ 0 \\ 6 \end{pmatrix}$

(a) $\cos \angle YXZ = \dfrac{\overrightarrow{XY} \times \overrightarrow{XZ}}{|\overrightarrow{XY}|\,|\overrightarrow{XZ}|} = \dfrac{3 + 0 + 24}{\sqrt{21}\,\sqrt{45}}$

$\angle YXZ = 28.6°$

(b) Area of $\triangle XYZ = \frac{1}{2}|\overrightarrow{XY}|\,|\overrightarrow{XZ}| \sin \angle YXZ = 7.35$ units^2.

3 (a) Direction of $\overrightarrow{AB} = \begin{pmatrix} 4 \\ 2 \\ -3 \end{pmatrix} - \begin{pmatrix} 3 \\ 4 \\ -5 \end{pmatrix} = \begin{pmatrix} 1 \\ -2 \\ 2 \end{pmatrix}$

Line AB has equation $\mathbf{r} = \begin{pmatrix} 3 \\ 4 \\ -5 \end{pmatrix} + t\begin{pmatrix} 1 \\ -2 \\ 2 \end{pmatrix}$ where t is a scalar parameter.

(b) Direction of $\overrightarrow{OC}$ is $\begin{pmatrix} 14 \\ 2 \\ -5 \end{pmatrix}$ and we note that

$\begin{pmatrix} 14 \\ 2 \\ -5 \end{pmatrix} \times \begin{pmatrix} 1 \\ -2 \\ 2 \end{pmatrix} = 14 - 4 - 10 = 0 \quad \Rightarrow \quad OC$ is at right angles to AB.

Take $t = \frac{5}{3}$, then $\mathbf{r} = \begin{pmatrix} 3 + \frac{5}{3} \\ 4 - \frac{10}{3} \\ -5 + \frac{10}{3} \end{pmatrix} = \frac{1}{3}\begin{pmatrix} 14 \\ 2 \\ -5 \end{pmatrix}$ which is C, and on AB.

4 (a) $\overrightarrow{PO} = \begin{pmatrix} -2 \\ -3 \\ -6 \end{pmatrix}, \quad \overrightarrow{PQ} = \begin{pmatrix} 0 \\ 1 \\ -2 \end{pmatrix}$

$\cos \angle OPQ = \dfrac{\overrightarrow{PO} \times \overrightarrow{PQ}}{|\overrightarrow{PO}|\,|\overrightarrow{PQ}|} = \dfrac{-3 + 12}{7\sqrt{5}} = \dfrac{9}{7\sqrt{5}}$

$\angle OPQ = 54.9°$

(b) $\overrightarrow{OR} \times \overrightarrow{PQ} = \begin{pmatrix} 5 \\ 12 \\ 6 \end{pmatrix} \begin{pmatrix} 0 \\ 1 \\ -2 \end{pmatrix} = 12 - 12 = 0$

$\therefore$ OR and PQ are at right angles.

(c) Equation of PQ is $\mathbf{r} = \begin{pmatrix} 2 \\ 3 \\ 6 \end{pmatrix} + \lambda \begin{pmatrix} 0 \\ 1 \\ -2 \end{pmatrix}$, equation of OS is $\mathbf{r} = \mu \begin{pmatrix} 5 \\ 12 \\ 6 \end{pmatrix}$

Equate x coefficients $\qquad 2 = 5\mu$ $\left.\right\}$ $\mu = \frac{2}{5}, \quad \lambda = \frac{9}{5}$
Equate y coefficients $\qquad 3 + \lambda = 12\mu$

Checking on Z coefficients $\qquad 6 - 2\lambda = \frac{12}{5}$ for PQ $\left.\right\}$
$\qquad\qquad\qquad\qquad\qquad 6\mu = \frac{12}{5}$ for OR $\left.\right\}$ $\therefore$ lines meet

Meeting point of lines $\overrightarrow{OS} = 2\mathbf{i} + \frac{24}{5}\mathbf{j} + \frac{12}{5}\mathbf{k}$

ANSWERS

1 (b) $8\mathbf{i} + 3\mathbf{j}$, (c) $35°$

2 (a) $28.6°$

(b) 7.35 units^2

3 (a), (b) see detailed working above.

4 (a) $54.9°$

(b), (c) see detailed working above.

11 Mechanics

HINTS AND OUTLINE SOLUTIONS

1 Apply Newton's second law to each stage

$45g - R_1 = 45 \times 3.5 \quad \Rightarrow \quad R_1 = 292.5$
$45g - R_2 = 45 \times 0 \quad \Rightarrow \quad R_2 = 450$
$45g - R_3 = 45(-5) \quad \Rightarrow \quad R_3 = 675$

The force exerted is $292.5\,\text{N}$, $450\,\text{N}$ and $675\,\text{N}$.

2 (a) Using $s = ut + \frac{1}{2}at^2$ with $s = 100, u = 0, a = 10$ then
$100 = 5t^2 \quad \Rightarrow \quad t = \sqrt{20}$. $\therefore$ Time to reach ground $4.5\,\text{s}$

(b) Using $v^2 = u^2 + 2as$ with $s = 100, u = 0, a = 10$, then
$v^2 = 2 \times 10 \times 100 \quad \Rightarrow \quad v = 44.7$
Time taken is $4.5\,\text{s}$ and speed of impact is about $45\,\text{m s}^{-1}$

(c) No air resistance.

3 Horizontally $(v\cos\alpha)0.4 = 12 \quad \Rightarrow \quad v\cos\alpha = 30$.
Vertically $(v\sin\alpha)0.4 - 5(0.4)^2 = 12 \quad \Rightarrow \quad v\sin\alpha = 32$.

(a) Hence $v = \sqrt{(30^2 + 32^2)} = 44$ (2 s.f.).

(b) $\alpha = \arctan\frac{32}{30} = 47°$ (2 s.f.).

(c) Greatest height $= \dfrac{v^2\sin^2\alpha}{2g} = 51.2\,\text{m}$.

4 Greatest speed $= aw = 0.6$ and greatest acceleration $= aw^2 = 2.4$
Solving simultaneously, $a = 0.15, w = 4$, $\therefore$ (a) amplitude $= 0.15\,\text{m}$

(b) period $= \dfrac{2\pi}{w} = \dfrac{\pi}{2} \quad \Rightarrow \quad$ Period is $1.57\,\text{s}$.

5 (a) Driving force = Resistance $\Rightarrow$ Power $= 870 \times 25$ W $= 21.75$ kW

(b) Driving force $= \dfrac{24\,000}{6}$ N $= 4\,000$ N

Driving force = Resistance + Gravitational component + Acceleration force

$$4\,000 = 870 + 640\,g \times \frac{1}{25} + 640\,a$$

Taking $g = 10 \Rightarrow a = 4.5$ (2 s.f.)

The acceleration is 4.5 m s^{-2}.

6 (a) Using the cosine rule

$$R^2 = 7^2 + 12^2 - 2 \times 7 \times 12 \cos 130°$$
$$\Rightarrow R = 17.3 \text{ (3 s.f.)}$$

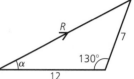

(b) Using the sine rule $\dfrac{\sin \alpha}{7} = \dfrac{\sin 130°}{R} \Rightarrow \alpha = 18°$ (nearest degree)

7 Using Newton's second law on each particle in turn

$P: \quad 3 - T = 0.3a$

$Q: \quad T - 2 = 0.2a$

Adding $\quad 0.5a = 1 \Rightarrow a = 2$ and $T = 2.4$

(a) Acceleration of P is 2 ms^{-2}.

(b) Tension in the string is 2.4 N.

(c) Force exerted on pulley $= 2T$ newtons $= 4.8$ N.

8 (a) X and Y collision $\quad mu = mv_1 + mv_2$ (Momentum)

$$eu = v_2 - v_1 \quad \text{(Newton)}$$

Hence, by solving $v_1 = \dfrac{u}{2}(1 - e), \quad v_2 = \dfrac{u}{2}(1 + e)$

(b) (i) Y and Z collision $\quad \dfrac{mu}{2}(1 + e) = mv_3 + mv_4$ (Momentum)

$$\frac{eu}{2}(1 + e) = v_4 - v_3 \quad \text{(Newton)}$$

Solving $\quad v_3 = \dfrac{u}{4}(1 - e)^2, \quad v_4 = \dfrac{u}{4}(1 + e)^2$

$$\frac{u}{4}(1 + e)^2 = \frac{9u}{16} \Rightarrow e = \frac{1}{2}.$$

(ii) Speeds of X, Y, Z after two collisions are $\dfrac{u}{4}, \dfrac{3u}{16}, \dfrac{9u}{16}$

Loss in $KE = \dfrac{1}{2}mu^2 - \dfrac{1}{2}m\dfrac{u^2}{16} - \dfrac{1}{2}m\dfrac{9u^2}{256} - \dfrac{1}{2}m\dfrac{81u^2}{256}$

$$= \frac{75}{256}mu^2$$

9 In equilibrium the tension is mg and by Hooke's law then, $mg = \dfrac{\lambda\left(\frac{l}{4}\right)}{l}$, hence, $\longrightarrow$

λ, the modulus of elasticity, is $4\,mg$.

When the particle comes to instantaneous rest after falling a distance x, gravitational PE lost = elastic energy gained by string

$$\Rightarrow mgx = \frac{1}{2}\lambda\frac{(x - l)^2}{l}$$

Since $\lambda = 4\,mg \Rightarrow 2(x - l)^2 = lx$

$$2x^2 - 5xl + 2l^2 = 0$$
$$(x - 2l)(2x - l) = 0$$

$\therefore$ The particle falls a distance $2l$ since clearly $x \neq \frac{1}{2}l$ which is less than the natural length of the string.

10 From the diagram we have

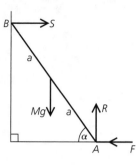

Vertical forces $\qquad\qquad\qquad\qquad\qquad R = Mg$

Horizontal forces $\qquad\qquad\qquad\qquad S = F$

Turning moments around $A \qquad S(2a\sin\alpha) = Mg\,a\cos\alpha$

$\therefore \quad S = F = \frac{1}{2}Mg\cot\alpha$

For equilibrium $\dfrac{F}{R} \leqslant \mu \quad \Rightarrow \quad \mu \geqslant \dfrac{1}{2}\cot\alpha$

$\qquad\qquad\qquad\qquad\qquad \Rightarrow \quad 2\mu \geqslant \cot\alpha$

11 (a) Impulse = Change in momentum $= 0.3[\mathbf{i} - 3\mathbf{j} - (13\mathbf{i} + 6\mathbf{j})]$

$\qquad\qquad\qquad\qquad\qquad\qquad\qquad = -0.3(12\mathbf{i} + 9\mathbf{j})$

Magnitude of impulse $= 0.3\sqrt{(12^2 + 9^2)}\,\text{Ns} = 4.5\,\text{Ns}.$

(b) Change in KE $= \left|\frac{1}{2} \times 0.3[1^2 + 3^2 - 13^2 - 6^2]\right|\text{J} = 29.25\,\text{J}$

12 (a) Moments about $A \quad \Rightarrow \quad 2T\cos 60° = 140\sin 60° \quad \Rightarrow \quad T = 121$ (3 s.f.).

(b) At A by resolving horizontally and vertically we have

$\qquad X_A = T, \quad Y_A = 140$

Magnitude of force at $A = 185\,\text{N}$ at $49°$ to horizontal.

13 (a) $\dfrac{\mathrm{d}x}{\mathrm{d}t} = e^{-\frac{x}{2}}$ and integrating $\quad \Rightarrow \quad \displaystyle\int e^{\frac{x}{2}}\,\mathrm{d}x = \int \mathrm{d}t$

$\qquad \left[2e^{\frac{x}{2}}\right]_0^x = [t]_0^t \quad$ since $x = 0 \quad$ at $\quad t = 0$

$\qquad \therefore \quad 2e^{\frac{x}{2}} - 2 = t \quad \Rightarrow \quad x = 2\ln\left(\dfrac{t + 2}{2}\right)$

(b) Remember $v\dfrac{\mathrm{d}v}{\mathrm{d}x}$ is acceleration, hence

$\qquad$ Acceleration $= e^{-\frac{x}{2}}\dfrac{\mathrm{d}}{\mathrm{d}x}\left(e^{-\frac{x}{2}}\right) = -\dfrac{1}{2}e^{-x}$

$\qquad$ At distance $x = 3$, acceleration $= -\frac{1}{2}e^{-3} = -0.025\,\text{ms}^{-2}.$

14 (a) $e = \dfrac{\frac{4u}{5}}{u} = \dfrac{4}{5}.$

(b) Using $v^2 = u^2 + 2as$ before the first bounce gives us

$\qquad\qquad u^2 = 2gs$ and after the first bounce

$\qquad \dfrac{16u^2}{25} = 2gh$ in rising to height h metres.

$\qquad \therefore \quad s = \dfrac{25}{16}h$

(c) Air resistance has been neglected. The marble has been taken as a particle.

15 Using conservation of energy we have

$$\frac{1}{2}m\left(\frac{7ga}{2}\right) = \frac{1}{2}mv^2 + mga\,(1 + \cos\theta) \qquad\qquad [1]$$

Also at instant when particle leaves surface $R = 0$, so using Newton's second law

$$mg\cos\theta = m\frac{v^2}{a} \quad \Rightarrow \quad v^2 = ga\cos\theta \qquad\qquad [2]$$

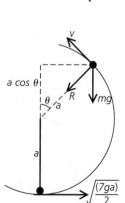

Combining [1] and [2]

$$\frac{7ga}{2} = ga\cos\theta + 2ga\,(1 + \cos\theta) \quad \Rightarrow \quad \cos\theta = \tfrac{1}{2}$$

Particle is at height $\dfrac{3a}{2}$ above projection point when it leaves the surface of the sphere.

1 292.5 N,   450 N,   675 N

2 (a) 4.5 s   (b) 45 ms^{-1}
   (c) Assumption: no air resistance

3 (a) $v = 44$ (b) $\alpha = 47°$,
   (c) 51.2 m

4 (a) 0.15 m,   (b) 1.57 s

5 (a) 21.75 kW,   (b) 4.5 ms^{-2}

6 (a) 17.3,   (b) 18°

7 (a) 2 ms^{-2},   (b) 2.4 N,   (c) 4.8 N

8 (b) (i) $\frac{1}{2}$,   (ii) $\frac{75}{256} mu^2$

9 2l

10 See detailed working above.

11 (a) 4.5 Ns,   (b) 29.25 J

12 (a) 121,   (b) 185 N at 49° to horizontal

13 (a) $x = 2\ln\left(\dfrac{t+2}{2}\right)$
   (b) $= -0.025$ ms^{-2}

14 (a) $\frac{4}{5}$ (b) $\frac{25}{16} h$
   (c) Air resistance neglected; marble
       taken as a particle.

15 See detailed working above.

12 Random variables and probability distributions

HINTS AND OUTLINE SOLUTIONS

1 (a) $p = 1 - (0.15 + 0.20 + p + 0.35 + 0.10) \quad \Rightarrow \quad p = 0.2$
   Remember, the sum of all the probabilities is 1.

   (b) Expected value $= \Sigma x_r P(x_r)$.
   $$\mu = E(X) = 1(0.15) + 2(0.20) + 3p + 4(0.35) + 5(0.10)$$
   $$= 3.05$$

   $\mu = 3.05 \quad \Rightarrow \quad$ need 0.35 and 0.10

   (c) $P(X > \mu) = 0.35 + 0.10 = 0.45$

2 (a) $P(B|A) = \dfrac{P(A \cap B)}{P(A)} \quad \Rightarrow \quad \dfrac{1}{10} = \dfrac{P(A \cap B)}{\frac{1}{5}}$

   $$\Rightarrow P(A \cap B) = \frac{1}{10} \times \frac{1}{5} = \frac{1}{50} = 0.02$$

   (b) $P(A \cup B) = P(A) + P(B) - P(A \cap B)$

   $$= \frac{1}{5} + \frac{3}{5} - \frac{1}{50} = \frac{39}{50} = 0.78$$

   P (Just one event A or B) $= 0.78 - \dfrac{1}{50} = 0.76$

   You may find a Venn diagram helpful.

3 (a) Since X and Y are mutually exclusive, $P(X \cap Y) = 0$, so
   $$P(X) + P(Y) = P(X \cup Y) \Rightarrow P(Y) = 0.7 - 0.2 = 0.5$$

   (b) A and B are independent, so $P(A) \times P(B) = P(A \cap B)$
   $$\Rightarrow P(A \cap B) = 0.25\, P(B)$$
   But $P(A \cup B) = P(A) + P(B) - P(A \cap B)$
   $$\Rightarrow 0.6 = 0.25 + P(B) - 0.25 P(B)$$
   $$\Rightarrow 0.75\, P(B) = 0.35 \quad \Rightarrow \quad P(B) = \tfrac{7}{15}$$

4 (a) Cumulative frequencies 4 856, 7 137, 8 562, 9 245. Remember, when plotting a cumulative frequency curve cumulative frequencies are plotted against corresponding upper class boundaries.

$$\text{Median corresponds to } 4\,623 \quad \Rightarrow \quad 21\,\text{yr}\ 9\ \text{months}$$
$$\text{Upper quartile corresponds to } 6\,934 \quad \Rightarrow \quad 25\,\text{yr}\ 7\ \text{months}$$
$$\text{Lower quartile corresponds to } 2\,311 \quad \Rightarrow \quad 18\,\text{yr}\ 3\ \text{months}$$
$$\Rightarrow \quad \text{IQR} = 7\,\text{yr}\ \ 4\ \text{months}$$

(b) Now having babies at an earlier age.

(c) Do not have to guess distribution for 32 years and over class which would be required for the mean and standard deviation.

5

x	$y = \frac{x - 22\,500}{3\,000}$	f	fy	fy^2
15 500	-4	3	-12	48
18 500	-3	7	-21	63
21 500	-2	21	-42	84
24 500	-1	98	-98	98
27 500	0	123	0	0
30 500	1	62	62	62
33 500	2	36	72	144
		350	-39	499

Notice how the coding reduces the work involved; but remember, $\bar{x} = M + c\bar{y}$

$\text{Var}(x) = c^2\,\text{Var}(y) \quad \Rightarrow \quad S_x = c\,S_y$ where, in this case, $c = 3\,000$.

(a) $\text{Mean} = 27\,500 - \frac{39}{350} \times 3\,000 = 27\,166 \approx 27\,000$

$$S_y^2 = \frac{1}{350}\left\{ 499 - \frac{(39)^2}{350} \right\} = 1.413 \quad \Rightarrow \quad S_y = 1.189$$

$$S_x = 3\,000 \times 1.189 = 3\,567 \approx 3\,570$$

(b) $\text{Mean} = 27\,000 + 1\,000 = 28\,000, \quad S_x \Rightarrow \text{None}.$

6 (a) $N(2.0,\ 0.01^2)$

$P(1.996 < x < 2.015)$

$P(-0.004 < z < 0.015) = \Phi(1.5) - \Phi(-0.4)$

$= 0.9332 - (1 - 0.6554) = 0.9332 - 0.3446$

$= 0.5886 \approx 0.589 \quad (3\ \text{s.f.})$

Alternatively, you may find it helpful to show the area required on a normal distribution curve

$\Rightarrow P(1.996 < x < 2.015)$

$= P\left(\dfrac{1.996 < 2.0}{0.01} < z < \dfrac{2.015 - 2.0}{0.01} \right)$

$= \Phi(1.5) - \Phi(-0.4)$, etc.

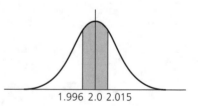

1.996 2.0 2.015

(b) Given rivet $>2.0\,$cm, then probability that the rivet is satisfactory is

$$\frac{0.9332 - 0.5}{0.5} = \frac{0.4332}{0.5} \approx 0.866$$

7 (a) Remember, both regression lines pass through $(\bar{x}, \bar{y})$.

$$\left. \begin{array}{l} \bar{y} = 1.5\,\bar{x} + 0.3 \\ \bar{x} = 0.6\,\bar{y} - 0.1 \end{array} \right\} \quad \Rightarrow \quad \bar{y} = 1.5(0.6\,\bar{y} - 0.1) + 0.3$$

$$\bar{y} = 0.9\,\bar{y} - 0.15 + 0.3 \quad \Rightarrow \quad \bar{y} = 1.5, \quad \bar{x} = 0.8$$

(b) Remember, $r = \dfrac{S_{xy}}{S_x S_y}$ and the gradients of the regression lines are such that

$$1.5 = \frac{S_{xy}}{S_x^2}, \quad 0.6 = \frac{S_{xy}}{S_y^2}$$

$$\Rightarrow \quad \frac{(S_{xy})^2}{S_x^2 S_y^2} = 1.5 \times 0.6$$

$$\Rightarrow \quad r^2 = 0.9 \quad \Rightarrow \quad r \approx 0.95$$

8 (a) $\lambda = 0.8 \quad \Rightarrow \quad P(0) + P(1) = e^{-0.8} + \frac{0.8}{1} e^{-0.8}$

$\Rightarrow \quad P(0) + P(1) = 0.4493 + 0.3594 = 0.8087$

$\Rightarrow \quad P(\text{At least two accidents per week}) = 1 - 0.8087$

$$\approx 0.191$$

Do show *all* of your working.

(b) For 4-week period the mean will be 4 times that of a 1-week period
$\Rightarrow \quad \lambda = 4 \times 0.8 = 3.2$.

$$P(3) = \frac{(3.2)^3}{3!} e^{-3.2} \approx 0.223$$

9 (a) $\begin{array}{rrrrrrrrrrr} d = & 1, & 2, & 0, & -3, & 2, & -1, & -1, & 2, & -1, & -1 \\ d^2 = & 1, & 4, & 0, & 9, & 4, & 1, & 1, & 4, & 1, & 1 \end{array}$

$$\Sigma d^2 = 26 \quad \Rightarrow \quad r_S = 1 - \frac{6 \Sigma d^2}{n(n^2 - 1)} = 1 - 0.1576$$

$$\Rightarrow \quad r_S \approx 0.842.$$

Null hypothesis $r_s = 0$.

(b) Using table, $n = 10$, $P(\Sigma d^2 \geqslant 30) = 0.0029$, i.e. 0.003. Very small indeed
$\Rightarrow$ reject $H_0 \quad \Rightarrow$ strong correlation between the managers.
(Do not forget to state both your null hypothesis and conclusion.)

10 (a) $\displaystyle\int_0^1 3x^\alpha \, dx = \left[\frac{3x^{\alpha+1}}{\alpha+1}\right]_0^1 = \frac{3}{\alpha+1} \quad \Rightarrow \quad \frac{3}{\alpha+1} = 1 \quad \Rightarrow \quad \alpha = 2.$

(Remember, the total area under the curve is 1.)

(b) $E(X) = \displaystyle\int_0^1 x \times 3x^2 dx = \left[\frac{3}{4}x^4\right]_0^1 = \frac{3}{4}.$

(c) $\sigma^2 = \displaystyle\int_0^1 x^2 \times 3x^2 dx - \left(\frac{3}{4}\right)^2 = \left[\frac{3x^5}{5}\right]_0^1 - \frac{9}{16} = \frac{3}{5} - \frac{9}{16} = \frac{3}{80}.$

(Do not forget the $-\left(\frac{3}{4}\right)^2$.)

(d) $\displaystyle\int_0^x 3x^2 dx = x^3 = 0.8$ when $x \approx 0.928.$

11 (a) Use the cumulative binomial probability tables for $n = 20$, $r = 7$.
(b) Use the cumulative binomial probability tables for $n = 20$ and $r = 7, 8$.

12 (a) Median is 21 reading, Q_1 the 10th reading, Q_3 the 32nd reading.
(b) Negative skew.

13 (a) $P(X < 75) = P(Z < -1) = P(Z) > 1 = 1 - 0.8413 = 0.1587.$

(b) $P(X \geqslant 90) = P(Z \geqslant 2) = 1 - P(Z) \leqslant 2 = 1 - 0.9772 = 0.0228.$

(c) $P(76 < X < 86) = P\left(\dfrac{76 - 80}{5} < Z < \dfrac{86 - 80}{5}\right) = P(-0.8 < Z < 1.2)$

$$= \Phi(1.2) - (1 - \Phi(0.8)) = 0.8849 - 0.2119 = 0.6730$$

14 (a) Do not forget to use a continuity correction.

$$X \sim N(30, 30) \quad \Rightarrow \quad P(X > 35.5) = P\left(Z > \frac{35.5 - 30}{\sqrt{30}}\right)$$

$$P(Z > 1.004) = 1 - P(Z < 1.004) = 1 - \Phi(1.004)$$
$$= 1 - 0.8423 = 0.1577.$$

Normal approximation can be used because the mean is sufficiently large.

15 (a) Number of degrees of freedom $= \nu = 2$.

(b) At 5% level critical value $= 5.991$.

(c) At $2\frac{1}{2}\%$ level critical value $= 7.378$.

16 Use a tree diagram.

(a) $0.5 \times 0.6 + 0.5 \times 0.45 = 0.525.$

(b) $0.5 \times 0.45 = 0.225.$

(c) $\dfrac{0.3}{0.3 + 0.5 \times 0.45} = 0.571.$

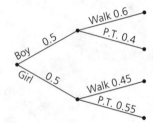

ANSWERS

1 (a) 0.2, (b) 3.05, (c) 0.45

2 (a) 0.02, (b) 0.76

3 (a) 0.5, (b) $\frac{7}{15}$

4 (a) Median 21 yr 9 months,
    IQR 7 yr 4 months

5 (a) Mean $= 27\,166$, $\sigma = 3\,567$
    (b) Mean $+ 1\,000$, σ None

6 (a) 0.589, (b) 0.866

7 (a) See detailed working above.
    (b) 0.95

8 (a) 0.191, (b) 0.223

9 (a) 0.842

10 (a) 2, (b) $\frac{3}{4}$, (c) $\frac{3}{80}$, (d) 0.928

11 (a) 0.416, (b) 0.180

12 (a) LQ 55, median 69, UQ 81.
    (b) Negative skew.

13 (a) 0.1587, (b) 0.0228,
    (c) 0.6730

14 (a) 0.158

15 (a) 2
    (b) (i) 5.991, (ii) 7.378

16 (a) 0.525, (b) 0.275, (c) 0.571

Timed practice papers with answers

Here you will find separate examination papers in Pure Mathematics, Mechanics and Statistics which will give you practice in timing yourself under examination type conditions. Answers and examiner comments are provided to these questions so that you can check your performance.

1 The volume $V\,\text{m}^3$ of water in a large tank when the depth of water is $x\,\text{m}$ is given by the formula

$$V = \tfrac{1}{3}\pi x^2(9 - x)$$

Water is pumped into the tank at a constant rate of $4\,\text{m}^3\,\text{s}^{-1}$. Calculate the rate at which x is changing when $x = 2$, giving your answer in ms^{-1} to 2 significant figures.

2

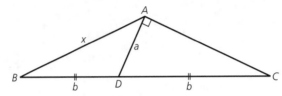

In the diagram, $\angle DAC = 90°$, $AB = x$, $BD = DC = b$ and $AD = a$.

(a) Show that $x^2 = 3a^2 + b^2$

(b) Given that $b = 3a$, calculate $\angle ABD$ giving your answer to the nearest $0.1°$.

3 In the binomial expansion of

$$(3 - 2x)(1 + ax)^9, \qquad a \neq 0$$

the coefficient of the x^4 term is zero.
Find (a) the value of a and (b) the coefficient of the x term in this expansion.

4 With O as origin, A is at $(-2, 2)$ and B is at $(3, 1)$. Find an equation for
(a) the line AB,
(b) the line perpendicular to AB passing through M, the midpoint of AB,
(c) the circle on AB as diameter.
(d) If A and B are opposite corners of a square, find the coordinates of the other two corners.

5 The finite region R is bounded by the curve $y = x^2 + 1$, the tangent to this curve at the point $P(2, 5)$ and positive x- and y-axes.
(a) Sketch the region R.
(b) Use integration to find the area of R.
(c) The finite region S is bounded by the curve $y = x^2 + 1$, the y-axis and the lines $y = 1$ and $y = 4$. The region S is rotated completely about the y-axis. Find the volume of the solid generated.

6 (a) Find those values of x in $(0, 360)$ to 1 decimal place for which

$$2\sec^2 x° - 4 = 3\tan x°$$

(b) Solve in radians for the internal $(-\pi, \pi)$ the equation

$$\sin y + \cos y + \sec y + \csc y = 0,$$

giving your answers to 2 decimal places.

7 $f(x) \equiv \dfrac{x(x-2)}{(x-4)(x-6)}$.

    (a) Find the set of values of x for which $f(x) > 0$.

    (b) By first expressing $f(x)$ in the form $A + \dfrac{B}{x-4} + \dfrac{C}{x-6}$ where A, B and C are constants, evaluate

$$\int_7^8 f(x)\,dx$$

    leaving your answer in terms of natural logarithms.

8 (a) The first, third and fifth terms of a geometric series are $t-4$, $2t-5$ and $4t+2$ respectively. Find the value of t and the sum of the first 20 terms of the series, given the common ratio is positive.

    (b) Find the sum of all those integers between 0 and 200 inclusive which are *NOT* divisible by 4.

9 (a) Calculate the values of x for which

$$\dfrac{d}{dx}\left(x^2 e^x\right) = 0.$$

    (b) Assuming that $x^2 e^x \to 0$ as $x \to -\infty$, sketch the curve with equation $y = x^2 e^x$. On your sketch show the turning points and their coordinates clearly.

    (c) Find $\displaystyle\int x^2 e^x\,dx$.

    (d) On your sketch shade in a region whose area is $\displaystyle\int_{-1}^{1} x^2 e^x\,dx$.

10 $f(x) \equiv 2\tan x - 3x$,   where x is measured in radians.

    (a) Show that the equation $f(x) = 0$ has a root α in the interval $\left[\frac{\pi}{4}, \frac{\pi}{3}\right]$.

    (b) Use linear interpolation on the interval $\left[\frac{\pi}{4}, \frac{\pi}{3}\right]$ and show that $\alpha \approx 0.92$ (2 decimal places) by this method.

    (c) Taking 0.92 as an approximation to α use the Newton–Raphson method once to find another approximation to α, giving your answer to 2 decimal places.

OUTLINE ANSWERS TO PURE MATHEMATICS PAPER

Examiner Comments

1 Given $V = \frac{1}{3}\pi x^2(9-x)$, $\dfrac{dV}{dt} = 4$

Required $\dfrac{dx}{dt}$ when $x = 2$.

$\dfrac{dV}{dt} = \dfrac{dV}{dx} \times \dfrac{dx}{dt} = 4 \quad \Rightarrow \quad \dfrac{dx}{dt} = \dfrac{4}{\dfrac{dV}{dx}}$

$V = \dfrac{1}{3}\pi\left(9x^2 - x^3\right) \quad \Rightarrow \quad \dfrac{dV}{dx} = \dfrac{1}{3}\pi\left(18x - 3x^2\right)$

$\Rightarrow \quad \dfrac{dx}{dt} = \dfrac{4}{\dfrac{1}{3}\pi\left(18x - 3x^2\right)}$

$x = 2 \quad \Rightarrow \quad \dfrac{dx}{dt} = \dfrac{4 \times 3}{\pi(36-12)} = \dfrac{1}{2\pi}$

$\dfrac{dx}{dt} = 0.16\,\text{cm s}^{-1}$

First write down the information given in the question. Then write down the requirement

Now connect $\dfrac{dV}{dt}$ with $\dfrac{dx}{dt}$, i.e. chain rule

To find $\dfrac{dV}{dx}$, first multiply out

Do not forget to look at the question to see how the answer must be given, i.e. to 2 s.f.

2

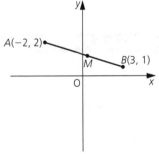

Draw the diagram and mark on it the given information. We need $\cos ADB$ and this can be obtained from $\triangle ADC$ right-angled at A.

(a) From $\triangle ABD \qquad x^2 = a^2 + b^2 - 2ab \cos ADB$

But $\cos ADB = -\cos ADC = -\dfrac{a}{b}$

$\Rightarrow \quad x^2 = a^2 + b^2 - 2ab\left(-\dfrac{a}{b}\right) = 3a^2 + b^2$

(b) From $\triangle ABD \quad a^2 = b^2 + x^2 - 2bx \cos ABD$

$\Rightarrow \quad a^2 = (3a)^2 + 12a^2$

$\qquad\qquad\qquad -2.3a \times 2\sqrt{3}a \cos ABD$

$\Rightarrow \quad \cos ABD = \dfrac{20a^2}{12\sqrt{3}a^2} = \dfrac{5}{3\sqrt{3}}$

$\Rightarrow \qquad ABD = 15.8°$

Remember,

$x^2 = 3a^2 + b^2 = 12a^2$

since $b = 3a$

Again, remember to give your answer to 1 d.p.

3 (a) $(3 - 2x)(1 + ax)^9 = (3 - 2x)\left\{1 + \dfrac{9}{1}(ax)\right.$

$+\dfrac{9 \times 8}{1 \times 2}(ax)^2 + \dfrac{9 \times 8 \times 7}{1 \times 2 \times 3}(ax)^3$

$+\dfrac{9 \times 8 \times 7 \times 6}{1 \times 2 \times 3 \times 4}(ax)^4\Big\}$

$= (3 - 2x)\{1 + 9ax + 36a^2x^2 + 84a^3x^3$

$\qquad +126a^4x^4 \ldots\}$

x^4 term $\quad 3 \times 126a^4 - 2 \times 84a^3 = 0$ when

$a = \dfrac{168}{378} = \dfrac{4}{9}$

Write out the expansion and do not forget to use brackets

If you are extra clever you will realise you only need the x^3 and x^4 terms, thus saving some work and time. Now pick out the x^4 term.

(b) x term $= 3(9ax) - 2x(1) = 10x \quad \Rightarrow \quad 10$

4

It is always helpful to draw a diagram

(a) Equation

$AB \quad \Rightarrow \quad \dfrac{y - 1}{2 - 1} = \dfrac{x - 3}{-2 - 3} \quad \Rightarrow \quad 5y + x = 8$

(b) $M \equiv \left(\dfrac{-2 + 3}{2}, \dfrac{2 + 1}{2}\right) \equiv \left(\dfrac{1}{2}, \dfrac{3}{2}\right)$

(Remember to add and not subtract.)

Gradient $AB = -\dfrac{1}{5} \quad \Rightarrow \quad$ gradient m where

$m\left(-\dfrac{1}{5}\right) = -1 \quad \Rightarrow \quad m = 5$

Equation required line is

$\left(y - \dfrac{3}{2}\right) = 5\left(x - \dfrac{1}{2}\right)$ or $y = 5x - 1$

(c) Circle on AB has diameter

$\Rightarrow \quad (y-1)(y-2) + (x-3)(x+2) = 0$

or $\quad x^2 + y^2 - x - 3y - 4 = 0$

Using $(y - y_1)(y - y_2)$
$-(x - x_1)(x - x_2) = 0$

(d) Meets $y = 5x - 1$ where

$x^2 + (5x - 1)^2 - x - 3(5x - 1) - 4 = 0$

$\Rightarrow \quad 26x^2 - 26x = 0$

$x = 0$ or $1 \quad \Rightarrow \quad$ coordinates $(0, -1), (1, 4)$

5 (a)

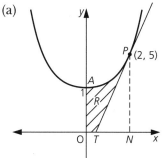

Mark clearly on your sketch
the region R. Then the
equation of the tangent at P is
required

(b) $y = x^2 + 1 \quad \Rightarrow \quad \dfrac{dy}{dx} = 2x$

$\Rightarrow \quad$ Tangent at $(2, 5)$ is $y - 5 = 4(x - 2)$ or
$y = 4x - 3$.

Meets x-axis at $x = \dfrac{3}{4} \Rightarrow TN = \dfrac{5}{4}$

Area $R =$ Area $APNO - \triangle PNT$.

Area $APNO = \displaystyle\int_0^2 (x^2 + 1)dx = \left[\dfrac{1}{3}x^3 + x\right]_0^2$

Area $= \displaystyle\int y\, dx$,

$= \dfrac{8}{3} + 2 = \dfrac{14}{3}$

Area $\triangle = \dfrac{1}{2}$ base $\times$ height

Area $\triangle PNT = \dfrac{1}{2} \times \dfrac{5}{4} \times 5 = \dfrac{25}{8}$

$\Rightarrow \quad R = \dfrac{14}{3} - \dfrac{25}{8} = \dfrac{37}{24}$

(c) Vol. rev. of $S = \pi \displaystyle\int_1^4 x^2 dy = \pi \int_1^4 (y - 1)dy$

Vol. revolution about
y-axis $= \pi \displaystyle\int x^2\, dy$

$= \pi \left[\dfrac{1}{2}y^2 - y\right]_1^4$

$= \pi \left[(8 - 4) - \left(\dfrac{1}{2} - 1\right)\right] = \dfrac{9\pi}{2}$

Remember, unless specified,
answers can be left in terms
of π.

6 (a) $2\sec^2 x° - 4 = 2(1 + \tan^2 x°) - 4 = 3\tan x°$.

$2\tan^2 x° - 3\tan x° - 2 = 0$
$= (2\tan x° + 1)(\tan x° - 2)$

$\tan x° = -\dfrac{1}{2}$ or 2.

$\tan x° = -\dfrac{1}{2} \quad \Rightarrow \quad x = 63.4, \quad 243.4$

$\tan x° = 2 \quad \Rightarrow \quad x = 153.4, \quad 333.4$

Convert to equation in $\tan x$
using $\sec^2 = 1 + \tan^2$
Solve quadratic in $\tan x$
Use your calculator to find a
value for x and keep adding
180 to obtain values in the
range.

(b) $\sin y + \cos y + \dfrac{1}{\cos y} + \dfrac{1}{\sin y} = 0$

$\sin y + \cos y + \dfrac{(\sin y + \cos y)}{\cos y \sin y} = 0$

$\Rightarrow \quad (\sin y + \cos y)\left(1 + \dfrac{2}{\sin 2y}\right) = 0$

$\Rightarrow \quad \sin y + \cos y = 0 \quad \text{or} \quad 1 + \dfrac{2}{\sin 2y} = 0$

$\sin y + \cos y = 0 \quad \Rightarrow \quad \tan y = -1$

$\Rightarrow \quad y = -\dfrac{\pi}{4} \quad \text{or} \quad \dfrac{3\pi}{4}$

i.e. $y = -0.79 \quad \text{or} \quad 2.36$

or $\sin 2y = -2$
But $\sin 2y$ must lie between -1 and $+1$
$\therefore$ No real solution

7 (a) $\dfrac{x(x-2)}{(x-4)(x-6)} > 0$

$\Rightarrow \quad x < 0 \text{ or } 2 < x < 4 \text{ or } x > 6$

x	$-$	$-$	0	$+$	$+$	$+$			
$x-2$	$-$	$-$		2	$+$	$+$	$+$		
$x-4$	$-$	$-$	$-$	$-$	4	$+$	$+$		
$x-6$	$-$	$-$	$-$	$-$		6	$+$	$+$	
$\dfrac{x-2}{(x-4)(x-6)}$	$+$	$-$		$+$		$-$		$+$	

$\quad\quad\quad\quad 0 \quad\; 2 \quad\quad 4 \;\; 6$

(b) $\dfrac{x(x-2)}{(x-4)(x-6)} = \dfrac{(x^2-10x+24)+8x-24}{(x^2-10x+24)}$

$\quad\quad\quad\quad\quad = 1 + \dfrac{8x-24}{(x-4)(x-6)}$

$\dfrac{8x-24}{(x-4)(x-6)} = \dfrac{-4}{x-4} + \dfrac{12}{x-6}$

$\displaystyle\int\left(1 - \dfrac{4}{x-4} + \dfrac{12}{x-6}\right)dx$

$\quad\quad = x - 4\ln(x-4) + 12\ln(x-6)$

$\displaystyle\int_7^8 dx \Rightarrow 8 - 4\ln 4 + 12\ln 2$

$\quad\quad\quad\quad -[7 - 4\ln 3 + 12\ln 1]$

$\quad\quad\quad = 1 - \ln 4^4 + \ln 2^{12} + \ln 3^4 + 0$

$\quad\quad\quad = 1 + \ln\left(\dfrac{2^{12} \times 3^4}{4^4}\right)$

$\quad\quad\quad = 1 + \ln\left(2^4 \times 3^4\right) = 1 + 4\ln 6$

Convert all terms to $\sin y$ and $\cos y$. Tidy up and factorise.

Remember
$2\cos y \sin y = \sin 2y$.

Form a table showing the signs of x, $(x-2)$, $(x-4)$, $(x-6)$

Divide or use nested multiplication to divide.

Use cover-up rule or any alternative method.

It is best to integrate first and consider the limits at the end. As the question is worded, there are various forms for the final answer.

8 (a) $(2t-5)^2 = (t-4)(4t+2)$ $\Rightarrow$ $6t = 33$

                                             $\Rightarrow$ $t = \dfrac{11}{2}$

For a GP, $\dfrac{T_3}{T_1} = \dfrac{T_5}{T_3}$

$\Rightarrow$ $T_3^2 = T_1 T_5$.

First term $= t - 4 = \dfrac{3}{2}$,

$r^2 = \dfrac{T_3}{T_1} = \dfrac{11-5}{\frac{3}{2}} = 4$ $\Rightarrow$ $r = 2$

$\Rightarrow$ $S_{20} = \dfrac{a(r^n - 1)}{(r-1)} = \dfrac{\frac{3}{2}(2^{20} - 1)}{2 - 1}$

$= \frac{3}{2}(2^{20} - 1)$

(b) $4, 8, 12, \ldots, 200$ (50 terms)

$S_{20} = 50 \times \dfrac{4 + 200}{2} = 5\,100$

$1 + 2 + 3 + \ldots + 200 = 200 \times \dfrac{1 + 200}{2}$

$= 20\,100$

$\Rightarrow$ Sum of integers

not divisible by $4 = 20\,100 - 5\,100$

$= 15\,000$

It is easier to sum all the integers divisible by 4 and then subtract this from the total sum.

Remember $S_n = n\left(\dfrac{a+l}{2}\right)$

9 (a) $\dfrac{\mathrm{d}}{\mathrm{d}x}\left(x^2 \mathrm{e}^x\right) = x^2 \mathrm{e}^x + 2x\,\mathrm{e}^x = x(x+2)\mathrm{e}^x = 0$

$\Rightarrow$ $x = 0$ or -2

(b) $y = x^2 \mathrm{e}^x$ $\Rightarrow$ $x = 0$, $y = 0$;

$x = -2$, $y = 4\mathrm{e}^{-2}$

Use the product rule.
Don't forget the $x = 0$.

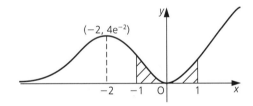

(c) $\displaystyle\int x^2 \mathrm{e}^2 \mathrm{d}x = x^2 \mathrm{e}^x - \int 2x\mathrm{e}^x \mathrm{d}x$

$= x^2 \mathrm{e}^x - \left[2x\mathrm{e}^x - \int 2 \times 1 \times \mathrm{e}^x \mathrm{d}x\right]$

$= \left[x^2 - 2x + 2\right]\mathrm{e}^x + c$

(d) See diagram above.

Make sure that you choose to integrate e^x and differentiate x^2

In this case do not forget the constant of integration. To do so may cost you a mark.

10 (a) $f(x) = 2\tan x - 3x$

$f\left(\dfrac{\pi}{4}\right) = 2 \times 1 - \dfrac{3\pi}{4} = -0.36$

$f\left(\dfrac{\pi}{3}\right) = 2\sqrt{3} - \pi = +0.32$

$\Bigg\}$ $\Rightarrow$ Root in $\left[\dfrac{\pi}{4}, \dfrac{\pi}{3}\right]$

(b)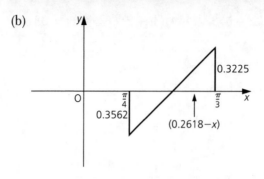

$$\frac{x}{0.3562} = \frac{0.2618 - x}{0.3225}$$

$$\Rightarrow \quad 0.6787x = 0.2618$$

$$x = 0.1374$$

$$\Rightarrow \quad \text{Root} = \frac{\pi}{4} + 0.1374 = 0.9227 \approx 0.92$$

(c) $f(x) = 2\tan x - 3x, \quad f'(x) = 2\sec^2 x - 3.$

$$f(0.92) = 2.6265 - 2.76 = -0.1335$$

$$f'(0.92) = 5.4493 - 3 = 2.4493$$

Newton–Raphson

$$\Rightarrow \quad 0.92 - \left(\frac{-0.1335}{2.4493}\right) = 0.97$$

In your linear interpolation do draw a diagram in order to make sure you get your ratios correctly with the similar triangles.

Question paper for
Mechanics

(Take $g = 10\,\text{ms}^{-2}$ if required)

Answer ALL the questions   **Time allowed:** $2\frac{1}{2}$ hours

1   A tube train covers 450 m from rest to rest in 1 minute. It accelerates at $\frac{1}{2}\,\text{ms}^{-2}$, then moves at uniform speed and finally retards at $1\,\text{ms}^{-2}$. Find the time taken in each stage of the journey and the distance covered at uniform speed.

2   A uniform plank PQ, of length 6 m and mass 50 kg, is supported in a horizontal position at P and R, where $PR = 4$ m. A girl, of mass 20 kg, stands on the plank at S, where $SQ = 4$ m. Find the magnitude of the force exerted by the plank on the support at P.

3   Particles, of mass m kg, are supported in turn by a light elastic string, of natural length l metres and modulus of elasticity λ newtons, from a fixed point O.
   When $m = 1.5$, the extension is 0.45 m.
   When $m = 2$, the string has a total length of 1.4 m.
   Find the values of l and λ.

4   A particle P moves at constant speed $V\,\text{ms}^{-1}$ in a horizontal circle of radius 1.2 m on the smooth inside surface of a fixed spherical bowl of internal radius 2 m.
   Find the value of V and the time taken by P to complete one orbit of the circle.

5   A particle A of mass $3m$ moving with speed $\dfrac{5u}{2}$ collides with a particle B of mass $2m$ moving with speed u in the same line and direction as A. After the collision, B moves with speed $2u$. Find
   (a) the coefficient of restitution between A and B,
   (b) the impulse exerted by A and B on the collision,
   (c) the loss in kinetic energy due to the collision.

6   A uniform wire of length $10a$ is bent, as shown, into the shape $ABCD$, where $AB = 5a$, $BC = 3a$, $CD = 2a$ and the angles at B and C are $90°$.
   (a) Find the distance of the centre of mass of the wire from
      (i) AB,   (ii) BC.
   (b) The wire is suspended freely from A and hangs in equilibrium. Find the angle made by AB with the vertical.

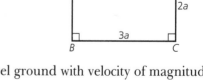

7   A player hits a ball from a point A on level ground with velocity of magnitude $25\,\text{ms}^{-1}$ at an angle of elevation of $50°$.
   (a) Find the greatest height of the ball above the ground and show that the horizontal range is about 61.5 m.
   (b) Show further that the ball can pass over a wall which is 11 m high and at a horizontal distance of 50 m from A with 0.2 m to spare.
   (c) State two assumptions that you have used in your solution to this question.

8   A particle P of mass m is moving along the positive x-axis towards the origin O and P is subjected to a force of magnitude mcx^2 towards O, where c is a positive constant. Initially $OP = a$ and P is at rest. Given that u is the speed of P when it first reaches O, show that $3u^2 = 2ca^3$.

9 A landrover of mass 1 500 kg pulls a caravan of mass 3 500 kg up a straight road, inclined at arcsin $\frac{1}{50}$ to the horizontal, at constant speed $12\,\text{ms}^{-1}$. Constant resistances of magnitudes 450 N for the landrover and 1 050 N for the caravan oppose their motion up the hill.

(a) Calculate the rate at which the engine of the landrover is working, giving your answer in kW.

(b) The power of the engine is suddenly reduced to 18 kW. Find the immediate retardation of the car and the thrust in the tow-bar at this instant.

10 Two particles A of mass 0.08 kg and B of mass 0.12 kg are tied at the ends of a light, inextensible string which is taut and passes over a smooth fixed pulley at the top of a double inclined plane, as shown.

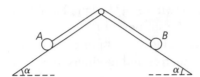

The plane on which A stands is smooth. The plane on which B stands is rough and the coefficient of friction between B and the plane is μ.

(a) Show that if equilibrium is maintained, $\mu \geqslant \frac{1}{3} \tan \alpha$.

(b) Given that $\tan \alpha = \frac{4}{3}$ and $\mu = 0.3$ and the particles are released from rest, find

   (i) the acceleration of A and the tension in the string,

   (ii) the magnitude of the force exerted by the string on the pulley while the particles are in motion.

OUTLINE ANSWERS TO MECHANICS PAPER

General Strategy

Draw neat freehand diagrams and place all given information on your diagram. Then form equations.

1 The time spent accelerating is twice that spent retarding.

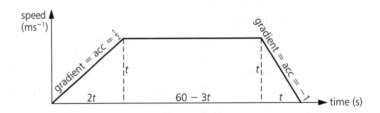

Since acc. $= \frac{1}{2}\,\text{ms}^{-2}$, after $2t$ seconds from rest, speed of train is given by

$$v = u + at \quad \Rightarrow \quad v = \frac{1}{2}(2t) = t$$

Now, area under speed–time graph = distance covered. Hence

$$\tfrac{1}{2} \times 2t(t) + t(60 - 3t) + \tfrac{1}{2}t \times t = 450$$

$$\Rightarrow \quad t^2 - 40t + 300 = 0 \quad \Rightarrow \quad (t - 10)(t - 30) = 0$$

$$t \neq 30, \text{ hence } t = 10$$

Time accelerating 20 s, at full speed 30 s, retarding 10 s. Distance covered at top speed $= 10(60 - 30)$ metres $= 300\,\text{m}$.

2

P — 2 m — 1 m — 1 m — R — 2 m — Q
R N ↑ (at P)
↓ 200 N
↓ 500 N
↑ (at R)

The diagram shows distances and forces in a simple way found from reading the question. The force R newtons at P is found from taking moments about R where the other supporting force acts, to give

$R \times 4 = 200 \times 2 + 500 \times 1 \quad \Rightarrow \quad R = 225$

Magnitude of force at $P = 225$ N

3 We need to use Hooke's law for each case. Let λ newtons be the modulus of elasticity of the string and l metres its natural length

$15 = \dfrac{\lambda(0.45)}{l}$ (since tension is $1.5g$ newtons)

$20 = \dfrac{\lambda(1.4 - l)}{l}$ (since tension is $2g$ newtons and *extension* is $(1.4 - l)$ metres)

Eliminating λ from these equations

$\dfrac{15l}{0.45} = \dfrac{20l}{1.4 - l} \quad \Rightarrow \quad 21 - 15l = 9 \quad \Rightarrow \quad l = 0.8 \quad \text{and} \quad \lambda = \dfrac{15 \times 0.8}{0.45} = 26\tfrac{2}{3}$

4

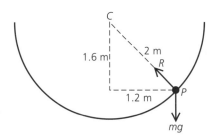

By Pythagoras, depth of P below level of C, the centre of the sphere, is $\sqrt{(2^2 - 1.2^2)}\,\text{m} = 1.6\,\text{m}$.

Resolving vertically $\Rightarrow$ $R \sin \theta = mg$. But $\sin \theta = \dfrac{1.6}{2} = \dfrac{4}{5}$

$\Rightarrow \quad R = \dfrac{5}{4}mg$

Using Newton's second law horizontally $\Rightarrow$ $R \cos \theta = m \dfrac{v^2}{1.2}$, that is

$\dfrac{5}{4}mg\left(\dfrac{3}{5}\right) = m\dfrac{v^2}{1.2}$

$\Rightarrow \quad v^2 = 0.75 \times 10 \times 1.2 = 9 \quad \Rightarrow \quad v = 3$

Time to complete one orbit $= \dfrac{\text{circumference}}{\text{speed}}$

$= \dfrac{2\pi(1.2)}{3}\,\text{s} = 2.51\,\text{s}$

5

Before ⟶ $\dfrac{5u}{2}$ ⟶ u

    (3m)   (2m)

After ⟶ v ⟶ $2u$

Mark your diagram clearly, as shown.

(a) Conservation of momentum $\Rightarrow (3m)\left(\dfrac{5u}{2}\right) + (2m)(u) = (3m)(v) + (2m)(2u)$.

That is

$v = \text{speed of } A \text{ after collision} = \dfrac{11u}{6}$

Newton's experimental law $\Rightarrow \quad e\left(\dfrac{5u}{2} - u\right) = 2u - \dfrac{11u}{6} \Rightarrow e = \dfrac{1}{9}$

(b) The impulse exerted by A on B = change in momentum of B

$$= 2m(2u - u) = 2mu$$

(c) The loss in KE $= \dfrac{1}{2}(3m)\left(\dfrac{5u}{2}\right)^2 + \dfrac{1}{2}(2m)(u)^2 - \dfrac{1}{2}(3m)\left(\dfrac{11u}{6}\right)^2 - \dfrac{1}{2}(2m)(2u)^2$

$$= \dfrac{4}{3}mu^2$$

6 (a) Let mass per unit length of the wire be m.

  (i) Let $\bar{x}$ be distance of G, the centre of mass, from AB. Moments about AB are

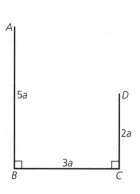

$$\dfrac{3a}{2} \times 3am + 3a \times 2am = (10am)\bar{x}$$

$$\Rightarrow \quad \bar{x} = \dfrac{21a}{20}$$

  (ii) Moments about BC, where G is $\bar{y}$ from BC, are

$$\dfrac{5a}{2} \times 5am + \dfrac{2a}{2} \times 2am = (10am)\bar{y}$$

$$\Rightarrow \quad \bar{y} = \dfrac{29a}{20}$$

(b) α is the angle required when wire is hung from A.

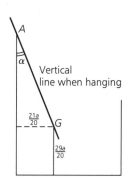

Vertical line when hanging

$$\tan\alpha = \dfrac{\dfrac{21a}{20}}{5a - \dfrac{29a}{20}} = \dfrac{21}{71}$$

$$\alpha = 16.5° \text{ (nearest tenth of a degree)}$$

7 (a) Greatest height $= \dfrac{25^2\sin^2 50°}{2g}\,\text{m} \approx 18.3\,\text{m}$

Range $= \dfrac{2 \times 25^2 \times \sin 50° \cos 50°}{g}\,\text{m} \approx 61.5\,\text{m}.$

(b) Ball is 50 m horizontally from A at time $\dfrac{50}{25\cos 50°}\,\text{s} \approx 3.11\,\text{s}$

At this instant, ball is at vertical height

$(25\sin 50° \times 3.11 - \tfrac{1}{2} \times g \times 3.11^2)\,\text{m} \approx 11.18\,\text{m}$

So ball does not pass over C.

(c) Assumptions: Ball modelled as a particle
                 No air resistance or wind

8 Use acceleration as $v\,\dfrac{dv}{dx}$ to form the differential equation $mv\dfrac{dv}{dx} = -mcx^2$ (from Newton's 2nd law). That is

$$v\dfrac{dv}{dx} = -cx^2$$

Integrating with respect to x $\Rightarrow$ $\tfrac{1}{2}v^2 = -\tfrac{1}{3}cx^3 + k,$ where k is a constant.

Now $v = 0$ when $x = a$ $\Rightarrow$ $k = \tfrac{1}{3}ca^3.$ Hence

$\tfrac{1}{2}v^2 = \tfrac{1}{3}c(a^3 - x^3)$

At 0, $x = 0$ and we have $v = u$ so

     $\tfrac{1}{2}u^2 = \tfrac{1}{3}ca^3$

$\Rightarrow \quad 3u^2 = 2ca^3$

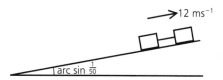

(a) Total resistance $= 450\,\text{N} + 1\,050\,\text{N} = 1\,500\,\text{N}$

Gravitational component $= (1\,500 + 3\,500)g \times \frac{1}{50}\,\text{N} = 1\,000\,\text{N}$

Workrate required $= (1\,500 + 1\,000)12$ watts
$= 30\,\text{kW}$

(b) Sudden reduction is $12\,\text{kW}$ at $12\,\text{ms}^{-1}$ so the *instantaneous* braking force is $\frac{12\,000}{12}\,\text{N} = 1\,000\,\text{N}$

On landrover, we have $\qquad T - 1\,000 - 450 = 1\,500a$

and on the caravan $\qquad -T - 1\,050 = 3\,500a$

by applying Newton's second law to each, where a is the acceleration and T the thrust in the tow-bar.
Solving gives

$a = \frac{2}{3}$ and $T = 3\,383$

Tension is $3\,383\,\text{N}$ and acceleration is $\frac{2}{3}\,\text{ms}^{-2}$.

10 (a) For A $\qquad 0.08g \sin \alpha = T$ $\left.\begin{array}{l}\\\\\end{array}\right\} \Rightarrow F = 0.04g \sin \alpha$
For B $\qquad 0.12g \sin \alpha = T + F$

$F \leqslant (0.12g \cos \alpha)\,\mu$ for equilibrium

$\Rightarrow (0.12g \cos \alpha)\mu \geqslant 0.4g \sin \alpha \Rightarrow \mu \geqslant \frac{1}{3}\tan \alpha$

(b) (i) Equations of motion for A and B when $\mu = 0.3$ are
For A $\qquad T' - 0.8 \sin \alpha = 0.08a$
For B $\qquad 1.2 \sin \alpha - T' - 1.2(0.3)\cos \alpha = 0.12a$
Solving these gives $T' = 0.682$ (3 s.f.) $\Rightarrow a = 0.52$.
Tension is $0.682\,\text{N}$ and acceleration is $0.52\,\text{ms}^{-2}$.

(ii) Force exerted by string on pulley $= 2T \sin \alpha$ newtons $\approx 1.09\,\text{N}$ (3 s.f.)

Question paper for
Statistics

Answer ALL the questions   **Time allowed:** $2\frac{1}{2}$ hours

1   Three unbiased cubical dice are thrown simultaneously
    (a) Calculate the probability that the scores on all of the dice are greater than 2.
    (b) Calculate the probability that the total score on the three dice is greater than 15.

2   A group of 70 children were given a spelling test which consisted of 20 words. The number of correct spellings obtained by the children is shown in the table below.

No. of correct spellings	7	8	9	10	11	12	13	14	15	16	17	18	19
No of children	1	3	4	3	5	7	6	9	14	8	6	3	1

   (a) For this distribution, (i) state the mode and calculate (ii) the median,
       (iii) the mean.
   (b) A parallel group of 40 children obtained a mean of 14.5 when performing the same test. Calculate the mean mark obtained by all 110 children.

3   An electrical shop sells on average three vacuum cleaners model XL, per week. It is found that the number sold in a week has a Poisson distribution. Find
    (a) the probability that the shop sells at least 2 of the particular brand of vacuum cleaner in a week,
    (b) the smallest number of the model that the shop should stock at the beginning of the week in order to have a 90% chance of being able to meet all demands for the cleaner during that week.

4   A random sample of 200 U2 batteries had a mean lifetime of 450 hours with standard deviation of 25 hours. A random sample of 250 P9 batteries had a mean lifetime of 575 hours and a standard deviation of 40 hours. Find approximate 95% confidence limits for the difference between the mean lifetimes of the populations of batteries, given that the populations from which both samples are taken are normally distributed.

5   The following table shows the number of minutes to the nearest minute that a group of children were late for school during the winter term

7	8	27	13	23	6	23	4	1	15
17	5	21	7	13	41	42	14	2	33
4	7	24	12	16	31	4	11	10	6
9	3	20	1	5	12	30	3	6	22
5	20	10	13	35	10	3	5	15	24

   (a) Construct an ordered stem and leaf diagram to represent these data.
   (b) Find the median and quartiles of these times.
   (c) Construct a box plot for these data.
   (d) Comment on the skewness of your distribution.

6   On a particular day a biscuit manufacturer produces a mixture of plain and chocolate biscuits for a market salesman. 60% of the biscuits are plain and 40% are chocolate. Random selections of 20 biscuits are placed in each packet.
    (a) Calculate the probability that in a packet chosen at random there are
        (i) an equal number of plain and chocolate biscuits,
        (ii) more plain biscuits than chocolate biscuits.

(b) The manufacturer also produces catering packs of 160 randomly selected biscuits. Use a suitable approximation to calculate the probability that a catering pack contains between 75 and 80 chocolate biscuits.

(c) If 5% of all the biscuits also contain a cream filling, find the probability that there are 6 such biscuits in a catering pack.

7 The marks obtained by 13 students in their pure mathematics examination and in their applied mathematics examination are given in the table below

Pure (x)	84	72	63	51	62	69	52	43	30	57	33	59	62
Applied (y)	80	64	75	33	67	56	29	54	40	56	43	45	60

(a) Draw a scatter diagram to represent the two sets of marks and state which 3 students appear to have performed differently from the rest of the group.

(b) Omitting these 3 students, calculate to 3 decimal places the product–moment correlation coefficient between the two sets of examination marks for the rest of the students

(You may assume $\sum xy = 36\,829$, $\sum x^2 = 40\,693$, $\sum y^2 = 34\,437$.)

8 At a WI meeting two judges were asked to place in order of merit 10 cakes ranking them 1, 2, 3 down to 10. The results were as shown in the table below.

	A	B	C	D	E	F	G	H	J	K
Judge I	8	1	4	7	2	5	10	9	6	3
Judge II	9	4	2	10	1	5	7	8	3	6

(a) Calculate the Spearman rank correlation coefficient between the two rankings.

(b) State clearly your hypothesis and using a 5% two-tailed test interpret your rank correlation coefficient.

9 A tyre firm claims that the average life of a particular tyre that it sells is 35 000 miles with a standard deviation of 1 700 miles. To test this claim a random sample of 100 of the tyres was taken and were found to have an average life of 34 500 miles. Stating clearly your hypotheses and using a 5% level of significance test the claim made by the firm using
(a) a two-tailed test,
(b) a one-tailed test.

10 A sample of 325 women from England, Wales and Scotland were asked which soap powder they preferred, Ultra, Ultra Extra, or Best Ultra, and their answers are shown in the table. Stating clearly your hypotheses, investigate whether or not there is any association between soap powder preference and regional environment. Use a 5% level of significance.

	Ultra	Ultra Extra	Best Ultra
England	35	40	55
Scotland	25	32	43
Wales	31	27	37

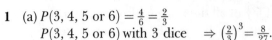

1 (a) $P(3, 4, 5 \text{ or } 6) = \frac{4}{6} = \frac{2}{3}$

$P(3, 4, 5 \text{ or } 6)$ with 3 dice $\Rightarrow \left(\frac{2}{3}\right)^3 = \frac{8}{27}$.

(b) To get total score >15 we need combinations of $6, 6, 6$ $6, 6, 5$ $6, 6, 4$ and $6, 5, 5$ i.e. $1 + 3 + 3 + 3 = 10$ possible throws $P(\text{score} > 15) = \frac{10}{6^3} = \frac{10}{216}$

Do show the examiner how you are thinking so that he may be able to allocate method marks if your answer is incorrect. An incorrect answer with no working shown gets no marks.

2 (a) (i) Mode $= 15$.

(ii) Median $= 14$.

(iii) Mean $= \dfrac{\begin{array}{c} 7 \times 1 + 8 \times 3 + 9 \times 4 + \\ \cdots + 17 \times 6 + 18 \times 3 + 19 \times 1 \end{array}}{70}$

$= \frac{953}{70} = 13.6$

(b) Combined mean $= \frac{1}{110}(953 + 40 \times 14.5)$

$= 13.94$.

Mode $=$ Most frequently occurring mark

Median $=$ Middle mark

3 (a) $\lambda = 3$.

$P(x \geqslant 2) = 1 - P(0) - P(1) = 1 - e^{-3} - 3e^{-3}$

$= 1 - 4e^{-3} = 1 - 0.19915 \approx 0.801$

(b) Need $P(X \leqslant n \mid \mu = 3) \geqslant 0.9$.

Using the cumulative Poisson probability tables

$P(x \leqslant n \mid \mu = 3) = 0.916$ for $n = 5$.

$\Rightarrow$ shop should stock 5 vacuum cleaners

Do not forget that at least 2 means $P(X \geqslant 2)$ not $P(X > 2)$

You can add $P(0) + P(1) + P(2)$ etc. until a probability >0.9 is obtained but it is much easier to use the cumulative tables

4 U2 $\Rightarrow$ $N(450, 25^2)$, P9 $\Rightarrow$ $N(575, 40^2)$

$\Rightarrow$ P9 $-$ U2 $\sim N\left(575 - 450, \frac{40^2}{250} + \frac{25^2}{200}\right)$

95% confidence limits

$\Rightarrow$ $(575 - 450) \pm 1.96\sqrt{\left(\frac{40^2}{250} + \frac{25^2}{200}\right)}$

$= 125 \pm 1.96\sqrt{(3.125 + 6.4)}$

$= 125 \pm 6.049 \Rightarrow (131.049, 118.951)$

Do not make the mistake of taking $\left(\frac{40^2}{250} - \frac{25^2}{200}\right)$.

5 (a)

0	112 333 444 5555 666 777 8 9	(21)
1	000 122 333 455 67	(14)
2	00 12 33 44 7	(9)
3	0 135	(4)
4	1 2	(2)

(b) Median $= \dfrac{11 + 12}{2} = 11.5$

$Q_1 = 5$, $Q_3 = 21$.

(c)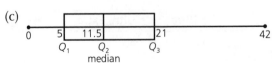

(d) Positive skew

Do not forget to keep a running total of each line so that you can ensure you have not missed out any values

For an even number of terms say $2n$, median $= \frac{1}{2}(T_n + T_{n+1})$.

6 (a) $P(\text{Plain}) = \frac{6}{10} = \frac{3}{5}$, $P(\text{Chocolate}) = \frac{4}{10} = \frac{2}{5}$.

    (i) $P(10, 10) = {}^{20}C_{10}\left(\frac{3}{5}\right)^{10}\left(\frac{2}{5}\right)^{10}$

           $= 0.872 - 0.755 \approx 0.117$

    (ii) Using the cumulative binomial
       probability tables
       P (More plain than choc) $= 0.755$.

  (b) Mean number chocolate biscuits $= 0.4 \times 160$

                           $= 64$

    Variance $= \sigma^2 = npq = 160 \times 0.4 \times 0.6$

                         $= 38.4$

    Normal distribution $N \sim (64, 38.4)$

    $P(74.5 \leqslant x \leqslant 80.5)$

        $= P\left(\dfrac{74.5 - 64}{\sqrt{38.4}} \leqslant Z \leqslant \dfrac{80.5 - 64}{\sqrt{38.4}}\right)$

        $= \Phi(2.663) - \Phi(1.694)$

        $= 0.99613 - 0.9549 \approx 0.0412$

  (c) n large

    $\Rightarrow$ Poisson mean $\mu = np = 160 \times 0.05 = 8.0$

    $P(x = 6) = \dfrac{8.0^6\, e^{-8}}{6!} = 0.122$

Using a binomial distribution.

Using the cumulative binomial probability tables for $n = 20$, $p = 0.4$ and $r = 10$ and $r = 9$, i.e. $P(r = 10) - P(r = 9)$.

Again using the tables for $r = 9$.

Continuity correction needed as a continuous distribution is used to approximate a discrete distribution

As n is large we use a Poisson distribution

---

7 (a) Scatter diagram shows that the students with $\binom{43}{54}$, $\binom{30}{40}$, $\binom{33}{43}$ performed differently.

  (b) $\sum x = 631 \quad \Rightarrow \quad \bar{x} = 63.1$

      $\sum y = 565 \quad \Rightarrow \quad \bar{y} = 56.5$

      $r = \dfrac{\sum xy - n\bar{x}\bar{y}}{\sqrt{\{(\sum x^2 - n\bar{x}^2)(\sum y^2 n\bar{y}^2)\}}}$

      $= \dfrac{36\,829 - 35\,651.5}{\sqrt{\{(40\,693 - 39\,816.1)(34\,437 - 31\,922.5)\}}}$

      $= \dfrac{1\,177.5}{\sqrt{(876.9 \times 2\,514.5)}} = \dfrac{1\,177.5}{1\,484.91} \approx 0.793$

Show clearly on the scatter diagram the three rejected sets of marks.

Do show the examiner what you are calculating. Do not just use your calculator and write down a final answer.

---

8 (a)

d	1	3	−2	3	−1	0	−3	1	3	3
d^2	1	9	4	9	1	0	9	1	9	9

    $\sum d^2 = 52 \quad \Rightarrow \quad r_S = 1 - \dfrac{6 \times 52}{10 \times 99} \approx 0.685$

  (b) Null hypothesis $\qquad\quad \rho = 0$,
    Alternative hypothesis $\quad \rho \neq 0$
    For $n = 10$ at 5% two-tail level, critical
    values are ± 0.6485. Since $r_S = 0.685 \Rightarrow$
    result is significant. Since $r_S = 0.685$ we do
    not accept the null hypothesis, i.e. there is
    evidence to suggest there is no relationship
    between the rankings of the two judges.

Again do show d at d^2

State your hypotheses

State your final conclusion.

9 $H_0 : \mu = 35\,000$, $\quad H_1 : \mu \neq 35\,000$ (two-tailed)

Always state your hypotheses.

(a) $\bar{Z} = \dfrac{34\,500 - 35\,000}{\dfrac{1\,700}{\sqrt{100}}} = -2.941$

But 5% level of significance with two-tailed test gives a critical region $|\bar{z}| > 1.96$ and hence we reject H_0 and conclude that the average lifetime is different from 35 000 miles.

(b) $H_0 : \mu = 35\,000$, $\quad H_1 : \mu < 35\,000$
For one-tailed test the critical region is $\bar{Z} < -1.645$ and as $\bar{Z} = -2.941$ we again reject H_0 and conclude that the average lifetime is less than 35 000 miles.

10 H_0: Regional environment and soap powder are associated, $\quad H_1$: Not associated.

State your hypotheses and set out your working clearly – it helps the examiner to see what you are doing and ensures you make fewer mistakes

	Ultra	Ultra Extra	Ultra Fresh	
England	35 36.4	40 39.6	55 54	130
Scotland	25 28	32 30.46	43 41.54	100
Wales	31 26.6	27 28.94	37 39.46	95
	91	99	135	325

$$\sum \frac{(O-E)^2}{E} \approx 1.538, \quad v = 4$$

Critical value 9.488 $\Rightarrow$ Cannot reject H_0
$\quad \Rightarrow$ Associated